OSHAWA PUBLIC LIBRARY

D0423287

APPROACHING AUSTRALIA

Papers from the
Harvard Australian Studies Symposium

35.⁰⁰
994
.0071
173
APP

APPROACHING AUSTRALIA

OSHAWA PUBLIC LIBRARY

Papers from the
Harvard Australian Studies Symposium

Edited by

HAROLD BOLITHO
&
CHRIS WALLACE-CRABBE

10 315621

OSHAWA PUBLIC LIBRARY

PUBLISHED BY
HARVARD UNIVERSITY
COMMITTEE ON AUSTRALIAN STUDIES

DISTRIBUTED BY
HARVARD UNIVERSITY PRESS
CAMBRIDGE, MASSACHUSETTS
LONDON, ENGLAND

For permission to use copyrighted material, consult the permissions
acknowledgments on page 251, which are hereby made
part of this copyright page.

Library of Congress Cataloging-in-Publication Data

Harvard Australian Studies Symposium (1997 : Harvard University)
    Approaching Australia : papers from the Harvard Australian
  Studies Symposium / edited by Harold Bolitho and Chris Wallace-Crabbe.
      p.   cm.
    Includes bibliographical references (p.) and index.
    ISBN 0-674-04189-5 (hardcover)   ISBN 0-674-04190-9 (paperback)
    1. Australia—Study and teaching (Higher)—United States
  —Congresses.   2. Australia—Relations—United States—Congresses.
  3. United States—Relations—Australia—Congresses.   4. Australia—
  Congresses.   5. United States—Congresses.   I. Bolitho, Harold.   II.
  Wallace-Crabbe, Chris.
  DU109.5.H37   1998
  994'.0071'173—dc21   98-26221
                                                                        CIP

3 9364 00675438 1

©1998 The President and Fellows of Harvard College
All rights reserved
Printed in the United States of America

Table of Contents

Acknowledgments

Both the symposium and the publication issuing from it represent the work of many hands. The symposium itself was assisted by the Embassy of Australia, Washington, D.C. We would, therefore, like to express our gratitude to the Embassy, and especially to Ms. Penelope Amberg, for that assistance. Our thanks are also due to the Honorable Andrew Sharp Peacock, Australian Ambassador to the United States, and to the Honorable Michael Baume, Australian Consul-General, New York. The organization of the symposium owes much to Bernard Bailyn, Helen Hardacre, and Judith Ryan, members of the Harvard University Committee on Australian Studies, who gave generously of their time and advice.

For the publication, thanks are first due to Jan Senbergs, Visiting Professor of Australian Studies at Harvard in 1989–1990, who kindly consented to the use of his "Circular Quay" for the dust jacket. Sarah Kimnach, project manager, and Javier Amador-Peña, designer, of Editorial Services of New England, Inc., should also be thanked for having seen the book safely through all the related technicalities.

Neither symposium nor book would ever have been possible without Janet Hatch, Coordinator of the Committee on Australian Studies, who gave unstintingly of her time and energy—at no small cost to herself—to both projects. To her go our very warmest thanks.

Foreword

ON JULY 4, 1976, the United States celebrated the bicentennial of the American Revolution. A little over three weeks later, on July 30, completing an initiative developed under the Whitlam government, Prime Minister Malcom Fraser signed a Memorandum of Understanding by which Harvard University was to receive a sum of money to fund a Chair of Australian Studies. It was a generous gift and, like the best gifts, had the potential of conferring benefit on both recipient and donor. On the one hand, it was an honor for Harvard to receive a new Chair. On the other, Australia also expected to gain something. In the language of the Memorandum, it was intended that the initiative should "maintain such teaching, research and publication as will help promote awareness and understanding of Australia in the United States of America."

Essentially the gift was an invitation. It was not an invitation to develop more trade and investment between the United States and Australia, nor to encourage more trans-Pacific tourism, nor to strengthen bilateral security— although any or all of these would have been welcome. It was an invitation to the United States to understand Australia, to move beyond the ruling clichés of surf and sunshine toward a recognition of what makes Australia distinctive, and to achieve this through scholarship. That was why Australia's gift to the United States was defined in intellectual terms and why it was offered to a major seat of learning.

Australia's expectations of the Harvard Chair were symbolized, perhaps unconsciously, in 1978. Manning Clark, who in 1975 had been intimately involved in initial discussions on the Australian Chair, arrived at Harvard in September of that year as the second Visiting Professor of Australian Studies. He came with a boomerang. This was not your ordinary souvenir-shop boomerang like those sold to tourists from Hobart to Darwin, but a businesslike throwing stick of a kind usually seen only in museums. It was long, slightly curved, roughly carved—and absolutely not the kind of object normally packed for a journey to the other side of the world.

In a sense it was an innocent piece of Australian exotica—exotic, at least, in American eyes. But it may also have been a metaphor for the Harvard Chair, since the boomerang, in Aboriginal society, has an equally well-defined and practical purpose. That, at least, is how I interpret it, because it was a gift for Henry Rosovsky, Dean of the Faculty of Arts and Sciences, who administered the Harvard Chair in its earliest years. Since then the boomerang, and the responsibilities that go with it, have passed to successive chairs of the Harvard committee which oversees the Harvard Chair, or, to use its formal title, the Chair in Australian Studies Advisory Committee. So from Rosovsky it went to the late John Clive, from Clive to Bernard Bailyn, and from Bailyn to me. All of us have taken the unspoken message of the boomerang, and the explicit obligation to promote awareness and understanding of Australia, with the utmost seriousness.

Our main duty has been to bring representatives of the very best of Australian scholarship to Harvard. From a list provided by a Nominating Committee in Australia, we invite a scholar to spend up to a year living and working in the Harvard community. Each is placed in the most appropriate academic department or program and is offered accommodation in one or other of Harvard's residential houses, so that they are brought into contact with a broad cross section of faculty and students, graduate and undergraduate. Flexible teaching obligations make it possible for them to travel for speaking engagements within the United States.

The smooth and efficient functioning of the Australian Chair has been our primary responsibility, but certainly not our only one. In the past we have sponsored Australian film festivals, and in 1990 we mounted an exhibition of Aboriginal art from the Holmes á Court collection. We also joined with others in the United States—notably Henry Albinski of the Australia–New Zealand Studies Center at Pennsylvania State University and John Higley of the Edward A. Clark Center for Australian Studies at the University of Texas at Austin—to help form the Australian Studies Association of North America (ASANA) in 1990. Since then we have encouraged ASANA in several significant ways. We joined with it in 1992 to sponsor a Conference on the Internationalization of Higher Education, which was held at Harvard, and the following year we hosted ASANA's first national conference, bringing several speakers from Australia to participate.

This volume speaks again to our efforts to promote awareness and understanding of Australia in the United States. In the spring of 1997, we brought together a group of Australian scholars for a symposium to celebrate the first twenty years of the Harvard Chair and invited those Americans concerned with Australian Studies to attend. We are proud to offer this collection of the papers given on that occasion. It is a record of an extremely successful scholarly meeting. It is also, in its way, a record of the Harvard Australian Chair as it has developed over the past two decades. Our aim was to offer a retrospective, embracing, as far as possible, previous incumbents and the areas of Australian Studies associated with them, but at the same time including the perspectives of other scholars of equal distinction. The emphasis in this collection is, therefore, on those aspects of Australian Studies most frequently addressed by those appointed to the Chair. Historians—La Nauze, Clark, Inglis, Blainey, Davison, Roe (and currently Rickard)—have held it more often than those in any other discipline. Archaeology-Anthropology would come next, with three scholars (Mulvaney, Hiatt, and Jones). Both fields are well represented here, with Alan Frost adding his voice to the History section. Unfortunately, circumstances precluded a panel on Economics, although it had also provided three incumbents. For Literature, Dame Leonie Kramer and Chris Wallace-Crabbe, both previous holders, were joined by Peter Steele and Kevin Hart, while Jan Senbergs, who combined theory and practice during his year at the Carpenter Center, spoke on Fine Arts. The social sciences are here represented by E. Gough Whitlam, who held the Chair in 1979, and two younger scholars, James Walter and Peter Beilharz.

By any yardstick this would have to be judged an idiosyncratic collection of papers. It could hardly be anything else. There is no single approach to the study of Australia; Australian Studies, however construed, is much too amorphous for that. Certainly no two-day symposium could hope to define it. For that matter, no small group of scholars—even as accomplished as these—is ever going to come up with a synthesis to satisfy everybody. But there is one important unifying principle: the Harvard Chair of Australian Studies, while it has veered over the humanities–social sciences landscape, and will soon range even further afield, has been held by scholars of great eminence and exceptional individuality. In their differing approaches to Australia, the papers in this collection reflect nothing less.

HAROLD BOLITHO

Introduction

AUSTRALIAN STUDIES is a most interesting congeries of institutional patterns and effects, not least on its own turf. Like its big sister, American Studies, it had grown up at first as a way of asserting our lack of Cringe, our refusal to tip the forelock forever and ever to the grand cultures of the Old World, even though we were obliged to base ourselves in the English language, that subtle and seductive tyrant.

Some disciplines in Australian universities had included native components for a long time—it would have been ridiculous to study botany, zoology, geology, or law without substantial attention to Australian conditions and examples. The teaching of our history and of our politics began to filter into courses during and after World War II, and three universities were teaching Australian literature courses by the end of the fifties. Three nationalist-heroic books from that decade, Russel Ward's *The Australian Legend*, A. A. Phillip's *The Australian Tradition*, and Vance Palmer's *The Legend of the Nineties*, laid out the territory where historical and literary studies could meet.

Academic study of Australian art, music, and film was still to come. So, too, were the feminist and transnational critiques of the Legend. By the time that Australian Studies centers and programs had been set in place in the eighties, the unitary sense of an Australian tradition, legend, or distinctive sensibility had already been dispersed. The stockyard had been feminized, or else set against G. A. Wilkes' polar opposite: the croquet lawn. Not that most debate was even binary: scholars had proceeded in directions akin to those of Benedict Anderson's *Imagined Communities* to focus on the web or tension of understandings that make up the nation-state. They had pluralized the arguments or, at times, dismantled and reinvented them. Above all, the silence that surrounded Australia's Aboriginal population became the focus for many kinds of investigation, including that of undergraduate study. It remains a major field of interest.

Accordingly, the Australian Studies centers that have appeared over the past decade and a half have constructed their courses and research projects in a climate that is feminist, postcolonial, and, above all, aware of ethnic issues. Structurally, most have had to begin by defining their relation to "parent" disciplines and exist within a parent department that makes funds, space, and students available to the new multidiscipline. Once freed from conservative skepticism within the campus, they have entered a field where national emphases are increasingly in doubt, even regarded as dodgy, stained with colonialism and its residues. There is no rest or calm available.

Australian Studies earns its nominal plural; it is not unified, has no one clear methodology. If this displeased conservative literary critics and historians in the mid-recent past, it has done so to many poststructuralist thinkers more recently. This chameleon promiscuity of approaches is partly camouflaged among holders of the Chair of Australian Studies at Harvard, because most have been firmly bedded down in one department or another, but back in Australia our fields of study have often been seen as not quite postcolonialist, not quite feminist, not quite postmodernist, and not quite Cultural Studies. Thus Meaghan Morris, the doyenne of Australian cultural theorists, has complained in these terms: "Australian Studies has slowly turned back towards the comfortable *de facto* union of literary and historical studies within which it was originally conceived." Morris sees something inherently conservative in our kinds of work.

For other modern theorists, Australian Studies can seem too much of a fox, too little of a hedgehog, to borrow the polarities of Archilochus; it knows many little things but lacks what we might call a unified field theory. But this is also true of Cultural Studies, surely, thus raising the question of why there often seems to be conflict between the two kinds of study. Angela Smith has recently claimed that such conflict also arises from confusion between interdisciplinary and multidisciplinary assumptions; whatever the case, the apparent conflict seems to be abating, of late.

As the contents of this book vividly show, Australian Studies at Harvard over the past twenty years has gone the way of the fox. Practitioners of many disciplines have come into Cambridge for a period and have added their tesserae to the whole developing design. Holistic yearners might see this as a piecemeal way to go about things, but it does, I believe, focus properly on the individual, the various, the richly significant, the remarkable, and the federated. Readers of the collection will go away with a sense of the many studies that Australia *is*. They will be reminded that there is no typical Australia, not even a charmingly battered crocodile hunter to represent us all.

From whatever department or institution, we are working critically in a field that has no ready center: the only thing that is typical may be our eccentricities, our ready freedom to pursue ideas that take off in many directions.

Like Australian cinema, our work is changing fast, vibrating oddly between metropolitan themes and regional ones. My kinetic understanding of Australian Studies, borne out by this book, could be characterized by Nietzsche's maxim *Against the Shortsighted:* "Do you think this work must be fragmentary because I give it to you (and have to give it to you) in fragments?" And the answer to his rhetorical question is, plainly enough, "Not bloody likely."

CHRIS WALLACE-CRABBE

PART I

Archaeology and Anthropology

1

Folsom and Talgai:
Cowboy Archaeology in Two Continents

RHYS JONES, DEPARTMENT OF ARCHAEOLOGY AND NATURAL HISTORY, RESEARCH SCHOOL OF PACIFIC AND ASIAN STUDIES, THE AUSTRALIAN NATIONAL UNIVERSITY, CANBERRA

Rain
Comes siding down,
Sharpening green knives,
Delving for flints in middens.
Like prehistorians
It fingers the grain of granite.

Rain picks out tunes
On tin roofs, praising
Lady Mungo, lithe as a heron,
And her Cretic sister,
La Parisienne,
Some millenniums younger.

The rain sides down.
Sideways they smiled at wayside men.
Old wounds are evergreen.
Rain, tell your lichened tales
To this year's girls.[1]

Harvard College celebrated its Tercentenary in September 1936 with three symposia in which the President and Fellows explicitly "called for the collaboration of scholars working in diverse fields of science and learning, and thereby cut across conventional academic disciplines." In this they were emulating the spirit of Robert Boyle's admiration of "that noble and improvable faculty which enables an Ingenious man to pry into the innermost

Recesses of Mysterious Nature," and which "points to the common basis of all our knowledge, and upholds its unity."[2]

Two hundred and fifty years previously, similar admiration had been expressed by Increase Mather, the Harvard divine (Class of 1656) who had met and studied with Boyle in London. In his *Remarkable Providences* in 1684, Mather wrote, "I have often wished that the Natural History of New England might be written and published to the world: the rules and method described by that learned and excellent person Robert Boyle Esq." The latter had proposed to the Royal Society in 1666 under the title of "General Heads for the Natural History of a Countrey" that topographic fieldwork be undertaken of both the natural and humanly made features, which marked the beginning of field archaeology in Britain. The archaeological historian Stuart Piggot has put it that "We are in a new world, that of the monuments of Roman and pre-Roman Britain."[3]

In 1712 some large bones which probably came from a mastodon were found near Cluverack, New England, and Mather communicated the discovery to the Royal Society of London. In his opinion they were the bones of gigantic men, "particularily a tooth which was a very large grinder, weighing four pounds and three-quarters, with a thigh-bone seventeen feet long."[4] Such antediluvians would have been consonant with the Mosaic record that "there were giants in those days," and bizarre though the identification may have been, it constitutes the first publication in a scientific journal concerning Pleistocene fossil fauna from America.

Increase's son, Cotton Mather (Class of 1678), in a sermon described ancient rock carvings on Dighton Rock near the Taunton River in Massachusetts which he published in 1690 in Boston under the title of "What the Indian people have engraved upon Rocks"; probably the first direct reference to any archaeological site in North America. In 1712 he sent drawings of these to the Royal Society, which were published in the *Philosophical Transactions* for 1714. He described a series of lines "each of them engraven with unaccountable characters, not like any known characters."[5] Seventy years later in 1783, the President of Yale, Rev. Ezra Stiles, in a sermon before the governor of Connecticut, was less diffident, confidently identifying them as being old Punic, "denoting that the Ancient Carthaginians once visited these distant regions," and with the moral lesson that the Indians, being descended from the accursed seed of Canaan, were preordained to fall away before the European descendants of Japhet (pp. 403–404).

Robert Boyle had a direct link with Harvard as the governor of the "Society for the Propagation of the Gospel in New England, and the parts adjacent, in America," which funded the construction of a building to house the Indian College, built in 1656, where it was the fourth structure within Harvard Yard and dedicated to the "education of Indian youth," a task specifically set out in the royal charter from Charles II to President Dunster in 1650.[6] A printery was set up in this building, and, in 1661, with funding from the Society, the evangelist John Eliot's translation of the New Testament, *Wushu Wutestamentum*, into the Algonquin language was published, followed two years later by a translation of the entire Bible. Boyle presented a copy of this to Charles, but history does not record how the monarch reacted to it, the first Bible ever printed in the New World (p. 347).

In 1665 Caleb Cheeshahteaumauck, a Wampanoag from Martha's Vineyard, became the first Native American to graduate from Harvard College. In 1663 he wrote a formal address in Latin to his *Honoratissimi benefactores*, "Most honored benefactors," which Governor Winthrop of Connecticut sent to Boyle as governor of the Society (p. 355) and which he in turn passed to the Royal Society in whose archives it still exists. Taking a metaphor from Ovid's *Metamorphoses,* the letter began with an account of Orpheus with his lyre obtained from Apollo, and of his moving stones and taming wild beasts through his songs, and of his journey and return from the underworld, which ancient philosophers interpreted as a symbol of the "force and virtue of learning and of civilized letters for altering the mind of barbarians." In the same way, learning and the Gospel had brought aid

> to us pagans, who were conducting our lives and raising our children in accordance with our ancestors. We were as naked in our minds as in our bodies, and we were alien to all humanity; having been led here and there in the desert and with various wanderings we lived.[7]

INDEPENDENCE, CONVERGENCE, AND BORROWING

Congregated in Harvard on the occasion in 1936 was what the *Boston Herald* (September 13) somewhat breathlessly described as the "World's wisest men." Some of these names can still create a frisson, such as Carl Jung, Bronislav Malinovski, Jean Piaget, and the biologist mathematician R. A. Fisher, inventor of the chi-squared test. But many of the others, alas, have, in a mere six decades, slipped into that respectable obscurity that is the fate of most scholars.

Representing the discipline of archaeology in this distinguished gathering was V. Gordon Childe (1892–1957), then the Professor of Prehistoric Archaeology at the University of Edinburgh. In a previous career, a graduate of the University of Sydney, he had been a prodigal son of Australian left-wing politics, who, having left his native country at the age of 30 with the fall of John Storey's Labor government in New South Wales in 1922, went on to become probably the single most influential prehistorian of the twentieth century. His *How Labour Governs* (1923) remains a central text in the moral conundrum of how the ideals of reform within a social democracy can be maintained within the potentially corrupting context of exercising real political power. Archaeologically, Childe defined a distinctive European personality within the prehistoric archaeological record, especially in his masterly *Dawn of European Civilization* (1925). The Soviet dissident archaeologist Leo Klejn has described how both students and the professor at Leningrad University, during a course on Bronze Age archaeology "were gripped by its clear construction, its all-embracing system, its unity." They understood the "shock that Western archaeologists experienced in the late 1920s and [which] we experienced in the late 1940s."[8]

Childe had been invited to participate in the symposium entitled "Independence, Convergence, and Borrowing in Institutions, Thought, and Art," which was intended to "trace the effect of the past upon the present and of neighbouring peoples upon each other."[9] He was conscious of "the privilege of speaking first on this day," but saw the honor, not only to himself, but rather to "the very youthful science which I represent." He was less coy about its potential impact, saying "Prehistoric archaeology has effected a revolution in man's knowledge of his own past, comparable in scale to the revolutions achieved by modern physics and astronomy . . . instead of the beggarly five thousand years patchily illuminated by written records, archaeology now offers the historian a vista of two hundred and fifty thousand years." Childe's view was that the practice of contemporary archaeological research was a revolutionary act and that it had the capacity to transform the field of inquiry of the human past. Late in his paper, he took the metaphor of the explorer, that the discovery of "Harappa and Mohenjo-Daro [in the lower Indus] has opened up a world no less new than that uncovered by Columbus to medieval Europe.[10]

DISCOVERY OF AMERICA
AND THE BIBLICAL CHRONOLOGY

The European discovery of the Americas also raised profound new questions about the deep past of human societies to Renaissance scholars, working as they had done within the geographical confines of Ptolemy and the chronological one of Genesis. First and most important was the question of whether or not these newly discovered peoples were fully human in the sense of having souls capable of salvation. This was resolved decisively by Pope Paul III in his Bull *Sublimis Deus* in 1537, which stated that "those Indians of the west, the south and elsewhere who had been discovered during our epoch [had been reduced to servitude] under the pretence that they were like brutish beasts incapable of receiving the Catholic faith." However, evidence from the Dominican missionaries had shown that "these same Indians are true men, not only finding themselves capable of receiving the

Christian faith, but [also] hasten towards this faith with promptitude."[11] The Dominican scholar and jurist Francisco de Vitoria began teaching at the University of Salamanca in Spain in 1538, and he was greatly influenced by the writings of Thomas Aquinas, who in the late thirteenth century had attempted to integrate the newly discovered works of Aristotle on physics and cosmology with the teachings of the medieval Church, both of which he considered the gifts of God.[12] Vitoria extended this inclusiveness between the divide of "pagan" and Christian, both within the remembered history of Europe and to the limits of the known world during his own time. In his *Relectiones de Indis,* he argued that the peoples of the New World should be considered like those of the Old, and subject to exactly the same laws of *jus gentium,* or the "laws of the nations."[13]

The reality of the colonial contact was of course brutal and devastating to the indigenous peoples, as was made graphically clear by Bartholomew de Las Casas in his *Brevissima Relacion de la Destruction de Las Indias,* which he read aloud to Emperor Charles V of Spain in a single sitting in 1541.[14] These depredations had been given a quasi-legal status, which were derived ultimately from Pope Alexander's granting in 1494 of sovereignty of newly discovered lands in different zones of the world, respectively to the crowns of Spain and of Portugal, by the formal reading of a *Requerimiento,* or "Requirement," which was codified in 1513, to those natives witnessing or opposing the landing. It stated that God "had created the heaven and the earth and one man and one woman of whom you and we, and all the men who have been or shall be in the world are descended"; and then it proceeded with a simple history of the world, that over a period of some five thousand years, humankind had been dispersed into different parts due to the pressure of population increase. However God had given charge of all these to "one man Saint Peter whom he constituted the lord and head of all the human race." From this was derived the authority of ownership, and the Indians were then required immediately to accept Christianity, the authority of the Pope, and the absolute sovereignty of His Majesty.[15] Thus embedded within this legal justification of European conquest was the first theory as to the origins of the peopling of the New World.

The narrow constraints of the Biblical chronology was no mere convention, but had exercised some of the best minds of the sixteenth and seventeenth centuries. Attempts to intercalate the chronologies of the Classical world with the text of the Hebrew Old Testament, so as to produce a unified calendar of events back to the earliest recorded times, required enormous erudition and engaged the attentions of such major scholars as Joseph Scaliger in his *Opus novum de emendatione temporum* in 1583 and after him, James Ussher in *Annales Veteris Testamenti, a Prima Mundi Origine* in 1650. Scaliger stated that "No Frankfurt fair goes by without its crop of chronologers,"[16] and the subject was deeply infused by astrological and metaphysical aspects, seized on by artists and humanists alike; of its fleeting quality, the unique occasion, the ever-recurring cycle. The task itself was difficult, involving calculations of the span of ancient calendars, so that as Iacobus Curio complained in 1557, "You will find it easier to make the wolf agree with the lamb, than to make all chronologers agree about the age of the world."[17] Isaac Newton devoted the last twenty years of his life to the problem, trying to use astronomical calculations to give absolute ages to events such as eclipses recorded in the ancient texts. His last book, published posthumously in 1728, was entitled *The Chronology of Ancient Kingdoms Amended,* and in it he argued, as a devout Christian, that the Scriptures were the oldest document of mankind, against which all other heathen chronologies were to be tested, and he also reaffirmed a chronology for the world of 4,000 years B.C.E.[18]

I find it interesting that Las Casas appeared before Charles V only two years before the publication of Copernicus's *De revolutionibus orbium celestium.* In the work of the great astronomers and physicists of the period, the earth was removed from the center of the universe, and in Newton's laws, a set of physical relationships between matter and motion had been proposed that were true in a spatially infinite world. Yet these very same people, for deep religious reasons, were intellectually entirely locked into a narrow constraint of time, derived not from any experiment or testing against nature, but from the authority of the written word. This straitjacket was to inhibit any serious investigations into the deep human past until the middle of the nineteenth century, and within some fundamentalist Christian communities it still does.

AMERICANS AS EXEMPLARS OF THE PAST

The impact of descriptions and illustrations of American Indians on the European consciousness was enormous and touched on every aspect of literature and thought.[19] In Britain comparisons were quickly made between their physical appearance, styles of body decoration, or artifacts with the putative state of the Ancient Britons. Martin Frobisher abducted some Nugumuit Eskimos from South Baffin Island, and these were later "exhibited" in Bristol in 1577. The artist John White was a member of this expedition and made watercolor drawings of them. These were seen by the antiquary William Camden, author of *Britannia,* who, referring to the blue paint on their faces, made the first direct comparison between Inuit body decoration and that recorded by Tacitus for the Ancient Britons. These analogies were developed further with White's drawings of southeastern Algonquin Indians when he was the artist on Walter Raleigh's Virginia expedition of 1585. In Theodor De Bry's *America* of 1590, engravings of these were used to illustrate not only Thomas Harriot's account of "the new found land of Virginia," but also in a separate section of what were claimed to be pictures of the Picts which "show how that the inhabitants of the great Bretannie have been in times past as savage as those of Virginia."[20] This definitive ethnographic comparison was greatly to influence subsequent depictions of the inhabitants of pre-Roman Britain, and soon genuine archaeological details such as twisted torques and globular bronze spear butts were combined to form a composite image, as in Speed's Ancient British man and woman in his *Historie of Great Britaine* (1611).

By the mid seventeenth century, the indigenous peoples of the Americas were routinely seen as exemplars of ancient society, and metaphors drawn from their ethnography were used to illustrate what were believed to have existed in earlier states of human society. Hobbes with his famous dismal view in the *Leviathan* (1651) of the state of primitive life as being unpleasant and short was followed by the observation that "the savage people in many places of America . . . live at this day in that brutish manner, as I said before."[21] Perhaps the most lasting metaphor was John Locke's in his *Second Treatise on Government* (1690); when discussing the origins of private property, he considered the situation at the beginning of human society when land was held in common and it was in the same condition as "the wild woods and uncultivated waste of America." It was only later with increase of population and the need to define boundaries that land was enclosed, and that "As much Land as a Man Tills, Plants, Improves, Cultivates, and can use the product of, so much is his Property. He by his labour does as it were, inclose it from the Common." His memorable phrase, "Thus in the beginning all the world was America," was profoundly to influence the later Enlightenment thinkers in their "conjectural histories" and progressive universalist schemes for human development.[22]

THE BEGINNING OF AMERICAN ARCHAEOLOGY

It was only within the fourth decade of the nineteenth century that archaeology began to develop its own systematic procedures for investigating the preliterate past from a study of the material remains of human actions and associated stratigraphic contexts. Largely from the work of Danish scholars on classifying museum collections and carrying out pioneering excavations in burial mounds and from within bogs, came the structure of the "Three Age System," with its successive periods of the Stone, Bronze, and Iron ages, defined according to characteristic artifacts, and seriated into a chronological series, supported by the field evidence. C. J. Thomsen's pioneering guide to the Copenhagen Museum was translated into English by Lord Ellesmere in 1848, under the title of *A Guide to Northern Archaeology,* and J. J. A. Worsaae's *Danmarks Oltid* (1843) was published in English in 1849 as *The Primeval Antiquities of Denmark.*[23] These profound developments stimulated direct archaeological surveys, excavations, and artifact typological studies in North America.

The first synthesis was Samuel Haven's *Archaeology of the United States,* published in 1856, just before the Civil War. This was significant since one of the burning issues of the day was that of polygenesis, or speculations about "pre-Adamite" man, whereby it was argued that the different races of man had been separately created by God. Louis Agassiz, as an extreme "splitter" in his concept of species, was a leading supporter of this view.[24] In terms of the issue of the antiquity of the peopling of the Americas, there was a political paradox: on the one hand, commentators from the slave-owning South tended to have less problems in supporting a high antiquity, since this would imply that the first ancestors of the American Indians had been on the continent before the time of the garden of Eden; and if Americans and Europeans were separate, so also the Africans. On the other hand, many scholars from the emancipationist North, who one might in the contemporary context regard as "progressive," argued strongly for a short chronology, since the more recent the time that people had got into the New World, the more likely it would be that all humans were closely related.[25] Haven admitted that his aim was "to record, not to reconcile opinions," a view endorsed by Lubbock, and archaeological data played a relatively minor part in his synthesis.[26] Nevertheless, he took a strong stand on the polygenesis issue, dismissing it; and also on the other critical question, namely, the ethnic identity of the Mound Builders.

A series of large mounds and other earth works had been found in the upper Mississipi and Ohio valleys, including the massive site of Cahokia, a short distance south of St. Louis, and these were the subject of a major survey by Squier and Davis published by the Smithsonian Institution in a 300-page monograph in 1847. The central question raised by these sites was not only their age but also the fact that they had been discovered on the river plains where the French and British had encountered only small-scale, mobile hunting and gathering Indian groups. As to their antiquity, the great British geologist Charles Lyell had visited the United States in 1841 and had inspected some of these mounds where he was shown a tree growing from the top of one, which when it had been cut showed eight hundred years of tree ring growth.[27] No less than a president of the United States (1841), General Harrison, made the ecologically prescient observation that, when discovered, these mounds were clothed in a complex vegetation of trees. Only "after a great number of centuries (several thousand years perhaps), that remarkable diversity of species characteristic of North America, and far exceeding what is seen in European forests, would be established" (p. 41). Having established a high antiquity for these mounds, the fundamental question still remained as to whether or not they had been built by Native Americans. A view developed that these mounds were the works of an ancient and lost civilization, far beyond the cultural capacities of the contemporary Indians or their ancestors; perhaps even some lost tribe of Israel. To counter this there was direct testimony from the archaeological record that pottery fragments and other artifacts found in the mounds were similar to those made by recent and contemporary Indians of the region. There was a unity also in the agricultural system which had supported the Mound Builders, based as it was on the American cultigens of maize and sunflowers. Haven's conclusion was that the culture of the Mound Builders was related to Meso-American societies and that they "differ less in kind than in degree from other remains concerning which history has not been entirely silent," a view endorsed by latter commentators.[28]

The émigré Scottish archaeologist Daniel Wilson, inventor in 1851 of the term "prehistory,"[29] took up a post as Professor of History at the University College of Toronto, and in 1857 established there an honors course on "ancient and modern ethnology," believed to be the first anthropology course in any English-language university. He carried out fieldwork on prehistoric copper workings on Lake Superior, on the American mounds, and also ethnographic studies with the Ojibwa. In 1862, he published the first edition of his major work *Prehistoric Man,* which was subtitled *"Researches into the Origin of Civilisation in the Old and the New World."* Within it many chapters were devoted to north and central America, including extended accounts of the Mound Builders, and linguistic and physical anthropological evidence. This was a genuine attempt at a world prehistory, the first ever written, and it sought to integrate the archaeological and ethnographic evidence from the Americas with that of Europe, central Asia, and elsewhere. It also was a product of its day, with a formally stadial view of cultural progression that he explicitly outlined a quarter of a century later in his contribution on "archaeology" for the *Encyclopaedia Britannica,* that "Everywhere man seems to have passed through the same progressive stages"; yet the evolutionists also advocated the unity of the human race since this alone is "consistent with the physical, mental, and moral characteristics common to savage and civilised man whether we study him amid the traces of palaeolithic osteology and arts, or among the most diverse races of living men."[30] Concerning the question as to the antiquity of humans in the New World, Wilson in 1865 wrote that "The Red Man it thus appears is among the ancients of the earth. How old he may be is impossible to determine, but among one American school of ethnologists, no historical antiquity is sufficient for him."[31]

PLEISTOCENE MAN

The publication of Darwin's *Origin of Species* in 1859 smashed the confines of the Genesis chronology. Within four years Lyell had published his

Geological Evidences of the Antiquity of Man, an American edition of which was published in the same year. Evidence was presented for past glacial periods, which extended back in time perhaps a million years or so within the Pleistocene period, a term that Lyell himself had proposed in 1839. These consisted of glacial moraines, till deposits formed on the edges of ice sheets, wind-blown loess, river terraces, and the evidence for sculpting of mountain cirques and ice gouging of rocks, et cetera. The Ice Age theory had been pioneered by the Swiss geologist Louis Agassiz in his *Studies on Glaciers* of 1840, and he would later make a name for himself as a founder of the teaching of natural sciences at Harvard, though he went to his deathbed denying Darwin's theory of evolution.

Evidence for humans as toolmakers in the form of flaked stone artifacts of various types, were shown to exist stratigraphically both in what was called the "drift" and also in cave deposits. Hand axes were found in Pleistocene sands and gravels within the valleys of the Somme as had been proposed by Boucher de Perthes in 1847 and confirmed by a famous visit of the British geologists Prestwich and Flower to the type sites at Amiens and St. Acheul in 1859. Within cave deposits in Belgium and Devon, stone artifacts had been found securely stratified with the bones of extinct animals, often sealed by thick layers of stalagmite—the species themselves sometimes indicating colder conditions, and in other levels a warmer climate. And finally from the caves of Engis in Belgium and Neanderthal in Germany, the skulls of the Pleistocene peoples themselves were found. Soon the "old stone age" or Paleolithic as proposed by Lubbock, would become subdivided into a series of successive cultures, the Acheulean, Mousterian, Aurignacian, and so on. And then came the realization that the Mousterian and earlier industries had been manufactured by Neanderthal man, a fossil human physically distinctive from modern *Homo sapiens.* The "descent of man," as Darwin had put it, extended back in an unbroken biological line to the other primates and to the rest of the animal kingdom. In the Old World, there was now evidence to show that human antiquity had to be measured in terms of hundreds of thousands of years.

The same question was soon asked in the New World. Lyell had devoted a chapter to glacial evidence in North America, where he said between the arctic circle and the 42nd parallel of latitude, there was evidence "of ice action on a scale as grand if not grander than in Europe," and that there were fossil remains of extinct animals such as the mastodon, indicating different climatic conditions.[32] While digging an excavation for a gas works near New Orleans in the 1840s, workers were reported to have found a human skeleton sixteen feet below the surface under four buried swamp beds. Dr. B. Dowler, who reported the find, considered the cranial features to be those of a Native American and proposed an age of some 50,000 years for it.[33] In another part of the Mississippi basin near Natchez, a human

pelvic bone associated with bones of mastodon and megalonyx were supposed to have been washed out of an alluvium from a depth of some thirty
feet. Lyell visited both sites in 1846 and made a detailed examination of the
deposits there. At Natchez he also found fossil bones of mastodon, megalonyx, and within the genera of *equids* and *bovids*, some extinct and some living species. Lyell concluded from geological evidence that the loam itself
and the fossil bones could be more than 100,000 years in age. He also
inspected the human bone and saw it to be of the same dark color as the others. However, he concluded that since it had never been seen *in situ*, and that
bones from Indian graves dug into the top peaty soil were often stained
black from the humus, there was a possibility that it had just fallen in from
the surface and been mixed up with the other fossils. Because of these critical uncertainties in the light of its potential significance as indicating "that
North America was peopled more than a thousand centuries ago by the
human race," Lyell judiciously returned a Scotch verdict of "not proven."[34]
The same went for a series of other claims, including human bones said to
have been associated with a raised coral reef in Florida and dated by Agassiz
to be about 10,000 years old.[35]

Nevertheless, the question was now an open one, and some workers
attempted to search into glacial gravels analogous to the European ones.
Perhaps the most serious claims were those of C. C. Abbott, a retired physician, who in 1872 claimed to have found Paleolithic implements from gravels
at Abbott Farm situated on the Delaware River bluff near Trenton, New
Jersey. Artifacts made from argillite, a metamorphosed mudstone, were
believed by him to be typologically similar to European Paleolithic tools, and
he also claimed to have found these within the "Trenton gravels," an outwash
of the last glaciation. He proposed that these were not the work of Indian
peoples who had arrived later, but of an earlier occupation by Paleolithic
man somewhat related to the Eskimo.[36] The thesis of Abbott's *Stone Age in
New Jersey* was supported by F. W. Putnam, the second director of the
Peabody Museum in Harvard, which financed its own long-term project here
run by Ernest Volk. The museum's archive store holds the large Abbott collection, which was placed on exhibition at the Peabody, arranged by Abbott
into his three cultures; the "paleolithic," the intermediate, and the modern
Indian. This body of evidence ran into heavy controversy that dragged on for
twenty-five years, involving European as well as American scholars. The critiques involved the validity of the typological comparisons; whether or not
the artifacts were genuinely *in situ* within the gravels, or had been washed
into slip deposits; and finally whether or not some were in fact humanly made
as opposed to being formed by natural processes in the gravels. Some of the
debate resembled the contemporary "eolith controversy" for Tertiary man in
Europe. The meeting of the American Association for the Advancement of
Science at Detroit in 1897 came to a general conclusion that the claims of a

glacial "Palaeolithic man" could not be maintained, though protagonists continued the debate with increasing acrimony for several years.[37]

By the beginning of this century, a deep reaction had set in due to the inconclusive or irreproducible nature of the evidence. It became asserted that there were no claims for a high antiquity for the peopling of the Americas. This view was led by Ales Hrdlicka from the Smithsonian, the leading American physical anthropologist of his day. Hrdlicka argued from osteological evidence that people had got to the Americas quite recently, and he proposed a date of no earlier than 1,000 B.C.E. Any dissent from that view was severely criticized, often with ridicule. The subject of early humans in America had become effectively taboo.

THE FOLSOM COWBOY

George McJunkin was born a slave in 1851 on a ranch in Midway, Texas. His father, a blacksmith and skilled farrier, carried the name Shoeboy. Working for cowboys in the spare time that was not due to his owner, he earned enough money to buy his freedom, and henceforth was called Mr. Shoeboy. George was freed by Union forces at age 14 on June 19, 1865, a date that he never forgot. He stayed three more years on the ranch where he learned to ride with Mexican *vaqueros* who worked on a neighboring outfit, and it was from them that he became fluent in Spanish. At the age of 17, he took part in one of the great cattle drives to Dodge City, Kansas, and assumed the surname of his old owner, John McJunkin. In those days it was dangerous to be a lone black man riding a horse, since accusations of theft or gratuitous racial thuggery could easily lead to a lynching. He went west, finally settling in the Dry Cimarron Valley in northeastern New Mexico, which in the Civil War had sided with the Union. He fell in love with this country, which, with its racially mixed population of Indians, Hispanics, and Anglos, had greater civil tolerance of a working black man than was the case in Texas, with its Jim Crow Laws. The word *cimarron,* too, was a Mexican Spanish name for a domestic animal that had run away—but with another layered meaning: it had been used in Texas to refer to a slave who had striven for freedom, had run away, had gone wild.[38] McJunkin eventually became foreman of the Crowfoot Ranch, situated near the small town of Folsom, and he gained the reputation of being one of the best cowboys in the county, with many Anglo and Hispanic station hands working under him. Once when he and a white cowboy named Gay Mellon went to a hotel in nearby Clayton to eat a formal lunch, they were told that the hotel did not serve blacks. Mellon took out his Colt 45 revolver, and pointing it at the manager, and said softly "Your policy has just been changed."[39]

Folsom was founded as a construction camp for the Denver, Texas, and Fort Worth Railroad in 1888. Its original name, Ragtown, was changed in honor of local girl Frances Folsom, who married President Cleveland in the White House. Now past its economic prime, Folsom, with its deep verandahs, its creaky wind pumps, and extensive backyards with corrugated iron sheds, reminds one of countless small Australian towns on the ends of rail sidings, out on the banks of the Darling River, or at the edge of wheat in South Australia. The landscape, with a 6,400-foot elevation and a semi-arid climate, has broad, sweeping, open valleys under yellow grass in summer and high hills with dark green woodland vegetation and bears an extraordinary resemblance to the Western Slopes or to the Monaro of New South Wales.

McJunkin was no ordinary cowboy. He was a fiddler of great skill, and he learned to read from the two sons of one of the ranchers he had worked for, in exchange for teaching them the skills of riding and roping. He was given a telescope by a U.S. army lieutenant that he had saved from an ambush by three outlaws, and he kept this in a scabbard on his saddle on the opposite side of his rifle. With the telescope he spotted cattle brands by day and looked at the stars by night. He read avidly, especially on subjects of natural history, and possessed a small library that included a Bible, books of geology, star maps, and an encyclopedia. From the latter he learned to manufacture small instruments to measure such phenomena as wind speed, and he was a skilled surveyor with a compass transit, often being asked to do boundary surveys for neighboring ranchers. Over the years he made a collection of stone artifacts, fossil bones, and a prehistoric Indian skull that were assembled as in a museum on the mantelpiece over the fireplace in his home, where he lived alone.

In 1908 there was an enormous flash flood that washed away half the town and drowned seventeen people. McJunkin, then aged 57, as part of breaking in a horse called Kalicrates, went to what he had called the Wild Horse Arroyo, since many of the brumbies went there, and found that it had torn an eight-foot-deep gully, smashing a barbwire fence. While fixing this, McJunkin noticed a bone exposed at its base. With a pair of wire clippers, he scraped the earth from around this bone. He recognized that these bones were of extinct animals, which, while resembling those of a bison, were much larger.[40] He returned to the site repeatedly and found more bones. Soon it became known locally as "McJunkin's bone pit." Reading *Deuteronomy,* which was his favorite book in the Bible, he noted the text "Giants dwelt therein in olden time, and the Ammonites call them Zamzummins" (Deut. 2:20); Increase Mather would have understood. A lighting bolt destroyed his log cabin and burned his entire collection. As an old and ailing man, he went to live in the Folsom Hotel, a square stone structure which still stands, and where his cowboy mates fed him raw bootleg whiskey which they fixed up with rubber tubing that allowed him to sip it from his bed. He died there in 1922, and his coffin was lowered to his grave on the lariats of his companions.

THE FOLSOM SITE

McJunkin wrote several letters about his finds, both to Carl Schwachheim, a blacksmith and amateur fossil bone collector in the nearby town of Raton, and also to F. Howarth, a local banker. In those days it would have required a two-day horse ride from Raton to Folsom, thirty miles away. Some six months after McJunkin's death, they decided to visit McJunkin's pit—aided by Howarth's purchase of a motor car, which reduced the travel time to that of an afternoon's outing—and from the site obtained a sackfull of bones. In 1926 Howarth wanted to deliver cattle to the stockyard in Denver, so he and Schwachheim took these bones to what was then called the Colorado Museum of Natural History. They entered the office of its director, Jesse D. Figgins, who recognized the bones as being those of an extinct Pleistocene bison *(Bison antiquus)*. Figgins was extremely interested in the site, particularly since he was one of the few scientists of his day who still believed in the possibility of Pleistocene man in America, and concerning a previous excavation report, had been savagely criticized by Hrdlicka for it. In March 1926 Figgins organized an excavation at the bone pit, with his son Frank and Schwachheim (p. 140). Under four to thirteen feet of clay and gravel, they uncovered a series of almost intact skeletons of the giant bison. They also discovered several bifacially flaked projectile points within the loose soil matrix. Figgins suggested that this was evidence that humans had killed the bisons, but critics dismissed the claims, saying that the artifacts were out of context and might have rolled into the deposit from a higher level. On July 14, Frank Figgins made the critical find of a projectile point fragment *in situ* in the clay that surrounded a rib of one of the animals. The solid block of matrix with these finds still in position was sent intact to the Museum at Denver, and the find was published by Jesse Figgins in *Natural History* in 1927. Hrdlicka was still not satisfied, and he criticized Figgins for not having invited other scientists to the site to see the evidence directly in the ground, the implication being that there had been some sort of incompetence.

Work at the site continued and, on August 29, 1927, Carl Schwachheim made the discovery that was to transform American archaeology. His field journal for that day reads, "I found an arrow point this morning, it is of a clear agate or jasper . . . It is not exposed the full length but is hollow on the sides . . . The point was near a rib in the matrix . . . Sent a letter to the boss today" (p. 143). What he had found was one of the distinctive points *in situ,* embedded in the matrix between the rib bones of a bison. All work at the site stopped, and Figgins telegraphed the leading institutions, inviting them to send representatives to view the evidence. Three responded, and they were all convinced of the genuine association of artifacts and the extinct animals and presented this conclusion at the next American Anthropological Association meeting. Yet entrenched views are not easily swayed: when Harold Cook, geologist at the Colorado Museum, published

The original Folsom Point, made from agate, discovered by Carl Schwachheim on August 29, 1927, at George McJunkin's "bone pit," in the Wild Horse Arroyo, Crowfoot Ranch near Folsom, New Mexico. Photograph by Rhys Jones, made available by Dr. Jim Dixon, Denver Museum of Natural History. Scale in centimeters.

a report on the discovery in *Scientific American* in 1928, the journal carried an editorial disclaimer for "claims concerning the proof of the antiquity of man in America."[41] Further excavations at the site by a joint American Museum of Natural History and Colorado Museum expedition finally clinched the argument.

PALEO-INDIANS

Once the conceptual dam had been breached, it was as if a floodgate was opened. Within a few years, dozens of parallel sites were quickly discovered, especially in New Mexico and along the Colorado Front Range of the Rocky Mountains.[42] Collectively they document the culture referred to as the Paleo-Indians. These people were mobile, big game hunters, and they lived off herds of species now mostly extinct on open plains at a time corresponding to the very end of the Pleistocene.[43] The distinctive bifacial Folsom points are delicately made with pressure flaking. They are about two inches long, thin, leaf-shaped, and with concave bases. A characteristic feature was the removal of a longitudinal flake on each face, so as to produce a fluted, hollow cross section. Folsom sites are usually associated with bison.

Clovis is situated in New Mexico near the border with Texas in an arid region of the *llanos estacados;* the "staked plains," so named by Francisco de Coronado on his journey in 1541, because on that vast flat landscape he set out a line of sticks so that he could find his way back. Here there are numerous old dry basins hollowed out by wind. In 1933 at one of these called Blackwater Draw, a different type of stone projectile point was found in association with mammoth bones.[44] Clovis points are long, bifacially flaked, lanceolate points, but they lack major fluting except close to their concave bases. Their makers hunted mammoth, and they were the direct antecedents of the Folsom people. Recent precise radiocarbon dating has established the age of Folsom to be between 10,250 and 10,950 years old, whereas Clovis is between 10,900 and 11,200 years old.[45] Until very recently it has been strongly argued that Clovis people were the first arrivals in North America, and the timing of this coincided with the melting of the ice sheets, allowing a corridor of access from the region of the Bering Straits and Alaska.[46] Paleo-Indians, using a variety of styles of projectile points, quickly occupied most of the continent. Finds as far south as the shores of the Straits of Magellan by about ten thousand years ago indicate an extremely rapid process of colonization. The sites are associated in time with the cascading collapse of the late Pleistocene megafauna, and a persuasive argument has been made that this process of extinction was at least partly caused by the explosive impact of the human predators with their advanced technology of hunting.[47]

The search for pre-Clovis sites has been an enduring theme of the past half century, with most claims eventually discarded. A site that might change this is at Monte Verde in southern Chile, where T. D. Dillehay has recently dated an occupation site to 12,500 years B.C.E. The authenticity of the site and of its artifacts were the subject of a field inspection in January 1997, led by a group of scientists including some of the foremost skeptics, in an event with evocations of the Folsom event seventy years earlier. It seems that the skeptics may be satisfied, and the implications of this are not just that a thousand years has been added to the chronology but also that being situated so far south, the site has implications for the rest of the continent.[48] Also, the economy seems to have been a broad-based one with plant food and wooden artifacts. In the Brazilian Amazon, recent evidence from Caverna da Pedra Pintada indicates the presence in a humid tropical environment of a broad-based economy of plant foraging, fishing, and collecting of small game such as turtles. Well dated to 10,500 years ago, this site was contemporaneous with the southwest U.S. Paleo-Indian sites.[49] Perhaps the Clovis were not the first people in America, and the distinctive big game hunting culture was one that developed internally within some regions of the Americas, rather than being brought in by the first colonists.

AUSTRALIA'S EMPTY LAND

The eighteenth-century voyages of discovery by Cook and French navigators into the Pacific and around the shores of Australia raised exactly the same kind of speculations as to origins and cultural status as had been the case with the Americas two hundred years previously. Samuel Johnson, in his tour of the Hebrides in 1775, now made use of an ethnographic analogy from the Pacific for prehistoric stone arrowheads found on the island and that locals believed were "elf bolts" used by fairies to shoot cattle. "They nearly resemble those which Mr. Banks has lately brought from the savage countries in the Pacific Ocean, and must have been made by a nation to which the use of metals was unknown." Almost a century previously, Edward Lhuyd, of the Ashmolean Museum in Oxford had made exactly the same kind of comparison but had referred to "the same chip'd flints the natives of New England head their arrows with at this day."[50] Some of the voyagers thought quite literally that with the Aborigines of Australia and Tasmania they were looking at the childhood of man. "The philosophical traveller who sails to the extremities of the earth," said the French Enlightenment scholar J.-M. Degérando in his ethnographic instructions to the voyage of Nicholas Baudin to map the shores of western and southern Australia in 1803, "traverses in effect the sequence of the ages: he travels into the past; each step he takes leaps a century."[51]

Cook's and Banks' description of the relationship of the Aborigines to the land followed classically Locke's definition of one of those "great Tracts of Ground . . . [which is] more than the people, who dwell on it, do, or can make use of, and so still lie in common." Joseph Banks saw the Aborigines as being randomly peripatetic, "wandering like Arabs from place to place"; they enclosed no land nor did they practice agriculture. To Cook, it was "in the pure state of Nature, the Industry of Man [having] nothing to do with it." This was according to eighteenth-century ideas, a *terra nullius,* a land belonging to no one, which could be possessed through proclamation followed by effective occupation; *quod nullius est, id ratione naturali occupanti conceditur,* "because it belongs to nobody, therefore natural reason concedes it to the [first] occupier" (Justinian's *Institutiones*). Having satisfied himself that no other European power had previously physically claimed this coast, Cook, just when he was about to leave it through Torres Strait in August 1770, took possession in the name of His Majesty George III. The establishment of the settlement of soldiers and convicts at Sydney, within a reasonable time period in 1788, asserted effective occupation, which confirmed possession. As an advisor to the Colonial Office put it in 1822, New South Wales was acquired by the British "neither by conquest nor cession, but by the mere occupation of a desert or uninhabited land."[52]

With the inland explorations of Australia in the middle of the nineteenth century, a subtle shift of attitude occurred in the way that the continent was perceived. From the optimistic mirage of Sturt's "inland sea," the reality was that the westward flowing rivers petered out into the ephemeral lakes and dunes of a great desert. The coastal debouchment of Spencer Gulf did not lead to a Mississippi, and even the Murray River ended its course in a brackish Lake Alexandrina, shielded from the sea by the Coorong, a hundred-kilometers-long barrier of sand. In 1827, when Sturt was carrying out the real job of the European discovery of the Murray, a fantasy map of the interior of Australia was produced in a book called *Friend of Australia,* by T. J. Maslen, an officer in the Indian survey corps who had never visited Australia but who drew some geographic speculations from reading the reports of explorers.[53] On his map he depicted a great drainage system, drawing its source from streams along the western slope of the Great Dividing Range from north Queensland to central New South Wales, and this flowed northwestward across the entire continent through what he optimistically called the "Delta of Australia," situated just north of present day Alice Springs. As the "Great River" or "The Desired Blessing," this putative stream had its mighty mouth in the region of King Sound near Derby in the northwest of Western Australia.[54] The reality was far harsher. John Eyre set off on his Northern Expedition from Adelaide in 1840, intending to cross the continent from south to north. Trying to negotiate past what seemed like an enfolding horseshoe of gigantic salt lakes, he wrote, looking at Lake Frome, that "on every side we were hemmed in by a barrier which we could never hope to pass," and gazing out at Lake Eyre, the prospect was "cheerless and hopeless," and he named his vantage point Mount Hopeless. It defined an image of a vast, harsh, and empty land.

THE LIVING STONE AGE

Within this dead red heart of the continent, there also lived people who were seen as an archetype for the origins of man. In 1894 the Horn Expedition set out from Adelaide for Central Australia, its aim to carry out fundamental scientific work in the fields of geology, botany, zoology, and also to study the culture of the Aboriginal peoples of the Center. In enlisting the services of Melbourne University zoologist Baldwin Spencer, and bringing him together with the telegraph postmaster at Alice Springs, Frank Gillen, a scholarly collaboration started which produced *The Native Tribes of Central Australia* in 1899, one of the great classics of the heroic age of anthropological literature.[55] Working with the Arunta (Arrente) people, they described something of the vast panoply of Aboriginal ritual—their concepts of the primal life forces that they believed had once made the world and that still exist in quiescence, to be brought out through human ceremonial acts. It was on the Horn expedition that the Aboriginal concept of the "Dreaming" was first introduced into English, via the Arunta word *Altyerre,* to dream.

> The natives explain that their ancestors in the distant past (*ulchurringa*), which really means in the dream-times, for this is the manner in which the natives always speak of the long ago, acquired the art of

urpmalla (fire making) from a gigantic *arrunga* (*Macropus robustus*)
... endowed with the gift of speech and while making fire chanted."[56]

Ironically, it was only the demonstration by Spencer and Gillen of the spec-
tacular artistic products of the Arunta that finally persuaded the French
archaeologists that the Upper Paleolithic people of Europe could also make
art, and thus authenticate the antiquity of the painted caves of Altamira.[57]
Yet we must also remember that the intellectual context of all of this
work was that Aborigines represented the survival of an ancient, perhaps the
most ancient, stage in human development. The leader of the expedition, W.
A. Horn, wrote in his introduction, "The central Australian aborigine is the
living representative of a stone age, who still fashions his spear-heads and
knives from flint or sandstone and performs the most daring surgical operations with them. His origin and history are lost in the gloomy mists of the
past . . . he has no private ownership of property . . . he cultivates nothing,
but lives entirely on the spoils of the chase . . . he builds no permanent habi-
tation and usually camps where night or fatigue overtakes him."[58] There was
also a view, which was regretted but deemed to be inevitable, that the
Aborigines would soon become extinct due to the selective forces of contact
with the outside world, that "Thanks to the untiring efforts of the missionary and the stockman, he is rapidly being 'civilized' off the face of the earth,
and in another hundred years the sole remaining evidence of his existence
will be the fragments of flint which he has fashioned so rudely" (p. *x*).
The Victorian naturalists A. R. Wallace and Thomas Huxley in their
writings had both assumed what they called a "geological" antiquity for the
Aborigines. Huxley considered that the peoples of the islands to the east and
south of the continent, such as parts of New Guinea, New Caledonia, and
Tasmania, had got there prior to a tectonic sinking of a putative land bridge
which he believed had connected them all together, and if this were so then
"the distribution of the Negroid and Australoid races of man is as strong evidence of his antiquity as the occurrence of his works in the gravels of Hoxne
and Amiens."[59] Huxley was also asked by Lyell to comment on the Engis and
Neanderthal skulls for his *Antiquity of Man.* Huxley compared the dimen-
sions and shapes of these ancient skulls with Australian Aboriginal ones. He
clearly cautioned that he was not making any specific relationships of a
racial nor ethnic nature, since the latter was to be measured by such factors
as skin color, hair, language, and so on. Yet he also felt that there was a
"marked resemblance between the ancient skulls and their modern
Australian analogues." This he considered had further implications when it
was remembered that

the stone axe is as much the weapon and the implement of the modern as of the ancient savage; that the former turns the bones of the

kangaroo and of the emu to the same account as the latter did the bones of the deer and the urus; that the Australian heaps up the shells of devoured shellfish in mounds which represent the . . . Kjokkenmoddings [kitchen middens] of Denmark; and finally, that on the other side of Torres Straits, a race akin to the Australians are among the few people who now build their houses on pile-works, like those of the ancient Swiss lakes."[60]

It might have been thought that this assumption of a deep past for the Australian Aborigines would have stimulated energetic programs of archaeological exploration on the continent. But with a few exceptions, this did not happen, as opposed to the contemporary situation in the United States.[61] An explanation for this paradox is partly due to the very assumption that lay behind the archetype; that as the living was a relict of the past, so also that past would be the same as the present. This was memorably stated by R. H. Pulleine at the 1928 Australian Association of the Advancement of Science meeting in Hobart, Tasmania, a year after Folsom, when he commented about the shell middens within the coastal caves at Rocky Cape, on the northwest coast of the island: "Here the Aborigines must have lived for ages . . . However it is to be feared that excavation would be in vain, as everything points to the conclusion that they were an unchanging people in an unchanging environment."[62] The Aborigines, representatives of the Stone Age, owning no land, living in a static country, in a strange way, also had no history.

TALGAI

In 1891 Eugene Dubois discovered fossil bones of a hominid on the banks of the Solo River, east Java, and he published this in Batavia in 1893. He described the fossil bones as *Pithecanthropus erectus,* "upright apeman," and believed that they represented of the "missing link" between ape and man that Darwin had postulated. This stimulated a belief at that time that the origins of man were to be found in the tropical region of southeast Asia rather than in Africa. Since Australia is geographically located only a few narrrow oceanic barriers southeast of the old low–sea level Sundaland continent, when Java was joined to the rest of mainland southeast Asia, there might be some chances of old finds there too.

East Talgai, a magnificent homestead built in 1868, is situated on the Darling Downs, rich agricultural country on a basalt soil in southeastern Queensland, and at the end of the last century it was owned by the Clark family. About 1884 William Naish, a contract fencer employed by the Clarks, was interrupted at work by an exceptional flood. Returning to the storm gully at Dalrymple Creek, he found that the water had exposed a carbonate encrusted human skull. For a long time it went unremarked, but after

The Talgai Skull from Darling Downs, southeast Queensland. Specimen in its original condition encrusted with a thick layer of calcium carbonate, as exhibited by Professor Edgeworth David at the Sydney Meeting of the British Association for the Advancement of Science, August 1914.

Dubois's discovery it reemerged, being described by the *Sydney Mail* in 1896 as "a petrified skull . . . a protruding jaw and low retreating forehead—indicates a nature of almost exclusively animal propensities," After a protracted period of negotiation with the owners, it was eventually acquired by the University of Sydney. At the eighty-fourth meeting of the British Association for the Advancement of Science, held in Sydney in August 1914, the significance of the skull was presented by the famous geologist and codiscoverer of the South Magnetic Pole on Shackleton's expedition, Professor Sir Edgeworth David. While acknowledging that the skull had been found adventitiously, it was also noted that it had the same degree of fossilization as the bones of the extinct giant marsupial *Diprotodon* found in adjacent parts of the Downs. A field visit to the site in the company of Naish persuaded David that "there is a strong possibility of this fossil being of Pleistocene age, perhaps early Pleistocene. . . Certainly it is far older than any Aboriginal skulls that have ever been obtained in Australasia, and it proves that in Australia man attained to geological antiquity."[63]

The first anatomical description of this skull was made by S. A. Smith in 1918, and he had the misfortune to become unwittingly ensnared by the Piltdown *Eoanthropus,* then the sensation of the age. He drew attention to what he thought were certain primitive characteristics in the dentition of Talgai by comparing them with Piltdown. Since that fraudulent composite skull had a mandible from an ape, it is not surprising that subsequent analyses of the Talgai teeth, including those by Dubois himself, did not confirm the claims for morphological primitivity. The significance of the skull became diminished, and excessively so according to the anatomist N. W. G. Macintosh, who reanalyzed it in the early 1960s, confirming its archaic physical character.[64]

In 1924 Edgeworth David assembled various types of evidence to propose that the human occupation of Australia went back to Pleistocene times. These consisted of finds of stone artifacts that supposedly had been made in gravels during alluvial tin mining operations; typological considerations; geomorphic evidence of raised beaches, fossil bone beds, and so forth; and biogeographic arguments concerning the arrival of the Tasmanian Aborigines on their island prior to the Post Glacial sea level rise, and the fact that the dingo, taken by man from Asia to Australia, was found throughout the continent but was absent in Tasmania. Soon, however, the brittle nature of the archaeological facts underlying the synthesis became apparent, and in a parallel with the American situation, a school of thought developed that argued that Aborigines had only been in Australia and Tasmania a few thousand years.[65]

In 1929 H. M. Hale and Norman Tindale of the South Australian Museum in Adelaide published their account of an excavation at the limestone rock shelter of Devon Downs on the banks of the lower Murray River. This, carried out to a high standard of stratigraphic control and analysis, was the first modern archaeological excavation in Australia. They proposed a sequence of three typologically defined "cultures" on the European model, Mudukian, Murundian, and Pirrian, which had small tools such as points and which extended back to mid Holocene times; and an older Tartangan, defined from artifacts dug from a nearby open site. Tindale later proposed a basal "culture," called Kartan, which he believed was of late Pleistocene age, based on similar biogeographical arguments as David had used, since core-tool and large flake artifacts of this type were found on Kangaroo Island off the present coast of South Australia. Mulvaney in 1961 subjected the archaeological validity of this sequence to critical scrutiny and the matter remained unresolved. Grahame Clark, from his Olympian perspective in Cambridge, concluded in the first edition of his *World Prehistory* in 1961 that "there is no convincing evidence for the immigration of man into Australia before Neothermal times."[66] Mulvaney, reviewing the state of knowledge in 1964, said that "Australia is the last inhabited continent to discover its prehistory and this provides an opportunity to learn from the errors of others."[67]

RADIOCARBON DATING

The critical new factor was a technical invention, itself a by-product of the Manhattan Project to build the atom bomb. An unstable isotope of carbon with an atomic weight of 14 had been created as a laboratory freak as far back as 1936, by irradiating nitrogen with slow neutrons.[68] During his research on the effects of cosmic rays on the outer atmosphere, it occurred to Willard Libby, then working at the Institute for Nuclear Studies at the University of Chicago, that carbon 14 was also being produced naturally in the outer atmosphere through the collision of cosmic ray neutrons on nitrogen atoms and, as carbon dioxide, would then enter the biosphere through plant photosynthesis.[69] To test this proposition, Libby carried out an experiment in, of all places, the Baltimore City sewage works, from which he obtained a sample of biogenic methane which was being sold as natural gas, and he compared the isotopes of carbon within this with another sample of methane obtained from petroleum. As predicted, the recent biogenic methane contained carbon 14, whereas the ancient methane did not. Since the half-life of carbon 14 was known to be about 5,500 years, it could be used as a method to date the time since death of commonly found materials within both archaeological and sedimentary contexts, such as wood, charcoal, and shells.

For this method to work with ancient samples, there was one further assumption that had to be tested, namely that the cosmic ray flux, and thus the rate of production of natural carbon 14 in the past, had been similar to the present situation. To test the method, the physicists turned to the archaeologists, who provided samples of material of known age. There was a piece of a wooden floor from a Hittite palace from Syria, a cedar fragment from an Egyptian funerary boat, and pieces of coffins from the collections of various American museums. In addition there were samples of dated tree rings. Libby and his coauthor, the chemist Jim Arnold, published their results in the December 1949 issue of *Science,* in what Grahame Clark called the "three-page article that was to shake the world."[70] It showed that the calculated carbon 14 results fitted closely to the historically known ages of the samples, and thus indicated that the basic assumptions of the radiocarbon age determination method were correct. Now there was a universal method which at one stroke gave archaeologists the ability to erect absolute and independent chronologies for their sites. It won for Libby a Nobel Prize, the only one ever awarded to archaeologically related research.

Yet this gift to archaeology might also have a double edge to it, as was presciently observed by Gordon Childe in his "Valediction" to archaeologists written in 1957 in Australia few weeks before he ended his own life in the Blue Mountains. Contemplating his own era in archaeological research with its cross-datings based on theories of cultural diffusion, he acknowledged that a more trustworthy chronology independent of any archaeological skills or historical assumptions may well have been provided by radiocarbon. Yet there was a downside that "archaeologists will abandon responsibility for chronology or themselves become nuclear physicists. In any case every prehistorian must master enough mathematics, physics and chemistry to appreciate the limitation of the information the latter can provide."[71]

Despite these chronological triumphs, it is also true that for much of the known prehistory of North America, and especially in Europe and the Middle East, radiocarbon tended either to confirm the existing chronologies or to change them only to a limited extent, as was the case with the dating of the Paleo-Indian sites. The age of the British Neolithic sites such as Stonehenge was extended by a factor of about a thousand years, which obviously had major ramifications in the details of regional prehistories, but which did not transform the entire picture. It is a credit to the rigor and autonomy of the traditional methods of archaeology that so much of the essential chronological edifice survived the radiocarbon examination.

PLEISTOCENE AUSTRALIANS

In Australia and neighboring regions of New Guinea and the western Pacific, radiocarbon was, however, to transform the field. In his 1961 synthesis, Mulvaney concluded that the oldest acceptable date in Australia was Tindale's date of 8,700 B.P. for stone artifacts in a coastal sand dune at Cape Martin, South Australia. The first breakthrough past the "Pleistocene barrier" of 10,000 years ago was made by John Mulvaney in 1962, when he obtained a date of 12,900 B.P. from a depth of seven feet from his excavation at Kenniff Cave in the southern Queensland highlands.[72] A year later he announced an older date of 16,000 years B.P. from further down the section at this site, with stone artifacts being located within older deposits.[73] These dates were measured at the National Physical Laboratory in Teddington, England, indicating the dependence of Australian archaeologists at that time on links with colleagues overseas. This changed with the establishment in the early 1960s of radiocarbon facilities within Australia itself, most notably in 1965 within the Australian National University under the direction of Henry Polach. By 1967 there were dates of about 20,000 years B.P. from the debris of underground flint mining in the huge underground Koonalda Cave on the vast arid Nullarbor Plain, with its limestone cliffs facing the Great Australian Bight. Similar ages were obtained from archaeological levels within sandstone rock shelters both on the coast of New South Wales, and importantly, from the Kakadu area of western Arnhem Land in the Northern Territory.[74] These latter sites, Malangangerr and Nawamoyn, excavated by Carmel Schrire, also presented a great surprise: in the basal layers there were small, beautifully fashioned edge-ground axes made out of volcanic or metamorphic rock, some with grooves on their sides presumably for hafting.[75] To have found the typologically-defining artifact of John Lubbock's "Neolithic" period, having a high antiquity within the continent of hunters was a pleasing paradox, made more so that at 22,000 years old, they were the oldest edge-ground tools in the world, being three times the age for similar tools associated with the earliest agriculture in the Middle East.

In Papua New Guinea, which prior to 8,000 years ago had been joined to tropical Australia as a single landmass due to glacial low-sea levels, parallel discoveries were being made. An open site at Kosipe dated to 26,000 years ago contained large lenticular core tools, some made on large cobbles and with opposed notches on their sides, referred to as "waisted blades." Similar tools were found in limestone rock shelters in the highlands of New Guinea, which have since been dated to the mid twenty thousands.[76] These tools were presumably used as hafted axe-adzes, possibly to ring-bark rainforest trees so as to break up the canopy and allow light to penetrate to the forest floor where so many of the food plants such as yams and other vines grow.[77] These were radical ideas concerning the possibilities of large-scale landscape manipulation being carried out by the late Pleistocene tropical peoples of New Guinea which led to increased food production, and which might have been the precursor to the horticulture of such plants as taro, yam, sago, and sugarcane. From the Kuk Swamp in the Wahgi Valley in the highlands, there was evidence for drainage associated with horticulture, the oldest system there being dated to about 9,000 years ago. Jack Golson made a broad comparison between the late Pleistocene edge-ground tools of northern Australia and New Guinea and similar ones from presumed late Pleistocene contexts from southeast Asia and Japan, concluding that the technology of grinding tools and stemming their sides for hafting them as axes had a high antiquity in this part of the world, a fact not previously recognized because of what he referred to as the "burden of Europe," whereby all typological developments had previously been seen as having to conform to the European model.[78] The new empirical data were smashing that nexus.

MUNGO

A critical discovery was made at Lake Mungo, a dry fossil lake bed in the arid zone of southwestern New South Wales. In 1968 geomorphologist Jim Bowler, working on the paleo-climatic history of the lake—based on studies of the long arcuate sand dune, called a "lunette" after the shape of a new moon, which was situated along its eastern edge—noticed a pile of burned bones heavily encrusted in calcium carbonate stratigraphically situated in one of the oldest units of the dune, which he had previously dated to between 26,000 and 30,000 years old. A field visit to this site by a combined group of archaeologists and geomorphologists in March 1969 proved to be one of the turning points of Australian prehistory.[79] The bone fragments were those of a human and, when later carefully removed from their carbonate and reconstructed by the anatomist Alan Thorne, were shown to be the calvaria of a young woman who had been cremated at this site; the bones having been smashed and then interred in a shallow pit. Morphologically, the skull was totally modern and gracile. Carbon-dated to 26,000–30,000 years ago, it was one of the oldest fully modern *sapiens* skulls in the world, and the evidence of cremation and subsequent burial indicated that the people of that time had religious ideas concerning death. Further research at this site showed a series of hearths with charred food remains in the core of the dune, indicating that the people fished for golden perch and Murray cod and collected mussels from the lake edge; and from the desert scrub behind, they collected emu eggs and a range of small marsupial game.

Flaked stone artifacts made from fine quality siliceous quartzite consisted of distinctive dome-shaped core tools called "horsehoof cores" with steep retouch around their perimeters and a variety of steep-edged scrapers formed with noses and notches for probable use as spokeshaves. These tools had such typological similarity to other Pleistocene assemblages across the continent including Tasmania and also New Guinea, that Harry Allen and I proposed a broad classification of the "Australian core-tool and scraper tradition"; the concept of "tradition" following the sense proposed by Harvard's Gordon Willey and Phillip Phillips in their influential *Method and Theory in American Archaeology.*[80] Despite its antiquity, ranking with that of the early Upper Paleolithic of western Europe, every aspect of the Mungo site also seemed to indicate fully modern human behavior. Indeed, in my analysis of the economic and cultural aspects of the site, I was consciously comparing the archaeological evidence against the ethnographic record, and apart from the absence of seed grinding technology, there seemed to be little of the behavior of the people at Mungo 26,000 years ago that was not consistent with that of their presumed distant descendants within the same region at the time of British contact. I am fully aware of the great danger in erecting a monolithic unchanging past for Aboriginal people and of uncritically imposing an ethnographic model as opposed directly to investigate the past through archaeological means. However, I have also felt that there were broad patterns of historical continuity on a continental scale linking the ethnographically observed Aboriginal societies to the earliest archaeological record, when even by 30,000 years ago "the distinctive Australian economy was already in train and that the major adaptations to the continent had been made."[81]

There were many profound changes within past Aboriginal societies, in particular those associated with the rapid spread of the Pama-Nyungan languages over most of the continent, except for western Arnhem Land and the Kimberleys about 5,000 years ago, which may be associated with changes in stone tool technology such as hafted points and are marked by changes in rock art styles.[82] Yet I believe that these developments were grounded on a core cultural system that probably had its roots in the Pleistocene.

Mungo was also important because geomorphological research was indicating that vastly different climatic conditions had occurred during the time that people had lived there. Some 30,000 years ago, before the last glacial maximum, the lake was full due to greatly wetter conditions in Australia than exist at present. Then, as the last ice age intensified, 18,000 years ago, Australia was much drier than now, with great counterclockwise winds reactivating the continental desert dunes and driving sand as far east as Canberra and even over the Great Dividing Range into the upper reaches of the Shoalhaven River which flows to the Pacific. This revelation of the past climatic history of Australia was occurring at exactly the same time as the unveiling of a deep human history, the two processes often going hand in hand within joint research projects. There was an interesting symbiosis that whereas the natural scientists from their research could create past landscapes, the archaeologists populated these with human witnesses. Mungo Lady, as she is referred to by the Barkunji people, whose traditional lands encompass the site, would have seen the shining waters of the lake ruffled by the westerly winds that blew up sand to form the dune on which she and her people lived.

Soon older dates were obtained from other sites in the Mungo lunette— the discovery of an extended burial of a man whose body in the grave had been covered with fine red ochre powder was dated to about 32,000 years ago[83]; shell middens were found that also dated to 37,000 years, and within the Mungo stratigraphic unit itself, stone artifacts were discovered *in situ* at a depth of over a meter below the original finds and with a small carbon sample that gave a value of about 40,000 years ago, although the sample size itself was very small.[84] Similar orders of antiquity were soon obtained from several sites situated in widely separated parts of the continent.[85]

NAPIER RANGE, THE KIMBERLEYS

At present the oldest conventional radiocarbon date for any archaeological site in Australia comes from Carpenter's Gap on the Napier Range in the southern Kimberley region of northwestern Australia. The Napier Range itself consists of a fossilized coral barrier reef of the Devonian age extending east-west over a distance of several hundred kilometers like a great pink and light gray vertical wall of fluted limestone about a kilometer wide, situated some twenty kilometers south of the edge of the King Leopold Range, which at that time formed the mainland for this fringing reef. Behind it is the Kimberley Massif consisting of Archaean rocks, with the oldest surface landscape in the world. Splitting the Napier Range at intervals are vertical-sided gorges such as Windjana Gorge, on the walls of which the structure of the original coral reef can clearly be seen. This is where Jandamarra, or "Pigeon," a local Bunuba man, led his armed revolt in the 1890s against the colonists who had brought their cattle up and established vast properties in the region. He had been a mounted police trooper himself during the bloody punitive reprisals that were carried out in response to spearing of cattle and raids on homesteads. "It would be a good time," editorialized the *North West Times* in March 1894, "for the Western Australian Government to shut its eyes for say three months and let the settlers up here have a little time to teach the nigger the difference between mine and thine . . . it would only have to be done once, and once done, could easily be forgotten."[86] Jandamarra shot dead his police sergeant in the doorway of Lillimooloora Station and fled with rifles to the range where he led an armed revolt, ambushing many police parties. He was eventually shot dead in a cave by one of his fellow kinsmen for having transgressed traditional rules of marriage law. Bunuba men today are the stockmen and drovers of the vast cattle stations of the Fitzroy River district. "They used to lasso calves just like you see cowboys do. We'd bronco them in the open in those days."[87] This is true McJunkin country.

The Carpenter's Gap site is a huge limestone rock shelter situated three kilometers from Windjana Gorge and was used on occasion by Jandamarra. Excavations by Susan O'Connor in 1994 obtained two accelerator mass spectrometer (AMS) carbon dates of 39,200 and 39,700 years ago from the base of one of her units associated with artifacts, and there were also stone artifacts within a stratigraphically distinct unit underlying this.[88]

TO THE LIMITS OF RADIOCARBON DATING

It seemed at one time that every year's research within the late 1970s would add another few thousand years to the antiquity of people on Australia. But this did not happen, rather a plateau appeared at about 35,000 to 37,000 years ago. Dates of that order of antiquity were obtained from many parts of the Australian continent, but further increases in antiquity were no longer attained.[89] A recent systematic review of the data by Smith and Sharp has indicated that there are now 170 sites in the region with human occupation having been dated to greater than 10,000 years.[90] Geographically, this region encompassed not only Tasmania and Papua New Guinea but also truly oceanic islands never joined to the Sahul continent such as New Britain, New Ireland, and the northern Solomons, all of which had Pleistocene occupation. Its latitudinal range from the equator to 42 degrees south is the same span as that from Boston to the Amazon. The limits of the prehistory of a continent had been attained, but what was its chronological limit?

The problem lay with the radiocarbon method itself, the very tool that had unlocked this history. Because of the nature of the exponential decay curve, at about 35,000 years old, only one percent of the original radiocarbon still exists. If one were to mix Carboniferous coal which has a zero signal with only one percent of modern carbon, then the counting machine will give a value for this at about 37,000 years old. Whereas the physics of counting is now so good that, theoretically, machines can be built that measure ages back to 50,000 years ago, the problem is one of the reality of the field conditions where most carbon samples are contaminated to a tiny extent, for example, with humic acids, or with fine particles having been carried down through the deposit, and so on. Effectively, there is a wall beyond which samples that in fact might be hundreds of thousands of years old all seem to give the same age at the order of 35,000–40,000 years. Here then was a conundrum: were we to interpret the array of dated sites as indicating that humans arrived in Australia at about 35,000–40,000 years ago, as the archaeologist Jim Allen has argued, or was this simply an artifact of the limitations of our dating method, which is what I suspected?[91]

I remember vividly being faced with this issue one afternoon in the dry season of 1981 while standing in the trench of an excavation at Nauwalabila, a sandstone rock shelter situated under the towering cliffs of Deaf Adder Gorge in Kakadu, Northern Territory. In front of me was a three-meter-deep section of sand within which there were stone artifacts within every level including a basal rubble. Charcoal persisted only to about two-thirds of the way down, where dates of about 25,000 years had been obtained, but beneath this there were artifacts that I could not date.[92] From other indications such as the degree of weathering on their surfaces, I guessed that they were old, but at that time I felt that I would never live to know how old.

BOYLE'S BELLY AND THE SHINING DIAMOND

A novel dating technique had, however, just been invented, and it was based on a phenomenon first described by Robert Boyle in 1663. Diamond merchants had noticed that diamonds, when heated, glowed for a brief period. Once this had happened, they never glowed again, and there was a certain mysticism associated with it, as if the stone, like the mythical *schwanengesang*, had one last song. Boyle obtained a diamond and described how he went to bed in a darkened room and placed it on his naked belly, totally covering himself with sheets. As the diamond slowly warmed with his body heat, he observed a pale light like that of a glow worm for about twenty minutes, which finally slowly faded away. On the following day, he read these results before the Royal Society as "Some observations about a diamond that shines in the dark."[93] He had discovered the phenomenon of thermoluminescence (TL).

LUMINESCENCE DATING

When a grain of quartz sand becomes buried, natural radiation displaces electrons into metastable traps within its crystal lattice. The longer the grain is buried, the more electrons are displaced until all of the traps become filled and the grain is then said to be "saturated." However, if this grain of sand becomes exposed to sunlight or is heated, the traps are emptied. The exposed sand is said to be "bleached," and the luminescence "clock," as it were, has been set to zero. If the sand is buried again, the quartz crystals once more accumulate trapped electrons. To measure the age of the deposit, two values have to be known: first, the total radiation dose within the sand grain that has been acquired since burial, called the "paleodose"; and second, the ionizing dose delivered to the sample from the surrounding soil together with any cosmic rays, called the "dose rate." In simple terms, the age of the sample since it was last exposed to sunlight is thus calculated as the paleodose divided by the dose-rate. Samples are collected in the field by driving small tubes into the deposit section and making sure that the sand in the tubes remains unexposed to sunlight by shielding the tube ends with black plastic. The dose rate is measured in the field using a gamma spectrometer and later measured again in the laboratory. In TL dating, the paleodose is measured in a darkened laboratory by slowly heating the sample within the $300°–500°C$ range and the stored charge is determined from the quantity of faint light emitted as the trapped electrons are evicted. The more sophisticated optically stimulated luminescence (OSL) method uses light to evict the traps, and the OSL signal has been shown to correspond to the light-sensitive $325°C$ peak, which obviates the problem of having a residual signal in the sample due to insufficient bleaching prior to burial of the sample.[94] Luminescence methods in typical Australian conditions can be used to date an age range of a few hundred years back to about 200,000 years and thus provide the critical new tool to explore the time period beyond the radiocarbon barrier.

ARNHEM LAND AND THE SECOND DATING REVOLUTION

By a lucky fluke, one of the first luminescence laboratories in Australia had been established by the Commonwealth in Kakadu National Park, a short distance away from some of the key archaeological sites of the tropical north. This was in order to date sand deposits in planning for a stable location for the waste dump from the Ranger uranium mine. Richard Roberts was working here researching the ages and formation of sand aprons that mantled the feet of the escarpment cliffs. A series of consistent TL dates had been obtained, extending back in time to about 120,000 years, but due to the absence of charcoal in any of his columns beyond a few centimeters below ground, there was no means of testing his TL dates against the other independent method of carbon dating. Within the deposits of archaeological campsites however, because so much firewood had been brought in and concentrated here by Aborigines in the past, there was enough charcoal to buffer some of these decomposing processes. A somewhat serendipitous collaborative project in the finest traditions of what I once called "cowboy archaeology" was planned to pair TL dates against the known C-14 chronology within the archaeological sequences, and if these matched, then to use TL to attempt to date the lowest deposits beyond the limits of charcoal.[95]

The first site at which we worked in 1988 and 1989 was Malakunanja II, which had previously been partially excavated.[96] This was a large rock shelter under a high-sloping wall of quartzite forming the western face 200 meters high of an outlier massif detached a few kilometers from the main Arnhem Land escarpment. At its foot was a gently sloping sand apron, formed by sand grains detached over the millennia from the cliff above. Excavation revealed a total depth of five meters of sand. Within all excavation units of the upper 2.5 meters of deposit there were numerous flaked stone artifacts, in total numbering several thousand. Yet within the entire bottom half of the deposit there were none. The top three TL samples conformed well with the C-14 chronology which extended back to about 22,000 years, indicating that the assumptions concerning the validity of the TL method had been met. Then beneath these, in a zone where charcoal was no longer preserved, two TL dates bracketed the zone of first occupation of this site as between 53,000–60,000 years. Underneath this were four further TL dates extending from 65,000 years back to 110,000 years ago, all dates being in the correct chronological order as compared with their stratigraphic positions.[97] In our paper presenting these results, we put forward two propositions; first, that humans were present on Australia some 53,000–60,000 years ago, and second, that they were not there before that time, since we regarded the entire absence of any human artifacts at this site over the previous 50,000 years as being highly significant. This was because of its strategic location at the first line of cliffs that would have greeted any migrant traveling south along the then exposed Arafura Plain. The gullies and gorges between the cliffs with their rainforest pockets and the pools and streams amongst the rocky terrain constitute one of the most biodiverse landscapes on the entire continent, and once found would never be relinquished.

Adding as they did a fifty percent increase to the antiquity of humans on the Australian continent, these results were subject to strong scrutiny, and there was a need to repeat the experiment. In 1992 we returned to the Nauwalabila site within Deaf Adder Gorge, which we previously could not sample due to restrictions following the burial of two senior Badmardi men who had worked with me on the original excavation.[98] By this time the OSL methodology had been invented and five OSL samples were dated. One at a depth of 1.10 meters gave a value of about 13,000 years ago, consistent with both the TL and radiocarbon results. Another at 1.70 meters at the very lowest level where charcoal survived gave an OSL date of about 30,000 years ago, reasonably consistent with the radiocarbon testimony. Below that the lowest artifacts, some 300 in number, were bracketed by OSL dates of between 53,000–60,000 years ago.[99] Work at other sites around the continent to try and replicate these results is proceeding.

"RUBBLE TROUBLE"

In late 1996 there was a major announcement of results of TL dating at the rock shelter site of Jinmium on the border of the Northern Territory and Western Australia where TL dates had been obtained for human occupation of this site between 120,000–160,000 years ago, and in addition, that there were carved pieces of rocks covered by deposit dated to between 50,000–70,000 years ago.[100]

This claim created a huge impact in the world's media, with major features in the *Sydney Morning Herald,* the *New York Times,* the *Times* of London, and became the subject of several Australian and British TV documentaries. However, there is a fundamental problem with these dates. This is due to the fact that within the deposit there is a friable rubble, so that grains of sand have become detached from *in situ* weathered bedrock or "saprolite" and become incorporated within the deposit. These grains, never having been bleached, contain a saturated TL signal and, therefore, being mixed up with the sand that was properly bleached, give a false old age. To solve this problem has required a radical miniaturization of the luminescence technology, which parallels the same research process within radiocarbon dating and the development of direct weighing of the various isotopes of carbon using an accelerator mass spectrometer (AMS). Normal luminescence dates are done on an array of some 2,000 grains of sand, but the ultimate is to be able to obtain separate dates from individual single grains of sand, and this has been achieved within the past two years in the luminescence research laboratories at the Australian National University and at La Trobe University, Melbourne. The pioneering work itself is done by physicists, yet the stimulation for it comes from an archaeological imperative, and this interaction of problem and of technical innovation I find compelling. The future technology, which is not quite yet available but which is already planned, is to automate single-grain OSL dating using a "charge coupled device" to count photons. I find it poetic that this instrument that is used by astronomers to measure the light from the most distant stars can also be deployed onto a tray of sand to measure the distant past of the human experience. It adds a new dimension to William Blake's *Auguries of Innocence*—"To see a World in a grain of sand . . . And Eternity in an hour."

A recently completed restudy at the Jinmium site, using an array of new dating techniques, including AMS C-14, and OSL single-grain methods, does not confirm the previous claims and indicates that the entire deposit was laid down only over the past 10,000 years.[101] Such a great deflation from its previous claims would, however, still place its first occupation as coeval with Folsom.

MEGAFAUNA

My present view is that people entered the Australian continent on the order of 53,000–60,000 years ago. This corresponded to what climatologists refer to as the end of Isotope Stage 4, prior to the main part of the last ice age, and at a time when far wetter conditions in Australia were beginning to dry out. These climatic changes may have had a profound effect on the Australian fauna, since a major phase of extinction of marsupial and other megafauna took place sometime during the Upper Pleistocene; though for over a century it has proved impossible to date this event or series of events. I suspect that this is because it also occurred beyond the range of radiocarbon, and now new methods are being deployed to try and resolve this and also whether or not it occurred at about the time humans arrived. The best record that we have of any extinction event has been obtained at Lake Eyre from the dating of eggshells of both emu and the giant extinct *Genyornis,* a bird twice the weight of the emu.[102] It has been shown that the *Genyornis* suddenly became extinct about 45,000–50,000 years ago, whereas the emu survived through all of the environmental changes in the area. People were present at that time, and it can be asked whether or not their predation was the new factor that triggered the extinction. At a swamp in western New South Wales at Cuddie Springs, hundreds of stone tools have been found in close stratigraphic association with numerous bones of both *Genyornis* and *Diprotodon,* a marsupial the size and shape of a large cow. The dates are 34,000 or more, and a major current project is aimed to see whether or not humans were predating on these animals.[103] The parallels with the Paleo-Indian sites of the American Southwest are arresting.

THE OLDEST ART

The techniques of miniaturization of the OSL method were designed to solve a particular problem, but the fascination of science is that a new technique can be used for a totally unplanned purpose. The corpus of rock art in northern Australia may be the most prolific in the world. Sustained studies over the past thirty years in Cape York, Kakadu, and the Kimberleys have established relative sequences based on superimposition studies that almost certainly extend back to the Pleistocene.[104] It is now the job of who Scaliger in 1605 called the "chronologists" to try and pin the points of this sequence to an absolute timescale. The older paintings are consistently covered with mineral skin. Analysis of these has shown them to include calcium oxalates, which formed under more humid conditions than at present by the fixing from algae of carbonic acid within rainwater. They contain carbon 14 and can be dated using the AMS techniques which only require a dust-sized grain of carbon to obtain a result. If you can date a grain of sand with OSL methods, then the way is open to determine the ages of fossilized wasp nests which commonly cover parts of the oldest art in the tropical north of Australia. Carried on the "feet" of the wasps, these grains would have been bleached during transport and then built into solid nests away from light and would be under exactly the same process of luminescence charging as buried sand. Recently, we dated a fossil wasp nest overlying a small solid human figure in ancient purple pigment from the west Kimberleys to between 17,000–20,000 years old.[105] I am convinced that OSL dating of wasp nests under- and overlying ancient rock art in the north of Australia will soon transform our knowledge about its antiquity. Ground hematite ochre is common in the very basal levels of most sites including Nauwalabila and Malakunanja down to fifty thousand years ago. Art was not invented in Australia, the first peoples brought these conceptual skills with them. It was a defining mark of modern humanity.

These issues are important, since, if fully modern people entered Australia some time at around 53,000–60,000 years ago, this was a short time after what most geneticists now believe to have been the explosive expansion of modern *Homo sapiens* out of Africa. The Australian data document one of the key early events of that first global colonization.

TWO CONTINENTS

It can be seen that for the Americas and Australia there have been great parallels in the ways in which, from a European perspective, the native peoples have been seen, in the speculations about their antiquity and in the ways in which archaeological investigations have tried to grapple with these. They share a unique character in that they were the only two continents to be initially colonized by biologically and behaviorally modern humans. In order to try and document the times of entry, the nature of the colonizing process, and to evaluate the ecological impacts of these profound events, a comparative perspective adds a richness to our analyses. Viewed from this perspective, there are deep similarities to their prehistories.

Daniel Wilson, at the conclusion of his opening chapter of *Prehistoric Man,* wrote that "the New World is a great mystery; and even glimpses into its hidden truths reflect some clearer light on the secrets of the older world."[106] According to the poet A. D. Hope, Australia is not a young country, but it is "the last of lands, the emptiest." The greatest emptiness which I believe he felt in the 1920s when he wrote this was the lack of history, not that extending over the last two hundred years since the arrival of the British settlers, but a deeper one, the one that encompassed the first peoples, the changes in the landscape and climate that had molded the human experience on the continent. Archaeological research involves an integration of the methods and perspectives of both the humanities and the sciences; it is a domain of inquiry that constantly seeks to bridge the two "cultures" that C. P. Snow identified. The concept of the "frontier" is steeped within the mythologies of both Americans and Australians. There is also a frontier of time. Archaeological research has transformed our knowledge about the deep ancestors of both Native Americans and Aboriginal peoples, and in so doing has given the possibilities of molding new senses of national identity in both countries.

Notes

1. David Campbell, *Words with a Black Orpington and other Poems* (Sydney: Angus & Robertson, 1978).
2. President and Fellows of Harvard College, "Preface," in *Independence, Convergence, and Borrowing*. Harvard Tercentenary Publications (Cambridge, Mass.: Harvard University Press, 1937), *v.*
3. Kenneth Ballard Murdock, *Increase Mather: The Foremost American Puritan* (Cambridge, Mass.: Harvard University Press, 1925), 263; Increase Mather, *Remarkable Providences Illustrative of the Earlier Days of American Colonisation,* 1856 ed., introd. George Offor (London: John Russell Smith, 1684), *xiii;* Stuart Piggott, *Ancient Britons and the Antiquarian Imagination* (London: Thames and Hudson, 1989), 26.
4. *Philosophical Transactions* 24 (1712): 85.
5. Daniel Wilson, *Prehistoric Man: Researches into the Origin of Civilisation in the Old and the New World*, 2d ed. (London: Macmillan and Co., 1865), 405.
6. Samuel Eliot Morison, *Harvard College in the Seventeenth Century*, Part 1. (Cambridge, Mass.: Harvard University Press, 1936), 346.
7. On December 2, 1995, the Harvard Native American Program asked me to arrange the translation for the first time from its original Latin the *"Honoratissimi benefactores"* address which Caleb Cheeshahteaumauck had written and sent to his "benefactors," including Robert Boyle in London in 1663. Together with Professor Thomas Figuera of the Department of Classics and Ancient History at Rutgers University, I was able to do this and prepare a small exhibit of the original Latin and the English translation, which together with a copy of evangelist John Eliot's first translation of the New Testament to the Algonquin language, *Wushu Wutestamentum* (1680 ed.) from the Widener Library, was displayed at the Tribal Courts Symposium on "American Indian Tribal Courts and Self-Governance," held at the Harvard Law School. This was opened by keynote speaker U.S. Attorney General Janet Reno, and participants also received a signed letter of support for its aims from President Bill Clinton.

8. Leo S. Klejn, "Childe and Soviet Archaeology: A Romance," in *The Archaeology of V. Gordon Childe: Contemporary Perspectives,* ed. D. R. Harris (London: University College London Press, 1994), 81.

9. Harvard Tercentenary Publications (1936), 2.

10. V. Gordon Childe, "A Prehistorian's Interpretation of Diffusion," in *Independence, Convergence, and Borrowing* (Cambridge, Mass.: Harvard University Press, 1937), 19.

11. P. I. André-Vincent, *Bartolomé de Las Casas, Prophète du Nouveau Monde* (Paris: Librarie Jules Tallandier, 1980), 255–256.

12. H. A. L. Fisher, *A History of Europe* (London: Edward Arnold, 1936), 283.

13. J. H. Parry, *The Spanish Theory of Empire in the Sixteenth Century* (Cambridge: Cambridge University Press, 1940), 20.

14. T. Todorov, *The Conquest of America: The Question of the Other* (New York: Haper and Row, 1982).

15. Parry, *The Spanish Theory of Empire,* 21–22.

16. J. Scaliger, *Opus novum de emendatione temporum,* in *Epistolae omnes quae reperiri potuerunt,* ed. D. Heinsius (Leiden, 1627 [1605]).

17. I. Curio, *Chronologicarum rerum* (Basle, 1557); Anthony Grafton, "From *De Die Natali* to *De Emendatione Temporum:* The Origins and Setting of Scaliger's Chronology," *Journal of the Warburg and Courtauld Institutes* 48 (1985): 102.

18. Frank E. Manuel, *Isaac Newton Historian* (Cambridge, Mass.: The Belknap Press of Harvard University Press, 1963), 49.

19. Hugh Honour, *L'Amerique Vue par L'Europe* (Paris: Musée de L'Homme, 1976); Piggott, *Ancient Britons,* 73–86.

20. De Bry in ibid., 76.

21. Thomas Hobbes, *Leviathan,* ed. Richard Tuck (Cambridge University Press, 1991 [1651]), 89.

22. Ronald L. Meek, *Social Science and the Ignoble Savage* (Cambridge: Cambridge University Press, 1976), 37–67.

23. Glyn Daniel, *A Hundred Years of Archaeology* (London: Duckworth, 1950), 78–79; Vincent Megaw and Rhys Jones, *The Dawn of Man* (London: Wayland, 1972), 22–23.

24. Stephen Jay Gould, *The Mismeasure of Man* (New York: W. W. Norton and Co., 1990), 30–72.

25. David J. Meltzer, "Separating Learning from Folly, Fancy from Fact: Samuel Haven and the First Synthesis of American Archaeology (1856)," *Abstracts of the 61st Annual Meeting of the Society for American Archaeology,* New Orleans, 1996, 186–187.

26. John Lubbock, *Prehistoric Times* (London: Williams and Norgate, 1865), 243.

27. Charles Lyell, *Geological Evidences of the Antiquity of Man* (London: John Murray, 1863), 41.

28. Lubbock, *Prehistoric Times,* 243.

29. Christopher Chippindale, "The Invention of Words for the Idea of Prehistory,"

Proceedings of the Prehistoric Society 54 (1989): 303–314; Alice B. Kehoe, "The Invention of Prehistory," *Current Anthropology* 32 (1991): 467.

30. *Encyclopaedia Britannica* (1878), s.v. "Archaeology."

31. Daniel Wilson, *Prehistoric Man: Researches into the Origin of Civilisation in the Old and the New World,* 2d ed. (London: Macmillan and Co., 1865 [1862]), 12.

32. Lyell, *Geological Evidences,* 351.

33. Wilson, *Prehistoric Man,* 47; Lyell, *Geological Evidences,* 43–44.

34. Lyell, *Geological Evidences,* 204.

35. Ibid., 44–45.

36. C. C. Abbott, *The Stone Age of New Jersey* (Trenton, N.J.: n.p., 1872).

37. Dorothy Cross, *Archaeology of New Jersey, Vol. 2, The Abbott Farm* (Trenton, N.J.: The Archaeological Society of New Jersey and the New Jersey State Museum, 1956).

38. Franklin Folsom, *Black Cowboy: The Life and Legend of George McJunkin* (Niwot, Colo. and Schull, West Cork, Ireland: Roberts Rinehart Publishers, 1992), 61.

39. Douglas Preston, "Fossils and the Folsom Cowboy," *Natural History* 2 (1997): 18.

40. Folsom, *Black Cowboy,* 126–127.

41. Preston, "Fossils and the Folsom Cowboy," 20.

42. H. M. Wormington, *Ancient Man in North America,* 4th ed. (Denver, Colo.: The Denver Museum of Natural History, 1957).

43. D. J. Stanford and J. S. Day, eds., *Ice Age Hunters of the Rockies* (Denver, Colo.: Denver Museum of Natural History and University Press of Colorado, 1992).

44. Wormington, *Ancient Man,* 48.

45. C. V. Haynes, R. P. Beukens, A. J. T. Jull, and O. K. Davis, "New Radiocarbon Dates for Some Old Folsom Sites: Accelerator Technology," in *Ice Age Hunters of the Rockies,* ed. D. J. Stanford and J. S. Day (Denver, Colo.: Denver Museum of Natural History and University Press of Colorado, 1992), 83–100.

46. David J. Meltzer, "Clocking the First Americans," *Annual Review of Anthropology* 24 (1995): 21–45; R. Esmée Webb and David J. Rindos, "The Mode and Tempo of the Initial Human Colonisation of Empty Landmasses: Sahal and the Americas Compared" in *Rediscovering Darwin: Evolutionary Theory and Archaeological Explanations,* eds. C. Michael Barton and Geoffrey A. Clark. Archaeological Paper of the American Anthropological Association (1997): 240–264.

47. C. V. Haynes, "Stratigraphy and Late Pleistocene Extinction in the United States," in *Quaternary Extinctions: A Prehistoric Revolution,* ed. P. S. Martin and R. G. Klein (Tucson, Ariz.: University of Arizona Press, 1984); Paul S. Martin, "The Discovery of America," *Science* 179 (1973): 969–974; Paul S. Martin, "Prehistoric Overkill," in *Pleistocene Extinctions: The Search for a Cause,* ed. P. S. Martin and H. E. Wright (New Haven, Ct. and London: Yale University Press, 1975), 75–120.

48. Meltzer, "Clocking the First Americans"; ibid., "Monte Verde and the Pleistocene Peopling of the Americas," *Science* 276 (1997): 754–755.

49. A. C. Roosevelt, M. Lima da Costa, C. Lopes Machado, M. Michab, et al., "Paleo-Indian Cave Dwellers in the Amazon: The Peopling of the Americas," *Science* 272 (1996): 373–382.

50. Piggott, *Ancient Britons,* 86.

51. J.-M. Degérando, "Considérations sur les Diverses Méthodes à Suivre dans l'Observations des Peuples Sauvages," 1800; republished in *Aux Origines de L'Anthropologie Française: Les Mémoirs de la Société des Observateurs de l'Homme en l'an VIII,* ed. J. Copans and J. Jamin (Paris: Le Sycomore Editions, 1978), 127–169; Rhys Jones, "Philosophical Time Travellers," *Antiquity* 66 (1992): 744–757.

52. Alan Frost, "New South Wales as *terra nullius:* The British Denial of Aboriginal Land Rights," *Historical Studies* 19 (1981): 513–523.

53. Paul Carter, *The Road to Botany Bay* (London: Faber and Faber, 1987), 57.

54. Ibid., figure 5.

55. D. J. Mulvaney, "A Splendid Lot of Fellows: Achievements and Consequences of the Horn Expedition," in *Exploring Central Australia: Society, the Environment, and the 1894 Horn Expedition,* ed. S. R. Morton and D. J. Mulvaney (Chipping Norton, N.S.W.: Surrey Beatty and Sons, 1996), 3–12.

56. F. J. Gillen, "Notes on Some Manners and Customs of the Aborigines of the McDonnell Ranges Belonging to the Arunta Tribe," in *Report of the Work of the Horn Scientific Expedition to Central Australia, Part IV, Anthropology,* ed. B. Spencer (London: Dulau and Co.; and Melbourne: Melville, Mullen, and Slade, 1896), 185.

57. D. J. Mulvaney, "The Australian Aborigines, 1606–1929: Opinion and Field Work," in *Historical Studies: Selected Articles,* ed. J. J. Eastwood and F. B. Smith (Melbourne: Melbourne University Press, 1964), 43; Rhys Jones, "From Totemism to Totemism in Palaeolithic Art," *Mankind* 6 (1967): 384–392.

58. W. A. Horn, "Introduction," in *Report of the Work of the Horn Scientific Expedition to Central Australia,* ed. Baldwin Spencer (London: Dulau and Co.; and Melbourne: Melville, Mullen, and Slade, 1896), ix.

59. T. H. Huxley, "On the Distribution of the Races of Mankind and its Bearing on the Antiquity of Mankind," *International Congress of Prehistoric Archaeology, Third Session* (London: Longmans, Green and Co., 1869): 92–97.

60. Huxley, cited in Charles Lyell, *Geological Evidences,* 89.

61. See David Horton, *Recovering the Tracks: The Story of Australian Archaeology* (Canberra: Aboriginal Studies Press, 1991).

62. R. H. Pulleine, "The Tasmanians and their Stone Culture," *Australian Association for the Advancement of Science* 19 (1928): 310.

63. T. W. E. David and J. T. Wilson, "Preliminary Communication on an Australian Cranium of Probable Pleistocene Age," *Report of the Eighty-fourth Meeting of the British Association for the Advancement of Science, Australia, 1914* (London: John Murray, 1915), 531.

64. N. W. G. Macintosh, "The Talgai Cranium: The Value of Archives," *Australian Natural History* 16 (1969): 190.

65. A. L. Meston, "The Problem of the Tasmanian Aborigines," *Papers and Proceedings of the Royal Society of Tasmania for 1936* (1937): 85–92.

66. N. B. Tindale, "Culture Succession in South Eastern Australia from Late Pleistocene to the Present," *Records of the South Australian Museum* 13 (1957): 1–49; D. J. Mulvaney, "The Stone Age of Australia," *Proceedings of the Prehistoric Society* 27 (1961): 56–107; Grahame Clark, *World Prehistory: An Outline* (Cambridge: Cambridge University Press, 1961.)

67. D. J. Mulvaney, "The Australian Aborigines, 1606–1929: Opinion and Field Work," 42.

68. T. W. Bonner and W. M. Brubaker, "The Disintegration of Nitrogen by Slow Neutrons," *The Physical Review* 49778 (1936); S. Ruben and M. D. Kamen, "Long-Lived Radioactive Carbon: C14," *The Physical Review* 59 (1941): 349–354.

69. W. F. Libby, "Atmospheric Helium Three and Radiocarbon from Cosmic Radiation," *The Physical Review* 69 (1946): 671–672.

70. J. R. Arnold and W. F. Libby, "Age Determinations by Radiocarbon Content: Checks with Samples of Known Age," *Science* 110 (1949): 678–680; Grahame Clark, *Prehistory at Cambridge and Beyond* (Cambridge: Cambridge University Press, 1989), 84.

71. V. Gordon Childe, "Valediction," 1957; reprinted in Sally Green, *Prehistorian: A Biography of V. Gordon Childe* (Bradford-on-Avon, Wilts, UK: Moonraker Press, 1981), 167.

72. D. J. Mulvaney, "Advancing Frontiers in Australian Archaeology," *Oceania* 33 (1962): 137; ibid., "The Pleistocene Colonization of Australia," *Antiquity* 38 (1964): 263–267.

73. D. J. Mulvaney and E. B. Joyce, "Archaeological and Geomorphological Investigations on Mt. Moffatt Station, Queensland, Australia," *Proceedings of the Prehistoric Society* 31 (1965): 147–212.

74. Rhys Jones, "A Continental Reconnaissance: Some Observations Concerning the Discovery of the Pleistocene Archaeology of Australia," in *A Community of Culture: The People and Prehistory of the Pacific*, ed. M. Spriggs, D. E. Yen, W. Ambrose, R. Jones, A. Thorne, and A. Andrews (Canberra: Australian National University, Dept. of Prehistory, Research School of Pacific Studies, 1993), 112–113; Josephine Flood, *Archaeology of the Dreamtime*, rev. ed. (Sydney and London: Collins, 1995).

75. Carmel Schrire, *The Alligator Rivers: Prehistory and Ecology in Western Arnhem Land* (Canberra: Australian National University, Dept. of Prehistory, Research School of Pacific Studies, 1982).

76. S. Bulmer, "Prehistoric Stone Implements from the New Guinea Highlands," *Oceania* 34 (1964): 246–268.

77. Les Groube, "The Taming of the Rain Forests: A Model for Late Pleistocene Forest Exploitation in New Guinea," in *Foraging and Farming: The Evolution of*

Plant Exploitation, ed. David R. Harris and Gordon C. Hillman (London: Allen Hyman, 1989), 292–304.

78. Jack Golson, "Both Sides of the Wallace Line: Australia, New Guinea, and Asian Prehistory," *Archaeology and Physical Anthropology in Oceania* 6 (1971): 129.

79. J. M. Bowler, Rhys Jones, Harry Allen, and A. G. Thorne, "Pleistocene Human Remains from Australia: A Living Site and Human Cremation from Lake Mungo, Western New South Wales," *World Archaeology* 2 (1970): 39–60; D. J. Mulvaney, *The Prehistory of Australia*, rev. ed. (Harmondsworth: Penguin Books, 1975), 147–153.

80. G. R. Willey and P. Phillips, *Method and Theory in American Archaeology* (Chicago: University of Chicago Press, 1958), 37.

81. Rhys Jones, "The Neolithic, Palaeolithic, and the Hunting Gardeners: Man and Land in the Antipodes," in *Quaternary Studies*, ed. R. P. Suggate and M. M. Cresswell (Wellington: The Royal Society of New Zealand, 1975), 28.

82. Nicholas Evans and Rhys Jones, "The Cradle of the Pama-Nyungans: Archaeological and Linguistic Speculations," in *Archaeology and Linguistics: Aboriginal Australia in Global Perspective*, ed. P. McConvell and N. Evans (Oxford: Oxford University Press, 1997), 385–417.

83. J. M. Bowler and A. G. Thorne, "Human Remains from Lake Mungo: Discovery and Excavation of Lake Mungo 111," in *The Origin of the Australians*, ed. R. L. Kirk and A. G. Thorne (Canberra: Australian Institute of Aboriginal Studies; and New Jersey: Humanities Press, 1976), 127–138.

84. F. W. Shawcross and Maureen Kaye, "Australian Archaeology: Implications of Current Interdisciplinary Research," *Interdisciplinary Science Reviews* 5 (1980): 123.

85. Rhys Jones, "The Fifth Continent: Problems Concerning the Human Colonization of Australia," *Annual Review of Anthropology* 8 (1979): 445–466.; ibid., "East of Wallace's Line: Issues and Problems in the Colonisation of the Australian Continent," in *The Human Revolution: Behavioural and Biological Perspectives on the Origins of Modern Humans*, ed. Paul Mellars and Chris Stringer (Edinburgh: Edinburgh University Press, 1989), 743–782; Flood, *Archaeology of the Dreamtime*.

86. Quoted in Howard Pedersen and Banjo Woorunmurra, *Jandamarra and the Bunuba Resistance* (Broome, Western Australia: Magabala Books, 1995), 90.

87. Paul Marshall, ed., *Raparapa: Stories from the Fitzroy River Drovers* (Broome, Western Australia: Magabala Books, 1989), 43.

88. Susan O'Connor, "Carpenter's Gap Rock Shelter I: 40,000 Years of Aboriginal Occupation in the Napier Ranges, Kimberley, WA," *Australian Archaeology* 40 (1995): 58–59.

89. Jones, "East of Wallace's Line."

90. M. A Smith and N. D. Sharp, "Pleistocene Sites in Australia, New Guinea, and Island Melanesia: Geographic and Temporal Structure of the Archaeological Record," in *Sahul in Review: Pleistocene Archaeology in Australia, New Guinea,*

and Island Melanesia, ed. M. A. Smith, M. Spriggs, and B. Fankhauser (Canberra: The Australian National University, Dept. of Prehistory, Research School of Pacific Studies, 1993), 37–59.

91. J. Allen, "When Did Humans First Colonize Australia? *Search* 20 (1989): 149–154; ibid., "Radiocarbon Determinations, Luminescence Dating, and Australian Archaeology," *Antiquity* 68 (1994): 339–443; J. Allen and S. Holdaway, "The Contamination of Pleistocene Radiocarbon Determinations in Australia," *Antiquity* 69 (1995): 101–112; Rhys Jones, "Ions and Eons: Some Thoughts on Archaeological Science and Scientific Archaeology," in *Archaeometry, an Australasian Perspective*, ed. W. Ambrose and P. Duerden (Canberra: The Australian National University, Dept. of Prehistory, Research School of Pacific Studies, 1982), 22–35; Richard G. Roberts, Rhys Jones, and M. A. Smith, "Beyond the Radiocarbon Barrier in Australian Prehistory," *Antiquity* 68 (1994): 611–616.

92. Rhys Jones and Ian Johnson, "Deaf Adder Gorge: Lindner Site, Nauwalabila I," in *Archaeological Research in Kakadu National Park*, ed. Rhys Jones. Special Publication no. 13 (Canberra: Australian National Parks and Wildlife Service, 1985), 182.

93. Robert Boyle, *The Works of the Honourable Robert Boyle, Volume 1*. A new ed. with pref. by Thomas Birch, (London: W. Johnston, S. Crowder, et al., 1772), 796–799.

94. Richard G. Roberts and Rhys Jones, "Luminescence Dating of Sediments: New Light on the Human Colonisation of Australia," *Australian Aboriginal Studies* 2 (1994): 2–17.

95. Jones, "The Fifth Continent," 447.

96. J. Kamminga and H. Allen, "Report of the Archaeological Survey," *Alligator Rivers Environmental Fact-Finding Study*, 1973.

97. Richard G. Roberts, Rhys Jones, and M. A. Smith, "Thermoluminescence Dating of a 50,000-Year-Old Human Occupation Site in Northern Australia," *Nature* 345 (1990): 153–156; Roberts and Jones, "Luminescence Dating."

98. Jones and Johnson, "Deaf Adder Gorge."

99. Richard G. Roberts, Rhys Jones, N. A. Spooner, M. J. Head, A. S. Murray, and M. A. Smith, "The Human Colonisation of Australia: Optical Dates of 53,000 and 60,000 Years Bracket Human Arrival at Deaf Adder Gorge, Northern Territory," *Quaternary Science Reviews* 13 (1994): 575–583; Roberts and Jones, "Luminescence Dating."

100. R. L. K. Fullagar, D. M. Price, and L. M. Head, "Early Human Occupation of Northern Australia: Archaeology and Thermoluminescence Dating of Jinmium Rock Shelter, Northern Territory," *Antiquity* 70 (1996): 751–773.

101. Richard, G. Roberts, Michael Bird, Jon Olley, Rex Galbraith, Ewan Lawson, Geoff Laslett, Hiroyuki Yoshida, Rhys Jones, Richard Fullagar, Geraldine Jacobsen, and Quan Hua, "Optical and Radiocarbon Dating and Jinnium Rock Shelter in Northern Australia," *Nature* 393 (1998): 358–362.

102. Gifford Miller, John W. Magee, and A. J. T. Jull, "Low-Latitude Glacial Cooling in the Southern Hemisphere from Amino-Acid Racemization in Emu Eggshells," *Nature* 385 (1997): 241–244.

103. J. H. Furby, R. Fullagar, J. R. Dodson, and I. Prosser, "The Cuddie Springs Bone Bed Revisited, 1991," in *Sahul in Review: Pleistocene Archaeology in Australia, New Guinea, and Island Melanesia*, ed. M. A. Smith, M. Spriggs, and B. Fankhauser (Canberra: Australian National University, Dept. of Prehistory, Research School of Pacific Studies, 1993), 204–212.

104. George, Chaloupka, *Journey in Time: The World's Longest Continuing Art Tradition* (Sydney: Reed, 1993.); G. Walsh, *Bradshaws: Ancient Rock Paintings of North-West Australia* (Geneva: The Bradshaw Foundation, 1994).

105. Richard, G. Roberts, A. Murray, J. Olley Walsh, Rhys Jones, M. Morwood, C. Tuniz, E. Lawson, M. Macphail, D. Bowdery, and I. Naumann, "Luminescence Dating of Rock Art and Past Environments Using Mud-Wasp Nests in Northern Australia," *Nature* 387 (1997): 696–699.

106. Wilson, *Prehistoric Man*, 13.

References

Abbott, C. C. *The Stone Age of New Jersey*. Trenton, N.J.: n.p., 1872.

Agassiz, L. *Etudes sur les Glaciers*. Neuchâtel: Privately published, 1840.

Allen, J. "Radiocarbon Determinations, Luminescence Dating, and Australian Archaeology." *Antiquity* 68 (1994): 339–343.

——. "When Did Humans First Colonize Australia?" *Search* 20 (1989): 149–154.

Allen, J., and S. Holdaway. "The Contamination of Pleistocene Radiocarbon Determinations in Australia." *Antiquity* 69 (1995): 101–112.

André-Vincent, P. I. *Bartolomé de Las Casas, Prophéte du Nouveau Monde*. Paris: Libraire Jules Tallandier, 1980.

Arnold, J. R., and W. F. Libby. "Age Determinations by Radiocarbon Content: Checks with Samples of Known Age." *Science* 110 (1949): 678–680.

Bonner, T. W., and W. M. Brubaker. "The Disintegration of Nitrogen by Slow Neutrons." *The Physical Review* 49778 (1936).

Bowler, J. M., Rhys Jones, Harry Allen, and A. G. Thorne. "Pleistocene Human Remains from Australia: A Living Site and Human Cremation from Lake Mungo, Western New South Wales." *World Archaeology* 2 (1970): 39–60.

Bowler, J. M., and A. G. Thorne. "Human Remains from Lake Mungo: Discovery and Excavation of Lake Mungo 111." In *The Origin of the Australians*. Edited by R. L. Kirk and A. G. Thorne. Canberra: Australian Institute of Aboriginal Studies, and New Jersey: Humanities Press, 1976.

Boyle, Robert. *The Works of the Honourable Robert Boyle, Volume 1*. A new edition with a preface by Thomas Birch. Published by W. Johnston, S. Crowder, et al. London, 1772.

Bulmer, S. "Prehistoric Stone Implements from the New Guinea Highlands." *Oceania* 34 (1964): 246–268.

Campbell, David. *Words with a Black Orpington and Other Poems*. Sydney: Angus & Robertson, 1978.

Carter, Paul. *The Road to Botany Bay*. London: Faber and Faber, 1987.

Chaloupka, George. *Journey in Time: The World's Longest Continuing Art Tradition*. Sydney: Reed, 1993.

Childe, V. Gordon. *The Dawn of European Civilization*. London: Kegan Paul, Trench, Trubner, and Co., 1925.

———. *How Labour Governs*. London: Labour Publishing Co., 1923.

———. "A Prehistorian's Interpretation of Diffusion." In *Independence, Convergence, and Borrowing*. Cambridge, Mass.: Harvard University Press, 1937.

———. "Valediction."1957; Reprinted in Green, Sally. *Prehistorian: A Biography of V. Gordon Childe*. Bradford-on-Avon, Wilts, UK: Moonraker Press, 1981.

Chippindale, Christopher. "The Invention of Words for the Idea of Prehistory." *Proceedings of the Prehistoric Society* 54 (1989): 303–314.

Clark, Grahame. *Prehistory at Cambridge and Beyond*. Cambridge: Cambridge University Press, 1989.

———. *World Prehistory: An Outline*. Cambridge: Cambridge University Press, 1961.

Cross, Dorothy. *Archaeology of New Jersey, Vol. 2, The Abbott Farm*. Trenton, N.J.: The Archaeological Society of New Jersey and the New Jersey State Museum, 1956.

Curio, I. *Chronologicarum rerum*, lib II. Basle, 1557.

Daniel, Glyn. *A Hundred Years of Archaeology*. London: Duckworth, 1950.

David, T. W. E. "Geological Evidence of the Antiquity of Man in the Commonwealth, with Special Reference to the Tasmanian Aborigines." 1924; *Papers and Proceedings of the Royal Society of Tasmania for 1923*.

David, T. W. E., and J. T. Wilson. "Preliminary Communication on an Australian Cranium of Probable Pleistocene Age." *Report of the Eighty-fourth Meeting of the British Association for the Advancement of Science, Australia, 1914*. London: John Murray, 1915.

Degérando, J.-M. "Considérations sur les Diverses Méthodes à Suivre dans l'Observations des Peuples Sauvages." 1800; Republished in Copans, J., and J. Jamin. *Aux Origines de L'Anthropologie Française. Les Mémoirs de la Société des Observateurs de l'Homme en l'an VIII*. Paris: Le Sycomore Editions, 1978.

Evans, Nicholas, and Rhys Jones. "The Cradle of the Pama-Nyungans: Archaeological and Linguistic Speculations." In *Archaeology and Linguistics: Aboriginal Australia in Global Perspective*. Edited by P. McConvell and N. Evans. Oxford: Oxford University Press, 1997.

Fisher, H. A. L. *A History of Europe*. London: Edward Arnold, 1936.

Flood, Josephine. *Archaeology of the Dreamtime*. Rev. ed. Sydney and London: Collins, 1995.

Folsom, Franklin. *Black Cowboy: The Life and Legend of George McJunkin*. Niwot, Colo., Schull, West Cork, Ireland: Roberts Rinehart Publishers, 1992.

Frost, Alan. "New South Wales as *terra nullius*: The British Denial of Aboriginal Land Rights." *Historical Studies* 19 (1981): 513–523.

Fullagar, R. L. K., D. M. Price, and L. M. Head. "Early Human Occupation of Northern Australia: Archaeology and Thermoluminescence Dating of Jinmium Rock Shelter, Northern Territory." *Antiquity* 70 (1996): 751–773.

Furby, J. H., R. Fullagar, J. R. Dodson, and I. Prosser. "The Cuddie Springs Bone Bed Revisited, 1991." In *Sahul in Review: Pleistocene Archaeology in Australia, New Guinea and Island Melanesia*. Edited by M. A. Smith, M. Spriggs, and B. Fankhauser. Canberra: Australian National University, Dept. of Prehistory, Research School of Pacific Studies, 1993.

Gillen, F. J. "Notes on Some Manners and Customs of the Aborigines of the McDonnell Ranges Belonging to the Arunta Tribe." In *Report of the Work of the Horn Scientific Expedition to Central Australia, Part IV, Anthropology*. Edited by B. Spencer. London: Dulau and Co., and Melbourne: Melville, Mullen, and Slade, 1896.

Golson, Jack. "Both Sides of the Wallace Line: Australia, New Guinea, and Asian Prehistory." *Archaeology and Physical Anthropology in Oceania* 6 (1971): 124–144.

Gould, Stephen Jay. *The Mismeasure of Man*. New York: W. W. Norton and Co., 1990.

Grafton, Anthony. "From *De Die Natali* to *De Emendatione Temporum:* The Origins and Setting of Scaliger's Chronology." *Journal of the Warburg and Courtauld Institutes* 48 (1985): 100–138.

Groube, Les. "The Taming of the Rain Forests: A Model for Late Pleistocene Forest Exploitation in New Guinea." In *Foraging and Farming: The Evolution of Plant Exploitation*. Edited by David R. Harris, and Gordon C. Hillman. London: Allen Hyman, 1989.

Hale, H. M., and N. B. Tindale. "Notes on Some Human Remains in the Lower Murray Valley, South Australia." *Records of the South Australia Museum* 4 (1930): 145–218.

Haven, Samuel. *The Archaeology of the United States, or Sketches, Historical and Biographical, of the Progress of Information and Opinion Respecting Vestiges of Antiquity in the United States,* 1847.

Haynes, C. V. "Stratigraphy and Late Pleistocene Extinction in the United States." In *Quaternary Extinctions: A Prehistoric Revolution*. Edited by P. S. Martin and R. G. Klein. Tucson, Ariz.: University of Arizona Press, 1984.

Haynes, C. V., R. P. Beukens, A. J. T. Jull, and O. K. Davis. "New Radiocarbon Dates for Some Old Folsom Sites: Accelerator Technology." In *Ice Age Hunters of the Rockies*. Edited by D. J. Stanford and J. S. Day. Denver, Colo.: Denver Museum of Natural History and University Press of Colorado, 1992.

Hobbes, Thomas. *Leviathan*. Edited by Richard Tuck. Cambridge: Cambridge University Press, 1991 (1651).

Honour, Hugh. *L'Amerique Vue par L'Europe* Paris: Musée de L'Homme, 1976

Horn, W. A. "Introduction." In *Report of the Work of the Horn Scientific Expedition to Central Australia*. Edited by Baldwin Spencer. London: Dulau and Co., and Melbourne: Melville, Mullen, and Slade, 1896.

Horton, David. *Recovering the Tracks: The Story of Australian Archaeology.* Canberra: Aboriginal Studies Press, 1991.

Hweley, T. H. "On the Distribution of the Races of Mankind and its Bearing on the Antiquity of Mankind," *International Congress of Prehistoric Archaeology, Third Session* (1868). London: Longmans, Green, and Co., 1869.

Jones, Rhys. "A Continental Reconnaissance: Some Observations Concerning the Discovery of the Pleistocene Archaeology of Australia." In *A Community of Culture: The People and Prehistory of the Pacific.* Edited by M. Spriggs, D. E. Yen, W. Ambrose, R. Jones, A. Thorne, and A. Andrews. Canberra: Australian National University, Dept. of Prehistory, Research School of Pacific Studies, 1993.

———. "East of Wallace's Line: Issues and Problems in the Colonisation of the Australian Continent." In *The Human Revolution: Behavioural and Biological Perspectives on the Origins of Modern Humans.* Edited by Paul Mellars and Chris Stringer. Edinburgh: Edinburgh University Press, 1989.

———. "The Fifth Continent: Problems Concerning the Human Colonization of Australia." *Annual Review of Anthropology* 8 (1979): 445–466.

———. "From Totemism to Totemism in Palaeolithic Art." *Mankind* 6 (1967): 384–392.

———. "Ions and Eons: Some Thoughts on Archaeological Science and Scientific Archaeology." In *Archaeometry, an Australasian Perspective.* Edited by W. Ambrose and P. Duerden. Canberra: Australian National University, Dept. of Prehistory, Research School of Pacific Studies, 1982.

———. "The Neolithic, Palaeolithic, and the Hunting Gardeners: Man and Land in the Antipodes." In *Quaternary Studies.* Edited by R. P. Suggate and M. M. Cresswell. Wellington, NZ: The Royal Society of New Zealand, 1975.

———. "Philosophical Time Travellers." *Antiquity* 66 (1992): 744–757.

Jones, Rhys, and Ian Johnson. "Deaf Adder Gorge: Lindner Site, Nauwalabila I." In *Archaeological Research in Kakadu National Park.* Edited by Rhys Jones. Special Publication no. 13. Canberra: Australian National Parks and Wildlife Service, 1985.

Kamminga, J., and H. Allen. "Report of the Archaeological Survey." *Alligator Rivers Environmental Fact-Finding Study.* Canberra, 1973.

Kehoe, Alice B. "The Invention of Prehistory." *Current Anthropology* 32 (1991): 467–476.

Klejn, Leo S. "Childe and Soviet Archaeology: A Romance." In *The Archaeology of V. Gordon Childe: Contemporary Perspectives.* Edited by D. R. Harris. London: University College London Press, 1994.

Libby, W. F. "Atmospheric Helium Three and Radiocarbon from Cosmic Radiation." *The Physical Review* 69 (1946): 671–672.

Locke, John. *Two Treatises of Government.* Edited by Peter Laslett. Cambridge: Cambridge University Press, 1960 (1690).

Lubbock, John. *Prehistoric Times.* London: Williams and Norgate, 1865.

Lyell, Charles. *Geological Evidences of the Antiquity of Man*. London: John Murray, 1863.

Macintosh, N. W. S., "The Talgai Cranium: The Value of Archives." *Australian Natural History* 16 (1969): 189–195.

Manuel, Frank E. *Isaac Newton Historian*. Cambridge, Mass.: The Belknap Press of Harvard University Press, 1963.

Marshall, Paul, ed. *Raparapa: Stories from the Fitzroy River Drovers*. Broome, Western Australia: Magabala Books, 1989.

Martin, Paul S. "The Discovery of America." *Science* 179 (1973): 969–974.

———. "Prehistoric Overkill." In *Pleistocene Extinctions: The Search for a Cause*. Edited by P. S. Martin and H. E. Wright. New Haven, Ct., and London: Yale University Press, 1975.

Mather, Increase. *Remarkable Providences Illustrative of the Earlier Days of American Colonisation*. 1856 ed. with an introduction by George Offor. London: John Russell Smith, 1684.

Meek, Ronald L. *Social Science and the Ignoble Savage*. Cambridge: Cambridge University Press, 1976.

Megaw, Vincent, and Jones, Rhys. *The Dawn of Man*. London: Wayland, 1972.

Meltzer, David J. "Clocking the First Americans." *Annual Review of Anthropology* 24 (1995): 21–45.

———. "Monte Verde and the Pleistocene Peopling of the Americas." *Science* 276 (1997): 754–755.

———. "Separating Learning from Folly, Fancy from Fact: Samuel Haven and the First Synthesis of American Archaeology (1856)." *Abstracts of the 61st Annual Meeting of the Society for American Archaeology*. New Orleans, 1996.

Meston, A. L. "The Problem of the Tasmanian Aborigines (1937)." *Papers and Proceedings of the Royal Society of Tasmania for 1936*.

Miller, Gifford, John W. Magee, and A. J. T. Jull. "Low-Latitude Glacial Cooling in the Southern Hemisphere from Amino-Acid Racemization in Emu Eggshells." *Nature* 385 (1997): 241–244.

Morison, Samuel Eliot. *Harvard College in the Seventeenth Century*. Part 1. Cambridge, Mass.: Harvard University Press, 1936.

Mulvaney, D. J. "Advancing Frontiers in Australian Archaeology." *Oceania* 33 (1962): 135–138.

———. "The Australian Aborigines, 1606–1929: Opinion and Field Work." In *Historical Studies: Selected Articles*. Edited by J. J. Eastwood and F. B. Smith. Melbourne: Melbourne University Press, 1964.

———. "The Pleistocene Colonization of Australia." *Antiquity* 38 (1964): 263–267.

———. *The Prehistory of Australia*. Rev. ed. Harmondsworth, England: Penguin Books, 1975.

———. "'A Splendid Lot of Fellows': Achievements and Consequences of the Horn Expedition. In *Exploring Central Australia: Society, the Environment, and the 1894 Horn Expedition*. Edited by S. R. Morton and D. J. Mulvaney. Chipping Norton, N.S.W.: Surrey Beatty and Sons, 1996.

————. "The Stone Age of Australia." *Proceedings of the Prehistoric Society* 27 (1961): 56–107.

Mulvaney, D. J., and E. B. Joyce. "Archaeological and Geomorphological Investigations on Mt. Moffatt Station, Queensland, Australia. *Proceedings of the Prehistoric Society* 31 (1965): 147–212.

Murdock, Kenneth Ballard. *Increase Mather: The Foremost American Puritan*. Cambridge, Mass.: Harvard University Press, 1925.

O'Connor, Susan. "Carpenter's Gap Rock Shelter I: 40,000 Years of Aboriginal Occupation in the Napier Ranges, Kimberley, Western Australia." *Australian Archaeology* 40 (1995): 58–59.

Parry, J. H. *The Spanish Theory of Empire in the Sixteenth Century.* Cambridge: Cambridge University Press, 1940.

Pedersen, Howard, and Woorunmurra, Banjo. *Jandamarra and the Bunuba Resistance*. Broome, Western Australia: Magabala Books, 1995.

Piggott, Stuart. *Ancient Britons and the Antiquarian Imagination*. London: Thames and Hudson, 1989.

President and Fellows of Harvard College 1937. "Preface." *Independence, Convergence, and Borrowing.* Harvard Tercentenary Publications. Cambridge, Mass.: Harvard University Press, 1937.

Preston, Douglas. "Fossils and the Folsom Cowboy." *Natural History* 2 (1997): 16–21.

Pulleine, R. H. "The Tasmanians and Their Stone Culture." *Australian Association for the Advancement of Science* 19 (1928): 294–314.

Roberts, Richard G., and Rhys Jones. "Luminescence Dating of Sediments: New Light on the Human Colonisation of Australia." *Australian Aboriginal Studies* 2 (1994): 2–17.

Roberts, Richard G., Rhys Jones, and M. A. Smith. "Beyond the Radiocarbon Barrier in Australian Prehistory." *Antiquity* 68 (1994): 611–616.

————. "Thermoluminescence Dating of a 50,000-Year-Old Human Occupation Site in Northern Australia." *Nature* 345 (1990): 153–156.

Roberts, Richard G., Rhys Jones, N. A. Spooner, M. J. Head, A. S. Murray, and M. A. Smith. "The Human Colonisation of Australia: Optical Dates of 53,000 and 60,000 Years Bracket Human Arrival at Deaf Adder Gorge, Northern Territory." *Quaternary Science Reviews* 13 (1994): 575–583.

Roberts, Richard, G., A. Murray, J. Olley Walsh, Rhys Jones, M. Morwood, C. Tuniz, E. Lawson, M. Macphail, D. Bowdery, and I. Naumann. "Luminescence Dating of Rock Art and Past Environments Using Mud-Wasp Nests in Northern Australia." *Nature* 387 (1997): 696–699.

Robers, Richard, Michael Bird, Jon Olley, R. Galbraith, Ewan Lawson, Geoff Laslett, Hiroyuki Yoshida, Rhys Jones, Richard Fullagar, Geraldine Jacobsen, and Quan Hua. "Optical and Radiocarbon Dating at Jinmium Rock Shelter in Northern Australia." *Nature* 393 (1998): 358–362.

Roosevelt, A. C., M. Lima da Costa, C. Lopes Machado, M. Michab, et al. "Paleo-Indian Cave Dwellers in the Amazon: The Peopling of the Americas." *Science* 272 (1996): 373–382.

Ruben, S., and M. D. Kamen. "Long-Lived Radioactive Carbon: C14." *The Physical Review* 59 (1941): 349–354.

Scaliger, J. *Opus novum de emendatione temporum.* In *Epistolae omnes quae reperiri potuerunt.* Edited by D. Heinsius. Leiden, 1627 (1605).

Schrire, Carmel. *The Alligator Rivers: Prehistory and Ecology in Western Arnhem Land.* Canberra: Australian National University, Dept. of Prehistory, Research School of Pacific Studies, 1982.

Shawcross, F. W., and Maureen Kaye. "Australian Archaeology: Implications of Current Interdisciplinary Research." *Interdisciplinary Science Reviews* 5 (1980): 112–128.

Squier, E. G., and E. H. Davis. *Ancient Monuments of the Mississippi Valley, Comprising the Results of Extensive Original Surveys and Explorations. Smithsonian Contributions.* Vol. 1. Washington, D.C.: The Smithsonian Institution, 1847.

Smith, M. A., and N. D. Sharp. "Pleistocene Sites in Australia, New Guinea, and Island Melanesia: Geographic and Temporal Structure of the Archaeological Record." In *Sahul in Review: Pleistocene Archaeology in Australia, New Guinea, and Island Melanesia.* Edited by M. A. Smith, M. Spriggs, and B. Fankhauser. Canberra: Australian National University, Dept. of Prehistory, Research School of Pacific Studies, 1993.

Stanford, D. J., and J. S. Day, eds. *Ice Age Hunters of the Rockies.* Denver, Colo.: Denver Museum of Natural History and University Press of Colorado, 1992.

Tindale, N. B. "Culture Succession in South Eastern Australia from Late Pleistocene to the Present." *Records of the South Australian Museum* 13 (1957): 1–49.

Todorov, T. *The Conquest of America: The Question of the Other.* New York: Harper and Row, 1982.

Walsh, G. *Bradshaws: Ancient Rock Paintings of North-West Australia.* Geneva: The Bradshaw Foundation, 1994.

Webb, R. Esmée and David J. Rindos. "The Mode and Tempo of the Initial Human Colonisation of Empty Landmasses: Sahul and the Americas Compared." In *Rediscovering Darwin: Evolutionary Theory and Archaeological Explanation.* Edited by C. Michael Barton and Geoffrey A. Clark. Washington, D.C.: Archaeological Paper of the American Anthropological Association (1997): 233–250.

Willey, G. R., and P. Phillips. *Method and Theory in American Archaeology.* Chicago: University of Chicago Press, 1958.

Wilson, Daniel. *Prehistoric Man: Researches into the Origin of Civilisation in the Old and the New World.* 2d ed. London: Macmillan and Co., 1865 [1862].

Wormington, H. M. *Ancient Man in North America.* 4th ed. Denver, Colo.: The Denver Museum of Natural History, 1957.

2

The Frontier and Anthropology: Reflections on the Australian and American Experience

JOHN MULVANEY, PROFESSOR EMERITUS, AUSTRALIAN NATIONAL UNIVERSITY

ON OCTOBER 24, 1861, the United States transcontinental telegraph line was joined at Salt Lake City and the first Morse code message was tapped across the continent, preceding the first railway by eight years. Strangely, many American historians barely mention this feat, highlighting instead the Pony Express, which the telegraph consigned to bankruptcy after only eighteen months of daring horsemanship.

Half a century had elapsed since Meriwether Lewis and William Clark crossed America, so subsequent exploration, settlement, and contact with and impact on Indian societies ensured that the American frontier was a complex series of linkages, not some inexorable westward push. The revisionist historians Lamar and Thompson, in their *Frontier in History,* justifiably assert, "we regard the frontier not as a boundary or line, but as a territory or zone of interpenetration between two previously distinct societies." They suggest in passing that "the history of the Australian frontier is similar to . . . the North American but was later starting, slower developing, and smaller in scale."[1]

My theme concerns the "frontier" in Central Australia where, despite the above opinion, developments were surprisingly rapid, and where striking parallels exist with American technological, racial, and social experiences. They merit much closer study than this impressionistic sketch. For this American audience, it is relevant to quote dates for comparative purposes.

It was 1862 when J. McDouall Stuart, a dour but thirsty Scot, traveled north from Adelaide and by July reached the continent's farthest shore. At a time when the railway from Adelaide had fingered north for only one hundred miles, construction of the Overland Telegraph commenced on September 15, 1870, essentially following Stuart's trail across almost two thousand miles of virtually unknown country. As the Line progressed, lesser explorers and surveyors sallied out in various directions across Aboriginal lands in order to secure timber and water supplies, but also with interests in noting suitable pastures.

The first full telegraphic message spanned the miles between Adelaide and Darwin on August 22, 1872; soon afterward, Australia possessed a submarine cable link with London. It was a dramatic result for a thinly populated colony, only settled in 1836, but whose technology sufficed to span the distance from Boston to the Rockies.

Some statistics show the magnitude of the task. The single-strand iron wire was strung along thirty-six thousand poles. Extensive arid lands lacked suitable timber, each wooden pole averaged several miles cartage. When iron poles became necessary in the tropics to prevent termite attack, they averaged transport of some three hundred and fifty miles.

Morse code technology required repeater stations along the route to boost weak signals, so twelve solid stone telegraph stations lined the route, providing enclaves of predominantly male white settlement. Alice Springs

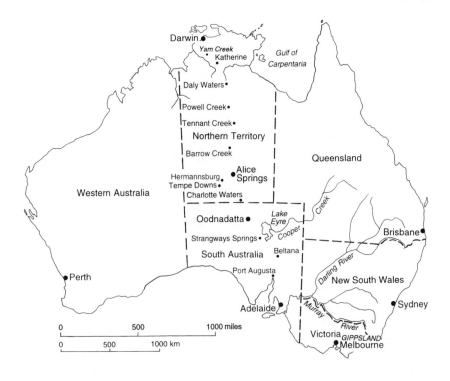

Map of the Overland Telegraph Line Indicating Repeater Stations

station was located at the midpoint, just north of the rugged Macdonnell Ranges. For our future attention, in 1875 a twenty-year-old Irish telegraphist, Francis James Gillen, was posted there. Unlike the United States of America, the optimistic colonial dream of a railway paralleling the Line never eventuated. Although it reached Oodnadatta by 1890, seven hundred miles from Adelaide, today it terminates at Alice Springs still only halfway to Darwin.

The South Australian government was unaware of problems, however, when it rapidly capitalized on prospects. Bureaucrats drew lines on the map enclosing hundreds of square miles. Australians termed such pastoral estates "runs," and they were open to takers. A lease would be issued provided that a run was stocked within three years. By 1873 the first runs were taken up near Alice Springs, some receiving leases in 1876. By the 1880s speculators grazed cattle across enormous areas, many of them totally unsuitable for stock. Enterprising men were presented with potential prospects which surely compared with their cowboy contemporaries in the Wild West.

Only ten years after Stuart's trailblazing, therefore, the continent was bisected by a boundary consisting of a single wire and associated track, linking watering points along an arid frontier. It functioned both as a lifeline for landtakers, along which they drove their stock, and as a safety net by explorers who penetrated regions outward from it, or trekked toward it from distant points east or west, secure in the knowledge that they must somewhere intersect with the Line. Already in 1872, D'Arcy Uhr, an enterprising Queenslander, drove four hundred cattle around the Gulf of Carpentaria to the expanding meat market along the northern sector of the Line. For, in the northern sector, when men dug holes for poles near Yam and Pine Creeks, they found traces of gold, so there were soon many prospectors to feed.

Despite jubilant colonial reactions to these discoveries and the elevation of explorers and pastoral pioneers to heroic status, this vast territory already was a discovered and inhabited land, but settlers, and until recently historians, virtually ignored the Aboriginal inhabitants in the saga of land settlement. I believe that I may claim the tardy honor of being the first to produce a book championing their forgotten history. My 1969 synthesis, *The Prehistory of Australia,* opened with the truism that "the discoverers, explorers and colonists of the three million square miles which are Australia, were its Aborigines."[2]

In America Patricia Nelson Limerick observed of historiographical concerns that slavery "was the domain of serious scholars . . . the subject of conquest was the domain of mass entertainment." In Australia, substitute convicts for slavery. It was anthropologist W. E. H. Stanner who wondered in 1958 whether Australians had a file marked "facts we would rather not know about"; later he castigated "the great Australian silence" concerning Aboriginal history. To John La Nauze, the first holder of the Harvard Chair,

Aborigines were noticed in our history only in a "melancholy anthropological footnote." James Axtell similarly noted that "American Indians were more invisible than blacks." Fred Alexander, who applied Frederick Jackson Turner's thesis to Australia in his *Moving Frontiers,* even blamed the indigenes for "the Australian frontier [failing] to produce a more vigorous local community life [which] is explained by the absence of strong aboriginal resistance comparable with that of the Red Indians."[3]

Today a vigorous school of historians is documenting the considerable extent of Aboriginal resistance, but at times this school's black armbands evidently blur its vision of other mitigating factors in crediting those who were humane colonists. James Axtell warned American historians that "bleeding-heart nativism will alienate the intelligent reader as quickly as anticolonial iconoclasm," and this is a factor today in the divisive land rights debate in Australia.[4] Historians of both continents have undergone profound rethinking, accepting that in culture contact situations consequences work both ways. When "savage" and "civilized" groups mutually experienced the shock of the new, they adopted and accommodated in diverse ways. Neither victor nor vanquished emerged unchanged. Self-determination was involved. As Cronon, Miles, and Gitlin emphasize, Indians "made their own choices about what to preserve and what to abandon from traditional ways." Francis Jennings aptly expressed the racial contact situation for both continents: "Europeans did not stay on one side of a line separating them from the awful savages—they mingled."[5]

Despite the human havoc that brutality, disease, and dispossession wrought on the indigenous populations of both continents, which contemporaries believed would exterminate those races, the truth is that their spiritual and cultural life sustained them more than it was deemed possible. Australian ethnographers judged Aboriginal culture "contaminated" by Europeans during the process of its decay. Yet in many cases, technological and social changes were conscious decisions and adaptations which produced positive results. Ironically, collectors of ethnographic specimens for museums a century ago rejected items which resulted from innovative adaptations to improve efficiency. Ernest Cowle, a policeman in Central Australia who collected for Melbourne's museum, for example, ensured that metal tips in admirably efficient woodworking chisels were replaced by stone flakes in order to make them "traditional."

Within this century innovative features that most white Australians believe typify Aboriginal culture actually are productive elaborations or adaptations to European models or markets. These include the proliferation of bark painting and basketweaving in Arnhem Land, dot-painted hardboard designs transferred from desert region ceremonial ground decoration, returning boomerangs, and the adoption of the didgeridoo as a national musical instrument.

Cronon et al. designate a more involuntary process of frontier change as "species shifting, the movement of alien organisms into ecosystems."[6] Lethal microorganisms and epidemiological disasters certainly followed the Overland Telegraph. Measles, whooping cough, respiratory, and venereal diseases cut a swathe through the indigenous population by 1900. The demographic impact of these diseases and related infertility was far more significant than the more publicized racial killings.

The Line was so much a man's world that even in 1900 it was said that only nine white women lived in Alice Springs. A contemporary photograph of the Alice Springs' annual race meeting has fifty-eight men and no women in view. Yet the white population soon depended on Aboriginal labor on the cattle stations, because Aboriginal men adapted readily to horse riding and they outnumbered white stockmen, though their role escaped mention in tales of European conquest of the land. It is significant that the black cowboy has been similarly omitted from the saga of the American West. In addition to Aboriginal labor force camps and their kin, the issue of rations also ensured that the races lived in proximity. Europeans seldom were as frank as W. H. Hardy, operator of the Arltunga goldfields stamp battery, east of Alice Springs: "Nearly every white man has his young lubra, who will toil away all day wood and water carrying, washing clothes etc." Night duties were not specified.[7]

One of white Australia's enduring social problems has been how to accept children of the resulting racial mixture. It was convenient a century ago to claim that evolutionary factors destined the Aboriginal race to extinction, while classifying half-castes as non-Aboriginal and devising eugenic engineering to "breed them white." Many Australians still believe that the last Tasmanian Aboriginal died in 1876. This is hard to reconcile with the claims of some three thousand descendants today who proclaim their Aboriginality.

The Overland Telegraph facilitated considerable species shifting, as domestic animals (horses, cattle, sheep, goats, and camels) spread across lands never previously compacted by cloven hooves, or where water resources were never drunk or muddied so prodigally. The release of cats, dogs, foxes, and rabbits all held profound consequences for the native flora and fauna. All these associated factors, together with the selection of the best water sources for European dwellings, ensured that indigenous people were forced to spear stock or were drawn to ration depots, in the one case inciting violent European reaction, and in the other, facilitating the spread of disease. Cronon et al. reached the heart of the matter with their dictum that "Ecology and Empire went hand in hand." The claim made by a pioneer anthropologist in 1880, A. W. Howitt, "that the advance of settlement has, upon the frontier at least, been marked by a line of blood," sadly has equal application.[8]

On this remote Australian imperial frontier there are many tales of atrocities, yet also others of initiative, endurance, and compassion. My favorite cowboy character is Tom Hamilton. As a youth in western Victoria, he raced against the celebrated poet and horseman, Adam Lindsay Gordon. During the early 1860s, Hamilton instructed and enthused young Aborigines on Bringalbert station on the game of cricket. Some of his team voyaged to England in 1868 to challenge Englishmen at their own game, but that is another story in Australian race relations.[9]

Spirited Hamilton was lured by the prospects of the Overland Telegraph. In 1872, aged 28, he drove a large mob of horses some two thousand miles from Victoria for sale in Darwin (as if from New Orleans to Halifax), dying of malaria a year later.

The cinematic potential of the Overland Telegraph saga has been ignored equally by Hollywood and local filmmakers. Like Australian artists and writers, films dwell instead on a prodigious contemporary failure—the Burke and Wills expedition across Australia. For Stuart was not the first European to reach the tropical shores. Burke and Wills set out from Melbourne in 1861 with a profligate cavalcade of men, supplies, and camels, which rashness and mismanagement reduced to four horsemen. They reached the northern coast a few months ahead of Stuart, but as three of them perished on the return journey, their efforts were futile.

An intelligent and well-educated stockman, Alfred William Howitt, rescued the survivor and retrieved the human remains. The grateful Victorian government rewarded Howitt by appointing him magistrate of that state's eastern district of Gippsland. There he achieved fame as a public servant, geologist, botanist, and the first major anthropologist of Aboriginal Australia.

Established now in Gippsland, the Overland Telegraph neared completion when Howitt read a notice in the *Australasian* newspaper, inserted by Lorimer Fison, a Wesleyan missionary from Fiji.[10] Fison had corresponded with Lewis Henry Morgan, the Rochester lawyer and ethnographer, whose *Systems of Consanguinity* was published in 1871.

In his advertisement Fison referred to Morgan's discovery of "the curious system of kinship among all the tribes of North America and among the Tamils" of India. Fison sought Australian collaborators to collect Aboriginal kinship data. Howitt evidently was the only reader to respond to Fison's appeal.[11] The origins of Australian and American anthropology therefore are closely linked.

Indeed, Fison and Howitt reacted so industriously to Morgan's constant encouragement that they completed a 366-page book by 1879. *Kamilaroi and Kurnai* was dedicated to Morgan, who contributed the introduction. Through his intercession the book was accepted for publication by the Smithsonian Institute, but because of long delays due to a publishing backlog, the authors withdrew their text and self-funded 550 copies in Australia. Morgan died before his offer to defray some of the cost could be taken up. Following his death in 1881, Howitt contributed a paper on Australian Group Relations to the 1883 Smithsonian Report, in which he stoutly defended Morgan's reputation against "violent attacks by certain critics . . . This confirmation of his conclusions will be gratifying to all who, like myself, admire his single hearted search after truth."[12]

This partnership among the trio of dedicated collectors of esoteric data is well documented in American anthropological literature. The repercussions of Morgan's inspiration on Aboriginal anthropology, even if misguided, were profound. Irrespective of the faults in his social evolutionary model, Morgan spurred Howitt to amass a corpus of data which, largely ignored by later anthropologists, is vital today in the cultural heritage of Aboriginal Australians. Significantly, the Australian Institute of Aboriginal and Torres Strait Islander Studies, reprinted (in facsimile) *Kamilaroi and Kurnai* in 1991, while Howitt's enormous compendium of 1904, *The Native Tribes of South-East Australia,* was published in facsimile in 1996. Meanwhile, Howitt's notes of an Aboriginal initiation ceremony which he attended in 1883 and sent to Edward Tylor at Oxford's Pitt Rivers Museum, in 1980 confirmed disputed Aboriginal oral traditions in southeastern New South Wales. The area was saved from devastating logging as a place of Aboriginal significance.[13]

In an earlier publication I labeled Howitt a postal anthropologist, because he specialized in distributing questionnaires to police, missionaries, and pastoralists across Australia. He was undaunted even though fewer than one in twenty recipients responded. Perhaps Howitt is better termed the "Cowboy anthropologist." He had circulars distributed the length of the Overland Telegraph through the assistance of his brother-in-law, the sheriff of Adelaide!

Even before he found Morgan, his interest in ethnography led him to "read through Lubbock *[Origin of Civilization]* riding across country . . . on the Great Dividing Range and High Plains." Late in 1873 Howitt wrote to Fison, explaining apologetically:

I have taken much interest in everything connected with the aboriginal natives . . . but . . . I have not much spare time and what I have has been for many years more than fully occupied by geological and mineralogical researches . . . when I say that I travel from 250 to 600 miles per month in the performance of my official duties and also . . . have been unravelling and illustrating by ground plates, sections as well as much contour survey about 54 sq miles round Bairnsdale. Add to this all my evenings occupied with examination of the metals, minerals etc of that district . . . I am at any rate not one of those who have spare time to devote to ethnological inquiry and do not avail themselves of it.[14]

Late in 1874 Morgan wrote directly to Howitt, so he then evidently rearranged his priorities, because the local Aborigines soon occupied Howitt's attention. Then in 1877 he received a copy of Morgan's *Ancient Society.*

> Have you received Ancient Society? [he asked Fison] But of course you have—Mr Morgan would be sure to send it to you. I have read it with the greatest satisfaction and interest. I think he has made out a very strong case and I find also that his views generally and mine seem to agree very closely. It has given me new ideas as to what I want to find out from our blacks here and I have already commenced.[15]

Writing to Morgan on February 28, 1876, Howitt reported "replies sent me from far to the northward on the Transcontinental Telegraph line," and hoped for more elaboration.[16] Although he failed to establish close links with officials on the Line, two decades later the Line focused international academic attention on the Arrernte (Arunta) people around Alice Springs.

It is time to record significant parallels again between the American and Australian frontier. On December 28, 1890, at least two hundred Indians lost their lives at Wounded Knee due to American Cavalry actions. Eight weeks later, on Tempe Downs cattle station, some one hundred twenty miles southwest of Alice Springs, Mounted Constable Willshire and his band of native police shot two Aborigines. While the evidence was being cremated, Willshire callously ate breakfast at the nearby homestead.

Willshire, based near Alice Springs, had not reckoned with the reaction of the local Post and Telegraph stationmaster, F. J. Gillen, Justice of the Peace. Gillen collected evidence and charged Willshire with murder, an unprecedented frontier action. South Australian pastoralists rallied to pay Willshire's legal costs, hiring an eminent barrister. Willshire was judged innocent at the trial, while Gillen was ridiculed in the press.

Yet among Aboriginal people, Gillen's brave action was a landmark event and henceforth he held the status of an Elder, fully trusted by them. In 1894 the Horn Scientific Expedition traversed the Center, ending its survey at Alice Springs. Baldwin Spencer, professor of biology at Melbourne University, was a member of that party. He and Gillen struck an amiable friendship, sustained by their mutual interest in Aborigines and whisky. Another congenial companion was Mounted Constable Ernest Cowle, who supplied Spencer with information over the following decade.

Spencer studied biology at Oxford during the early 1880s, but attended anthropology lectures by Edward B. Tylor, later assisting him to house the collections in the new Pitt Rivers Museum. His interest in marsupial fauna shifted to anthropology centered on Alice Springs people. The Spencer and Gillen classic, *The Native Tribes of Central Australia,* was published in 1899. It was dedicated to Howitt and Fison, supported by Tylor, and proofread by James Frazer, so its social evolutionary credentials were solid; it revisited themes pioneered by Lewis Henry Morgan.

This unfashionable evolutionist taint resulted in an unfortunate neglect of all Spencer and Gillen works by most twentieth-century social anthropologists. Howard Morphy and I have edited some 180,000 words of correspondence written by Gillen to Spencer. We believe that it establishes that their research was based on more than an evolutionary model. Another facet of their work revealed by the letters is the essential role that the Overland Telegraph played in their fieldwork. Through the cooperation of the South Australian Postmaster-General, Sir Charles Todd, who supervised the Line's construction, they had access to services and hospitality along that Line. Gillen's network of contacts meant that every repeater station from Charlotte Waters to Tennant Creek contributed data and ethnographic collections. In 1901 they traveled much of the length of the Line during a year's fieldwork. Nobody in Australia had attempted such extended participant observation fieldwork. Their correspondence reveals the extent to which data was cross-checked and their awareness that linguistic comprehension was an essential component of reliability. They both took a multitude of photographs, experimented with movie film, and recorded sound using unwieldy wax cylinders.[17]

There is time neither to investigate the richness of Gillen's correspondence, nor to explore the intelligent letters which Cowle sent Spencer from his isolated Illamurta police post. At a period in Australian history when the white community is divided on the claims of Aborigines to a stake in the land, and the significance to them of many places is disputed, it is appropriate to conclude by quoting the opinions of both men, with Gillen first:[18]

> I *think* a great deal of trouble with the Luritcha [Luritja tribe] is due to their being excluded from some of the best camping and hunting grounds on the run . . . At all our Telegraph stations along this line sheep and cattle have been bred without trouble from the blacks and I attribute this solely to the fact that we have never interfered with their camping grounds—With your knowledge of their traditions you will understand how a certain piece of country—perhaps the very piece from which he is excluded—means to the Nigger—It is hopeless to try to hammer this into the heads of Pastoralists who, when they take up a piece of country, appropriate the best portion for the exclusive use of their stock and relegate the Nigger to the barren wastes which are often destitute alike of game and tradition."

Listen now to Mounted Constable Ernest Cowle, a cynical character, who described *The Native Tribes of Central Australia* as "the 'Grimm's Fairy Tales' up to date by S & G."

> I believe that every water hole, Spring, Plain, Hill, Big Tree, Big Rock, Gutters, and every peculiar or striking feature in the Country, not even leaving out Sandhills, *without any exception whatsoever* is connected with some tradition and that, if one had the right blacks at that place, they could account for its presence there."[19]

Across Australia, as in the United States, there exists a similar sorry story of insensitive dispossession and a failure to comprehend the essentially spiritual relationship between people and landscape. In Australia this remains an essential problem today confronting the entire population.

Notes

1. H. Lamar and L. Thompson, eds., *The Frontier in History* (New Haven, Ct.: Yale University Press, 1981), 7, 310.
2. D. J. Mulvaney, *The Prehistory of Australia* (London: Thames & Hudson, 1969).
3. P. N. Limerick, *The Legacy of Conquest* (New York: Norton, 1987), 18–19; W. E. H. Stanner, *White Man Got No Dreaming* (Canberra: Australian National University, 1979), 46, 214; J. La Nauze, "The Study of Australian History, 1920–1959," *Historical Studies of Australia and New Zealand* 9 (1959): 11; J. Axtell, *The European and the Indian* (New York: Oxford University Press, 1981), ix; and Fred Alexander, *Moving Frontiers* (Melbourne: Melbourne University Press, 1947), 36.
4. Axtell, *The European and the Indian,* 15.
5. W. Cronon, G. Miles, and J. Gitlin, *Under an Open Sky: Rethinking America's West* (New York: Norton & Co., 1992), 10; F. Jennings, "A Growing Partnership: Historians, Anthropologists, and American Indian History," *Ethnohistory* 29 (1982): 29.
6. Cronon et al., *Under an Open Sky,* 11.
7. *Adelaide Observer,* July 16, 1898.
8. Cronon et al., *Under an Open Sky,* 12; L. Fison and A. W. Howitt, *Kamilaroi and Kurnai* (Melbourne: George Robertson, 1880), 182.
9. D. J. Mulvaney, *Cricket Walkabout* (Melbourne: Melbourne University Press, 1967), and with R. Harcourt, *Cricket Walkabout* (South Melbourne: Macmillan, 1988).
10. *Australasian,* June 15, 1872.
11. M. H. Walker, *"Come Wind, Come Weather": A Biography of Alfred William Howitt* (Melbourne: Melbourne University Press, 1971), 223.
12. The Howitt-Fison-Morgan letters are held in the Tippett collection of St. Mark's Library, Barton, Australian Capital Territory. The letters cited are

archived as TB3/11/7, 9, 14. Other details: number of print run—10 Apr. 1880; Morgan's offer of funding—21 Mar. 1880, 1 Aug. 1880. Fison Collection, National Library of Australia, MS 7080, 26 Mar. 1880—Morgan offered to cover part of any loss on *Kamilaroi and Kurnai*, one year after date of publication. Presumably he had died by that time. Quote from Howitt, *Australian Group Relations* (Washington: Government Printer, 1885), 28.

13. D. J. Mulvaney, *Encounters in Place* (St. Lucia: University of Queensland Press, 1989), 220–224.
14. Howitt to Fison, December 29, 1873.
15. Howitt to Fison, July 24, 1877.
16. B. J. Stern, "Selections from the letters of Lorimer Fison and A. W. Howitt to Lewis Henry Morgan," *American Anthropologist* 32 (1930): 259.
17. D. J. Mulvaney, H. Morphy, and A. Petch, *My Dear Spencer, The letters of F. J. Gillen to Baldwin Spencer* (South Melbourne: Hyland House, 1997).
18. Gillen to Spencer, May 1, 1896.
19. Cowle to Spencer, 28 May 1900. Mulvaney, Morphy, and Petch are editing E. C. Cowle's letters for publication. The letters are held in the Pitt Rivers Museum, Oxford.

References

Alexander, Fred. *Moving Frontiers*. Melbourne: Melbourne University Press, 1947.

Axtell, J. *The European and the Indian*. New York: Oxford University Press, 1981.

Cronon, W., G. Miles, and J. Gitlin. *Under an Open Sky: Rethinking America's West*. New York: Norton & Co., 1992.

E. C. Cowle letters. Pitt Rivers Museum. Oxford.

Fison Collection. National Library of Australia.

Fison, L., and Howitt, A. W. *Kamilaroi and Kurnai*. Melbourne: George Robertson, 1880.

Howitt-Fison-Morgan letters. Tippett collection of St. Mark's Library. Barton, Australian Capital Territory.

Jennings, F. "A Growing Partnership: Historians, Anthropologists, and American Indian History." *Ethnohistory* 29 (1982): 21–34.

Lamar, H., and L. Thompson, eds. *The Frontier in History*. New Haven, Ct.: Yale University Press, 1981.

La Nauze, J. "The Study of Australian History, 1920–1959." *Historical Studies of Australia and New Zealand* 9 (1959): 1–11.

Limerick, P. N. *The Legacy of Conquest*. New York: Norton, 1987.

Mulvaney, D. J. *Cricket Walkabout*. Melbourne: Melbourne University Press, 1967.

———. *Encounters in Place*. St. Lucia: University of Queensland Press, 1989.

———. *The Prehistory of Australia*. London: Thames & Hudson, 1969.

Mulvaney, D. J., and R. Harcourt. *Cricket Walkabout*. South Melbourne: Macmillan, 1988.

Mulvaney, D. J., H. Morphy, and A. Petch. *My Dear Spencer, The letters of F. J. Gillen to Baldwin Spencer*. South Melbourne: Hyland House, 1997.

Stanner, W. E. H. *White Man Got No Dreaming.* Canberra: Australian National University, 1979.

Stern, B. J. "Selections from the Letters of Lorimer Fison and A. W. Howitt to Lewis Henry Morgan." *American Anthropologist* 32 (1930): 257–279.

Walker, M. H. *"Come Wind, Come Weather": A Biography of Alfred William Howitt.* Melbourne: Melbourne University Press, 1971.

3

....

Mutant Message Down Under: A New Age for an Old People

L. R. HIATT, AUSTRALIAN INSTITUTE OF ABORIGINAL AND TORRES STRAIT ISLANDER STUDIES

INTRODUCTION

*I*N SEPTEMBER 1994 HarperCollins published a book called *Mutant Message Down Under*, written by an American woman named Marlo Morgan. It quickly hit the U.S. best-seller lists and within months was receiving the attention of Hollywood scriptwriters. Early in 1995, not long after the book's release in Australia, an Aboriginal cultural organization in Perth called Dumbartung took action to have it withdrawn from sale.[1] Representatives were dispatched to numerous Aboriginal communities on a north-south axis through Central Australia, successfully enlisting many of them in the campaign. In due course a delegation of elders traveled to the United States to protest against the book and to attempt to prevent its being made into a film. Their trip was financed by the ATSIC, an elected body representing Aborigines throughout Australia. Opposition to the book was based on three main charges: (1) that, although claiming to be inspired by the author's personal experiences in Australia, it is almost entirely a fabrication; (2) that its contents are deeply offensive to Aboriginal people; and (3) that it appropriates and exploits Aboriginal culture for monetary gain.

SUMMARY OF MUTANT MESSAGE

The story is told in first person, as an adventure of the author, Marlo Morgan, a 50-year-old chiropractor and acupuncturist from Kansas City. During a professional visit to Australia, she joins a tribe of desert Aborigines and walks with them across Australia. They call themselves the "Real

People" and are the last indigenous inhabitants to hold out against incorporation into European society. Moreover, she is the first white person to be allowed into their midst. In this summary I omit the author's contrivances to explain how she was invited to join the tribe, numerous episodes and adventures, her preoccupation with the state of her feet, her body odors, past life, and other details, in order to focus on the lifestyle of the Real People, their place in the history of the universe, and the contingent significance of her own role in relation to them.

The Real People take from the environment only what they really need. After fifty thousand years, they have destroyed no forests, polluted no water, endangered no species, and caused no contamination. At heart they are vegetarians. It was only after they were driven from the coast into the desert that they were forced to kill and eat animals. The Real People do not compete with each other. Individuals have different talents that they develop for the benefit of the tribe as a whole. The talents of each are honored by all. They are never dishonest and regularly communicate with each other by telepathy. They heal illness by communicating with the afflicted organ and reminding it of its true function. At the beginning of each day, the tribe forms a semicircle, faces east, and says thank you to Divine Oneness. The Real People believe that the universe was created when the loving power of Divine Oneness expanded outwards in all directions from its nucleus. The first Real People learned that anger, worry, greed, lust, lies, and power were things not to be cultivated. Ancestors who came to grief because of these evils were often metamorphosed as hills, rocks, and so forth, to remind later generations of their dangers.

The Real People of today are the last remaining representatives of the first true human beings who learned to live in love and peace. This happened when there was only a single landmass on the earth's surface and continued in an unbroken tradition in Australia after the formation of separate continents. Elsewhere, especially in the cooler northern continents, people resorted to aggression and competitive individualism in adapting to new conditions. They abandoned ancient wisdom, their skins turned a lighter shade of color, and they became mutant offshoots of original humanity.[2]

The modern arrival of Mutants in Australia was an unmitigated disaster for the Real People. Their land was stolen, their sacred sites were pillaged, many of them died in battle or from disease and poverty, and, with few exceptions, those who survived were forced into slavery. About twelve generations ago, the one remaining tribe of Real People established their headquarters in a secret cave in the desert. Morgan's admission to it forms the climax of her narrative. To her amazement she found that it contained a garden, a meditation room lined with opals, and a time-keeping device enabling records of births and deaths to be made in terms of years, seasons, and positions of the sun and moon. On the wall she found a carving indicating a birth at the exact time as her own. The babe was named Regal Black Swan, now known simply as the Tribal Elder. Later she obtained an audience with Regal Black Swan, who told her that many years ago he had been made aware of a spiritual partner among Mutants living in the northern hemisphere. She had been sent for now because ecological disturbances brought about by Mutant technology had made physical survival impossible for the Real People and they were leaving the planet. Having religiously nurtured the Earth Mother since the beginning of time, they were now bequeathing that trust to the Mutants. Morgan was their chosen messenger. The outlook was bleak, but signs of a new consciousness among the young gave cause for hope. She must do her best.

ELABORATION OF DUMBARTUNG CHARGES

(1) Fact or Fiction?

In a postmodernist age, when anyone's truth is said to be as true as anyone else's, it is refreshing to witness a vigorous attempt to demonstrate that at least one text is downright false. Working in the positivist tradition, Western Australian Aborigines traveled through the Australian outback seeking corroboration of Morgan's narrative. Not a single Aboriginal person could be found who had heard of her, let alone seen her. Dumbartung noted the following infelicities in the text itself: (a) Aborigines do not walk over spinifex grass but around spinifex clumps; (b) Desert people do not use water to cook food, nor do they collect dung for fuel; (c) Numerous customs and concepts described in the book derive from North American Indian culture and are not in fact found among Aborigines (e.g., personal names like Secret Keeper, Sewing Master, Medicine Man; feathered headdresses; statues of wood and stone; and ceremonial pipe smoking).

(2) Offense to Aboriginal People

The most offensive aspect of the book is said to be that it presents cultural knowledge as being freely shared between men and women. In Aboriginal society, certain domains of knowledge are restricted to men, and others to women. Disclosure of secrets is subject to severe penalties. While it is true that *Mutant Message* does not reveal actual Aboriginal secret knowledge, since the book is a total fabrication, nevertheless the mere suggestion that an Aboriginal male would (or could) describe birthing procedures to a white woman, or that women could see the same sacred ceremonies as men, is in itself deeply offensive. A spokesman for one community said Morgan deserved the death penalty. The assertion that the secret cave of the Real People is the only sacred site left in Australia, following the depredations and appropriations of white invaders, is classified as denigratory as well as false. Last, but not least, the book denigrates urban Aborigines by referring to them as "half-castes," by implying that they have sold out to official policies, and by claiming that some of them evinced a wish to "breed out" their Aboriginal blood.

(3) Appropriation and Exploitation

Dumbartung was established in 1987 to promote Aboriginal visual, performing, and literary arts. It sees itself as an agency with the right to control the artistic use of Aboriginal cultural material, at least in the state of Western Australia. Given the mass circulation of Morgan's book and the apparent credence given to her claim to be an official spokesperson for the Real People, heads of Aboriginal organizations meeting under the auspices of Dumbartung in Perth agreed that it had become imperative to expose her as an impostor. Dumbartung states that Aboriginal people have never needed anthropologists, lawyers, doctors, or nonindigenous authors to tell their story. It notes as a matter of regret that readily accessible writings by such people may have provided Morgan with a framework for her falsehoods. The time has come for indigenous peoples throughout the world to protect their cultures against further exploitation.

COMMENTARY ON DUMBARTUNG CHARGES

However regrettable the existence of an anthropological corpus, recourse to it was made in the form of a report commissioned by Dumbartung from Dr. John Stanton of the Berndt Museum of Anthropology. A more exhaustive examination of the record than Dr. Stanton was able to make might even have persuaded Dumbartung that an empirical investigation among desert tribes was unnecessary, for nothing remotely like Morgan's account of Aboriginal cosmology and sacred technology is to be found anywhere in the reputable literature published since the establishment of the British colony in 1788. If the Real People really exist, they are recent arrivals from outer space pretending to be Aborigines and, for whatever purpose, using Morgan as their agent. If she really traversed the Australian continent on foot without shoes at an average of twenty miles a day in midsummer, she may even be one of them. Anything is possible. For the time being, the safest bet is that the Real People are products of the imagination of a naturopath from Kansas City and that *Mutant Message Down Under* is a New Age parable inscribed on the palimpsest of the author's fleeting impressions of Australia and its indigenous inhabitants.

On returning to America, Morgan produced a manuscript and published it herself when no one else seemed interested. Presented as a documentary account of her journey, it sold 275,000 copies through New Age outlets before Rupert Murdoch heard the good news, after which a further 350,000 copies were produced for a still-eager market. Although the back cover described the new edition as "the fictional account of the spiritual odyssey of an American woman in Australia," it included an equivocal foreword in which the author still maintained that the book was "written after the fact." A curious figure given in a report by Susan Wyndham in *The Australian Magazine* late in 1994, though not explained there or discussed in other commentaries, is that Morgan actually gave away some 85,000 copies of the first edition.[3] This would be hard to reconcile with her alleged cupidity and clearly points to a higher purpose; viz. to spread glad tidings. Conversely, the avidity of her readership reflects not an addiction to travel romance but exhilaration on being told that the central values and aspirations of the New Age movement are enshrined in the world's oldest surviving culture. If this is a correct interpretation of Morgan's motivation, we can reasonably infer that whatever offense *Mutant Message* gave to Aboriginal sensitivities, it was not intentional. On the contrary, the manifest purpose of the narrative is to elevate Aboriginal wisdom, values, and practice to the highest plane, where they can be contemplated as an exemplary alternative to the materialistic, competitive, and unhealthy lifestyles of the industrialized world. Admittedly, some Aborigines might be peeved by the assertion that they too have been infected by modernity. But it would be a hard charge to deny; and, perhaps accordingly, Dumbartung decided to give primacy to the offense of suggesting that Aboriginal men and women keep no secrets from each other. While one can acknowledge that such offense may be genuinely felt, the ethos rendering individuals susceptible to it would not necessarily be an object of universal admiration. To put the matter another way, it is unlikely to have occurred to Morgan that, in representing openness between the sexes as a characteristic of Aboriginal culture, she was in fact demeaning it.

The most remarkable feature of the section of the Dumbartung document cataloging the falsehoods of *Mutant Message* is that, while it attends to trivialities like spinifex grass and kangaroo dung, it remains almost totally silent on what a New Age readership would regard as the central assertions: that Aborigines in their pristine state communicate by telepathy, can heal by touch, are vegetarians by preference, have never endangered any species, are never dishonest, live with each other in love and peace, record births and deaths by an elaborate time-keeping system, attribute mystical significance to synchronicity, worship Divine Oneness, are direct descendants of the first beings, and have lived in Australia since the beginning of human history. Every one of these propositions could be challenged on the basis of the scientific record. Why then, if Dumbartung is concerned to show that the book is completely without foundation, have they been allowed to stand?[4] It may be hard to say so, but Dumbartung seems less concerned with the truth of statements about Aboriginal culture, especially if they are congenial, than with the right to make them.

The salability of Aboriginal culture is now widely established in the marketplace, and, not unnaturally, Aborigines themselves are seeking a fair return. No fair-minded person could be against it. The difficulty is to distinguish between cultural appropriations and free exchanges of ideas; or between custodianship and censorship. It would rightly be regarded as intolerable if black writings could be published and sold in bookshops only after a committee had agreed that they contained nothing offensive to whites. Anyone who ridiculed Aborigines for modernist pretensions in assimilating elements of Christianity into their traditional religion would properly be accused of racism.

While Aborigines should receive every encouragement to present and interpret their culture to outsiders, there are serious dangers in fostering the notion that this should be an exclusive prerogative. Dumbartung's censorious attitude to *Mutant Message Down Under,* with demands for suppression and muted hints of a death-sentence *fatwa,* may be no more than an overreaction to a trespassing Yankee goldminer. More likely, it signifies a developing mood in Aboriginal politics on the definition and control of cultural property.

If the notion of cultural appropriation is to gain intellectual and legal respectability, it obviously needs to be applied evenhandedly.[5] The dilemmas engendered by this requirement, as well as the sophistry used to resolve them, are exemplified in a recent article on *Mutant Message* by Gareth Griffiths, Professor of English at the University of Western Australia. In 1995 Griffiths gave some lectures at Guelph University (Ontario) on the works of Sam Watson, an Aboriginal activist whose recent book *The Kadaitcha Sung* spins a tale of racial hatred and revenge. Watson's works, according to Griffiths, provide a powerful example of "the synergic force which can result from the blending of traditional indigenous narrative elements and contemporary forms such as science fiction, video games, and other contemporary media."[6] After his lectures he was dismayed when a Native American graduate student expressed admiration for *Mutant Message Down Under* and put it to him that in principle Marlo Morgan and Sam Watson were doing much the same thing. Here is his reply:

> I tried my best to draw a distinction between the creation of a text by an indigenous writer, which incorporated and appropriated Western contemporary narrative to dismantle the historical and narrative assumptions in Western representations of indigenous culture, such as Watson's, and Morgan's creation of a fictional "tribe" whose magical powers were claimed to represent the "true" world of the Aboriginal people, whose purpose, it reveals, is to lead us, the white mutants, towards a recovered truth and new wholeness of being.[7]

Let me assure you that Watson's writings are as replete with attributions of magical powers to Aborigines as Morgan's. Professor Griffiths' distinction is to be understood wholly in terms of political correctness: it is justifiable for a native writer to appropriate Western forms in order to deconstruct the imperialist and racist attitudes embedded in them; it is not justifiable for a Western writer to extract a message from an indigenous culture for the betterment of her own people. The former is a heroic critique of colonialist exploitation, the latter a self-indulgent perpetuation of it.

Whether Griffiths managed to convince his student is not reported, but it soon became evident that she was not an isolated case. With growing horror (I use his own words) he realized that, in spite of the many demonstrations of the falsity of *Mutant Message,* the book was still being taken seriously not only by decadent and weak-brained members of the American middle classes but by the indigenous communities of North America and those who support them in their struggles. How could this be explained? Griffiths's secular militancy leads him to suppose that Native Americans have adopted *Mutant Message* in order to further their own interests through a tactical alliance with the Green lobby. He concedes that there may well be advantages in such a strategy, especially "where values which critique the oppressive, technological nature of modern social institutions look to other cultures for alter/native visions of what human life might be about."[8] But (perhaps remembering that this is precisely the ideological purpose of *Mutant Message Down Under)* he immediately warns of the dangers inherent in a strategy that links threatened indigenous cultures with the "world of the extra-terrestrial and the supernatural."[9]

The trouble with this is that the cultures referred to are already deeply immersed in such a world and have been from time immemorial. When Griffiths speaks derisively of the metaphysics of the New Age, he does not seem to realize that consistency would require him to speak just as disparagingly of the metaphysics of the Stone Age.[10] A spiritual and mystical conception of the universe is what they have in common, and that is precisely why they are interested in each other. Their mutual affinities not only unite them in opposition to Western materialism but distinguish them in significant ways even from Western religion: a lack of interest in sin and redemption, mystical animism instead of anthropomorphic monotheism, geophilia, and so on. Whereas Christian missionaries consistently despised the superstitions of tribal people and attempted to replace them with their own, contemporary New Agers embrace them in the name of a universal spirituality.

The history of the New Age movement has recently been set out with admirable detachment by Peter Washington in his book *Madame Blavatsky's Baboon.* This enables us to see that an amalgam of astrology, occultism, orientalism, mysticism, and quasi science promoted by the Theosophical

Society in the early years of the twentieth century has reemerged, along with an augmented ecological consciousness, toward the end of it. However variously the ingredients are weighed and mixed in individual minds, the general appeal of the movement for people whose religious traditions have been undermined is evidently quite powerful. While the most dynamic centers at the moment are located in the spiritually destabilized populations of the West, a diffusion of New Age ideas and values to culturally disoriented indigenous populations of the postcolonial Fourth World has begun, and it will be a matter of considerable interest to see how they fare and to what uses they are put.

In Australia the received view in academic circles, formulated in a seminal essay by Professor Julie Marcus some ten years ago, is that New Age interests in Aboriginal culture are extractive and exploitative in much the same sense as mining interests. Having depleted their own spiritual resources, European pilgrims are now trying to tap metaphysical sources of energy in the Australian outback. Their ventures ride roughshod over the distinctive features of Aboriginal religious beliefs and practices, which are wrenched out of context, incorporated into synthetic rituals, and later homogenized and transformed for consumption in New Age markets of white Australia, Europe, and North America. Aborigines receive little or nothing in return. Even worse, by representing indigenous peoples as repositories of transcendental wisdom and happiness, New Age ideology distracts attention from their earthly sufferings under European domination and their political struggles for liberation and equality.[11]

While there may be elements of truth in this viewpoint, it strikes me as basically unfair. First, New Age pilgrims (like any pilgrims) seek to better themselves, but not at the expense of the host culture. There are profits to be made from pilgrims, as well as from believers in the countries from which they originate, but, in general, rank-and-file New Agers are not profiteers. Second, probably alone among European visitors to Aboriginal Australia, New Agers think of themselves and their hosts as coreligionists and fellow animists. Politicians, academics, even miners, nowadays, may pay lip service, but either they owe allegiance to Christianity or are crypto-atheists. Third, New Age preoccupations with the transcendental do not necessarily remove adherents from the mundane world of politics, as witnessed by Annie Besant's efforts on behalf of Indian Independence in the heyday of Theosophy and the present-day involvement of her heirs with the Green movement. Conversely, Aborigines are beginning to support their political aspirations in modern Australia with religious ideologies that, if not directly inspired by New Age doctrines, are at any rate highly compatible with them. This happened in the Hindmarsh Island case, appears ubiquitously in the doctrine of "Mother Earth," and is evident in recent Aboriginal reworkings of the writings of anthropologists.[12] Similar processes are occurring among

Native Americans, and it is not implausible to suggest that New Age spirituality may end up contributing as much to a unifying framework for indigenous Fourth World peoples as dialectical materialism or secular humanism. Because materialists and humanists are unable to take the metaphysical doctrines of the New Age seriously, they understandably find it difficult to conceive its adherents as potential allies in a noble cause. Nevertheless, it is poor politics to snub a common aspiration. As Washington notes in *Madame Blavatsky's Baboon:*

> For a brief, glorious decade from 1919 to 1928 [the Theosophical Society] flourished among the world's youth as a sort of junior League of Nations. For what appealed to young people was not Theosophy's ceremonial and the psychic mumbo-jumbo but its humanitarian, pacifist and international ideals, embodied in the summer camps and the fetching person of Krishnamurti himself . . . Krishnamurti stood, apparently, for freedom, happiness, mutual tolerance and self-fulfilment.[13]

If something of the same spirit persists in contemporary New Age circles, its transmission to Aborigines could hardly be regarded as a bad thing, either for themselves or their Fourth World compatriots. On the final page of *Mutant Message Down Under,* Morgan published a letter written to her by an Aboriginal elder named Burnum Burnum, which reads in part:

> [The book] portrays our value systems and esoteric insights in such a way as to make me feel extremely proud of my heritage . . . . In the seventeenth century the English explorer William Dampier wrote of us as being the "most primitive, wretched people on the face of the earth." *Mutant Message* uplifts us into a higher plane of consciousness and makes us the regal and majestic people that we are.[14]

The encomium is reproduced in the Dumbartung document under the heading "Divide and Rule." Yet any attempt to represent Burnum Burnum as a white man's dupe would need to dispose of some awkward facts: (a) that, after studying law in Tasmania, he applied pressure on the Royal Society Museum to hand over the physical remains of Truganini[15] for appropriate last rites; (b) that he was actively involved in the Tent Embassy outside Parliament House in Canberra; (c) that he was sacked for using official time and a government vehicle to attend antilogging protests in northern New South Wales; and (d) that on the occasion of the bicentenary of the colonization of his native land, he planted the Aboriginal flag on the white cliffs of Dover and claimed England in the name of the indigenous people of Australia. It is true that, immediately afterward, he made a pilgrimage to Salzburg, birthplace of his favorite composer. It is also true that he was an adherent of Bahaism, a movement seeking universal peace and affirming the essential oneness of all peoples and all religions.[16]

To be sure, *Mutant Message Down Under* is as much a romance as the libretto of *The Magic Flute*. Yet, if we hope to understand why Native Americans give credence to its message, we would do better to heed Burnum Burnum than those who treat it as an opportunity to advocate parochialism and thought control. The emancipation of indigenous peoples, not only from colonial subordination but from the constraints of tribalism in both its modern and traditional forms, may ultimately depend less on rational, coordinated, and centralized policy making than on shifting alliances between strange bedfellows.

Notes

1. I am basing this account on a set of documents published by the Dumbartung Aboriginal Corporation under the title *Bounuh Wongee (Message Stick): A Report on* "Mutant Message Down Under." The coordinator of the documents is Robert Eggington. I have also consulted newspaper reports, as well as Robert Eggington's "Statement on the Marlo Morgan Affair" and "Interview with Robert Eggington, May 1996" in *Ulitarra* 9 (1996): 73–75.
2. Cf. Ted Berk's notion of an LSD-induced "mutant consciousness," discussed by James Webb, "The Occult Establishment," p. 78, in *Not Necessarily the New Age,* ed. Robert Basil (Buffalo, N.Y.: Prometheus Books, 1998), 54–83.
3. Susan Wyndham, "The Mystery of Marlo Morgan Down Under," *The Australian Magazine,* 29–30 October 1994, 50–53.
4. Dr. Stanton's report, though more detailed than Dumbartung's own critique, is hardly less irrelevant on the matter of the central assertions. The closest it comes to skepticism is a description of some of them (e.g., telepathy) as "popular stereotypes." A lacuna on the central empirical issues likewise appears in a comment on *Mutant Message Down Under* by Aboriginal writer Jackie Huggins ("Trancing into the Desert: An Interview with Jackie Huggins," *Thamyris* 3, no. 1 [1996]: 5–17). To her great credit, Huggins acknowledges that one of the main reasons why people found the book offensive was that it had made a lot of money. She praises *Mutant Message Down Under* for opening up "a space and knowledge about Aboriginal people" and affirms that Marlo Morgan donated a sum of money for the support of Aboriginal women writers.
5. Julie Marcus's definition of cultural appropriation as "the processes by which meanings are transformed within a political hierarchy" is presumably intended to exempt borrowings by the weak from the strong ("The Journey Out to the Centre: The Cultural Appropriation of Ayers Rock," p. 254, in *Aboriginal Culture Today,* ed. A. Rutherford [Sydney: Dangaroo Press, 1988], 254–274).

6. Gareth Griffiths, "Mixed Up Messages Down Under: The Marlo Morgan 'Hoax': A Textual Travesty of Aboriginal Culture," *Ulitarra* 9, (1996): 76–85.

7. Griffiths, "Mixed Up Messages," 81.

8. Ibid., 84.

9. Ibid.

10. Article 7 of the *United Nations Draft Declaration on the Rights of Indigenous People* states: "Indigenous peoples have the collective and individual right not to be subjected to ethnocide and cultural genocide, including prevention of and redress for. . . (e) Any form of propaganda directed against them." If this were to be interpreted to include protection against ridicule, it would certainly be a right not available to proponents of the New Age. For a more general critique of the *Draft Declaration,* see Ron Brunton, "The Human Wrongs of Indigenous Rights," *IPA Backgrounder* 9, no. 1 (1997).

11. Julie Marcus, "The Journey Out to the Centre." See also Julie Marcus, "New Age Consciousness and Aboriginal Culture," *Thamyris* 3, no. 1 (1996): 37–54; Denise Cuthbert and Michele Grossman, "Trading Places: Locating the Indigenous in the New Age," *Thamyris* 3, no. 1 (1996): 18–36.

12. See Chris Kenny, *Women's Business* (Sydney: Duffy and Snellgrove, 1996), 97; Ron Brunton, "The Human Wrongs of Indigenous Rights"; Jim Everett, foreword to *Aboriginal Men of High Degree* (new ed.), by A. P. Elkin (Rochester, Vt.: Inner Traditions, 1993).

13. Peter Washington, *Madame Blavatsky's Baboon* (New York: Schocken Books, 1993), 270.

14. Marlo Morgan, *Mutant Message Down Under* (New York: HarperCollins, 1994), endpage.

15. Truganini was the last of the fully indigenous people of Tasmania. Shortly after her death in 1876, her remains were exhumed and given to the Royal Society of Tasmania. From 1904–1947 her articulated skeleton was on display in the Royal Society's museum. After representations from the Aboriginal community, the Tasmanian government agreed to Truganini's cremation with appropriate rites on the centenary of her death.

16. Sadly, Burnum Burnum died shortly after I presented this paper at Harvard. I offer its final passages as a tribute to his memory. For me, the most eloquent manifesto for the objectives of reconciliation remains *Burnum Burnum's Aboriginal Australia: A Traveller's Guide,* published in the year of the Australian Bicentenary (Sydney: Angus & Robertson, 1988).

References

Brunton, Ron. "The Human Wrongs of Indigenous Rights." *IPA Backgrounder* 9, no. 1 (1997).

Cuthbert, Denise, and Michele Grossman. "Trading Places: Locating the Indigenous in the New Age." *Thamyris* 3, no. 1 (1996): 18–36.

Dumbartung Aboriginal Corporation. *Bounuh Wongee (Message Stick): A Report on* "Mutant Message Down Under."

Eggington, Robert. "Statement on the Marlo Morgan Affair, May 1996." *Ulitarra* 9 (1996): 73

———. "Interview with Robert Eggington." *Ulitarra* 9 (1996): 73–75.

Everett, Jim. Foreword to *Aboriginal Men of High Degree* (new ed.), by A. P. Elkin. Rochester, Vt.: Inner Traditions, 1993.

Griffiths, Gareth. "Mixed Up Messages Down Under: The Marlo Morgan 'Hoax': A Textual Travesty of Aboriginal Culture." *Ulitarra* 9, (1996): 76–85.

Huggins, Jackie. "Trancing into the Desert: An Interview with Jackie Huggins." *Thamyris* 3, no. 1 (1996): 5–17.

Kenny, Chris. *Women's Business*. Sydney: Duffy and Snellgrove, 1996.

Marcus, Julie. "New Age Consciousness and Aboriginal Culture." *Thamyris* 3, no. 1 (1996): 37–54.

———. "The Journey Out to the Centre: The Cultural Appropriation of Ayers Rock." In *Aboriginal Culture Today,* edited by A. Rutherford. Sydney: Dangaroo Press, 1988.

Morgan, Marlo. *Mutant Message Down Under.* New York: HarperCollins, 1994.

Stewart, D. (ed). *Burnum Burnum's Aboriginal Australia: A Traveller's Guide.* Sydney: Angus & Robertson, 1988.

United Nations. *United Nations Draft Declaration on the Rights of Indigenous People,* Article 7.

Washington, Peter. *Madame Blavatsky's Baboon*. New York: Schocken Books, 1993.

Webb, James. "The Occult Establishment." In *Not Necessarily the New Age,* edited by Robert Basil. Buffalo, N.Y.: Prometheus Books, 1998.

Wyndham, Susan. "The Mystery of Marlo Morgan Down Under." *The Australian Magazine,* October 29–30, 1994, 50–53.

PART II

Literature and Fine Arts

4

The Past: Burden or Asset?

DAME LEONIE KRAMER, UNIVERSITY OF SYDNEY

Hear the voice of the Bard!
Who present, past and future sees[1]

could have been the text for W. Jackson Bate's 1969 Alexander lectures, given at the University of Toronto, because Blake is a special exemplification of Bate's thesis in *The Burden of the Past and the English Poet*. Bate's lectures are, however, *my* text for this paper, which also, in an oblique way, pays homage to Harvard and the Chair whose twentieth anniversary brings us together.

I had read *The Burden of the Past* long before I came to Harvard because of a particular interest in the mid-eighteenth century, which went back to undergraduate days. I read it again here, largely because Bate himself was a presence in Warren House, and one with whom I had quite frequent and enlightening conversations. At that time, his book began to puzzle me. Its learned and compelling thesis is that, in the period between the English Renaissance and the Victorians and near-moderns (1660–1830), the "full weight" of the burden of the past pressed first on the poet. Underlying the argument is a pervasive sense of melancholy. It's almost a temperamental problem, and it persists to the very end in his statement that

> the arts mirror the greatest single cultural problem we face, assuming that we physically survive: that is, how to use a heritage, when we admire and know so much about it, how to grow by means of it, how to acquire our own "identities," how to be ourselves.[2]

His thesis becomes a plea that we "reground our thinking, in turning back again to the essential to discover what next to do" (p. 134). I need not draw attention to how many questions that leaves us to contemplate. Sixteen years ago, at Harvard, I began to think about where we might look for answers.

Bate, with his depth of learning and remarkable capacity to distill and clarify knowledge, has much to say about the interplay between the poet's need to be different, the sense that certain creative forms are exhausted, and the feeling of "fatigue and depression" characteristic of the second half of the twentieth century. The challenge of the great poem to eighteenth century poets contemplating Homer and Virgil, the temptation to substitute novelty for originality and to imitate rather than renew traditional forms—all these signify, in Johnson's words, "superstitious reverence of the dead" (p. 77).

Curiously, Johnson's own words are a substantial contribution to answering Bate's many questions. Johnson writes about the constantly changing nature of "the living world." Human passions might remain constant, but their objects will change, and there is, therefore,

> a fund from which those who study mankind may fill their compositions with an inexhaustible variety.[3]

Further (since renewing the language as well as finding new subject-matter is what is needed), "the mutability of mankind will always furnish writers with new images" (p. 78).

Bate does not follow up Johnson's lead, principally, I suspect, because he confines himself to "the English poet," but the enigmatic ending to his last lecture suggests where some answers might be found. Speaking of Johnson, he comments that "in whatever direction you happened to be going, you met him on the way back" (p. 134).

In *The Burden of the Past,* there is a footnote—the only one that includes a reflection by the author—that points to a way out of Bate's more somber predictions of the future of poetry, and a means of achieving that "regrounding" of which he writes. In it he draws attention to the group of Scotsmen (which included Hume and Adam Smith) who from the middle of the eighteenth century commented on the course of English literature ("as a kind of Greek chorus"). Bate describes them as "less crushed than the English themselves by the weight of the great English past" (p. 100 n.).

To Bate

> much of the fascination of the group is that they serve as the prototype of what still remains unexplored in any really comprehensive sense (the subject is unique to English as contrasted with every other European literature): the relation, during the last century and a half, of the vastly expanded English-speaking world (in population now twenty times that of the Britain of 1800) to the vertically long, if geographically confined, creativity of English letters from the beginning to at least the mid-nineteenth century. (p. 100 n.)

In the nearly thirty years since his Alexander lectures, literature in English has flourished throughout the former colonies, and has demonstrated that, in the past, we all have an asset that, far from constraining our imaginative possibilities, actually helps us to define and release them. Some of the discussion of postcolonial experience, to the extent that it dwells on the burden of the past instead of recognizing its value, has distorted our perspective on literary history. Writing in English outside England kept alive the tree from which it branched.

In less than 210 years of settlement, Australia has developed a literature of remarkable richness and variety. How could that have occurred without a long tradition of literary experiment and achievement on which to draw? Before Les Murray's poetry became known abroad, Australia was better known for its fiction, partly because of film and TV. But poetry is and always has been Australia's real strength, and it provides a strong counterargument to Bate's analysis. My brief journey, therefore, takes me away from the English poet, to the poet who writes in English, and specifically to the beginnings of Australian poetry, and some of its later adventures.

The phrase "the shock of the new" perhaps best captures the impact of the mythical Great South Land on its first settlers. This is vividly described in a recent speech by Robert May, the physicist turned biologist, in an account of Captain Arthur Phillip's journey to establish the new colony:

> With its heat and storms, its forbidding terrain, its immense black nights and new stars, it must have seemed very far indeed from home and the rule of civilised society. It was a country populated by strange animals and insects. Here was a kind of Eden. Phillip had the task of establishing social routines and maintaining the importance of the ordinary—of building a settlement with ordered street plans and established farms.[4]

All the novelty, strangeness, and mystery of the hitherto unknown forms of life are expressed in one of the worst imaginable poems, redeemed only by its witness to the struggle for a form and language to describe its subject— *The Kangaroo*, by Barron Field. The burden of the past is evident in its epigraph from the *Aeneid*, and in rhetorical references to the sphynx, mermaid, centaur, Minotaur, Pegasus, the hippogriff, and chimeras. Field comes to the quite reasonable conclusion that this animal can only be the result of Nature's ability to reconcile differences, by joining together the squirrel and the "bounding hart." The kangaroo is a "divine mistake" put together when Nature was taking a day off from the labors of creation. Nonetheless, Field finds the strange animal "graceful," even "ethereal," and, with unnecessary exaggeration, also finds that it redeems the "fifth part of the earth" from "utter failure."[5] From *The Kangaroo* to Les Murray is indeed a leap, but

Field's earnest endeavors to deal with a new subject would have been utterly frustrated had he lacked a verse form and a range of reference to mythical creations which, at least, allows him to give some impression of his subject for an English audience.

The colonial poets, in various ways, exemplify the benefits of an inherited and shared literary tradition. Of these, the most interesting is Charles Harpur, born in 1813 of convict parents. Harpur immersed himself in English poetry, and he was especially indebted to Dryden, Pope, and Byron (for his satirical verse) and to Milton, Wordsworth, and Coleridge for his descriptive and meditative poems. He also made adaptations from Goethe and Schiller and from Cowper's translation of the *Iliad.*

There is a curious paradox here. For Harpur himself, intimate knowledge of the major English poets was an indispensable base from which to begin the search for his own poetic voice. Yet commentators and editors have taken an opposite view. Elizabeth Perkins, the editor of his *Collected Poems* (relatively few of which were published in his lifetime), remarks:

> Harpur believed he was innovative and original to the limits of poetic freedom, but his passionate respect for the traditions of the best English poetry circumscribed his creativity in form and technique. He would have shown a more truly creative genius had he produced poetry in which form and tone were more closely related to the milieu in which it was written, or to the ruggedness of his own mind.[6]

This argument is similar to that used about early colonial painters. It was advanced by Bernard Smith in *European Vision and the South Pacific,*[7] despite the fact that there are very few early painters who do not exhibit a clear-sighted response to the new landscape, even when they use the techniques of contemporary or earlier European painters. The same is true of those painters influenced by French impressionism. Their view of the landscape is mediated through impressionistic techniques, but their individual perceptions are readily distinguishable.

Perkins's criticism of Harpur's failure to relate form and tone to the milieu or to his own mental qualities is a serious misrepresentation of Harpur's persistent search for a distinctive language. Sometimes he is frustrated by the sheer difficulty of the attempt, as when, in "A Mid-Summer Noon in the Australian Forest," he drops into archaisms to preserve the metrical form. Yet what characterizes the poem is not these lapses, but the hard-won achievements. The echo of Marvell in the opening and closing stanzas does not suggest an unwelcome weight from the past, but a recognition of a shared experience of solitary meditation.

Similarly, "A Storm in the Mountains" is indebted to Wordworth's description of the storm on the lake in "The Prelude." In both poems the observer is an eleven-year-old boy, watching in fearful awe the natural world in turmoil, but Harpur's language captures the landscape of the Blue Mountains, not that of the Lake District:

> *These huge-piled ledges, ribbing outward, stare*
> *Down into haggard chasms; onward, there,*
> *The vast-backed ridges are all rent in jags,*
> *Or hunched with cones, or pinnacled with crags.*
> *A rude peculiar world, the prospect lies*
> *Bounded in circuit by the bending skies.*[8]

Harpur's characteristic mix of a fading poetic diction and a strong distinctive voice reveals the way in which he puts the poetic tradition to work in a place that offers an entirely new landscape for the expression of the constants of human experience. It's extraordinary that, even now, Harpur receives very little recognition for his understanding of what it is to use the past to transmit individual insights into the present.

The difficulty here is the strength of idea of originality, which, as Bate points out, began to take hold in the mid-eighteenth century. With some sharpness, he comments that

> some of the least original minds were beginning to prate constantly of "originality," thus setting a precedent with which the intellectual has since been condemned to live.[9]

Originality also came to be associated with an individual's identity, the concept of which has now, of course, assumed major proportions in our thinking about culture and nationhood. The demand for originality is an obstacle to accurate analysis and understanding of the relationship between tradition and the individual talent. Indeed, I would argue that it has encouraged a false reading of much colonial literature—both poetry and fiction. Colonial novels have been criticized for their debts, in particular to Dickens and Scott, and for their use of melodrama and plots of romance and adventure, even when, as in the case of Henry Kingsley, they are full of close observations of colonial social and political life, and of considerable knowledge of local botany and geology. The flaws in much colonial fiction are obvious, but they cannot be attributed to the narrative traditions on which their authors drew. It would be much more helpful to our understanding of early colonial writing if it were to be seen as exploratory and experimental, as was the work of Arthur Phillip.

Bate's speculative explanation of the rise of the concept of "pure poetry" leads to some important comments on the status of the epic and the longer forms of poetry. Poe described a long poem as a contradiction in terms, but many poets whose most valued achievements have been lyrics or other forms of short poems, have, nevertheless, felt that to write a long poem is the real test of one's poetic talent. Yet it is in attempting the epic form, or even the extended narrative, that the burden of the past is likely to be unbearably heavy. The Romantics and Victorians were not entirely unsuccessful in their attempts to escape from the achievements of Homer, Virgil, and Milton. But how can the modern poet challenge them?

There are some interesting examples of Australian poets testing themselves against the challenges of those epic subjects—such as heroism, the struggles, failures and triumphs of great enterprises, the battle between good and evil, the mysteries of human aspirations, or the origins and history of a civilization.

At the beginning of the century, Christopher Brennan, a man of great scholarship in classical, French, and German literature, began his *Poems 1913*, the form of which is related to Mallarmé's concept of the *livre composé*. His theme is mankind's search for Eden, though it includes many passages of distilled and mythologized personal experience. The goal is sought through love and self-knowledge which confronts the mythical figure of Lilith, the source of both desire and fear. The journey ends with the wandering spirit's abandonment of the search, and its resolution is a peaceful resignation to reality.

It is abundantly clear from Brennan's attempt at a substantial poetic epic of man's search for a lost paradise that he lacks the architectural powers that the writer of the classical epic and its Miltonic variation possesses. The way in which *Poems 1913* grew is itself an example of the tension between his lyrical gift (much influenced by the French symbolists) and his desire to make a more comprehensive poetic statement. Its often dense and tortured language reflects the difficulty of the subject matter, but out of the struggle for meaning emerge some poems of pure lyrical utterance. Once again, as with Harpur, it is difficult to see how such a sequence of poems could have been conceived without knowledge of "the tradition"—in his case, as for the eighteenth century poets, encompassing the classics as well as the English Renaissance.

Johnson's point about "the alterations which time is always making in the modes of life,"[10] is well illustrated by some major themes of Australian experience, beginning with the search for and discovery of the country itself. When James McAuley in the late 1950s began his narrative epic *Captain Quiros*, he was conscious of writing against the spirit and values of the time. The poem describes the expeditions of the Portuguese navigator in his search for the Great South Land. This is indeed an epic subject, and the most ambitious of a group of poems by various poets dealing with voyages of discovery.

At the beginning of Quiros's final voyage in search of Australia del Espíritu Santo, the narrator expresses Bate's sense of the battle to be fought:

Therefore I have less care who shall approve;
For poems in this kind are out of fashion,
Together with the faith, the will, the love,
The energy of intellectual passion
That build the greatness which we have resigned.
I play a match against the age's mind:
The board is set; the living pieces move.[11]

The final failed voyage sails under the stars of the southern skies, as the poet seeks to "make that inward vision/of spiritual cosmography" (p. 42).

The narrator's awareness of the mismatch between the present and the past has, I suppose, been verified by the fact that *Captain Quiros* has had a small audience, even though it is very effective as a spoken poem. Nevertheless, one could not possibly argue that McAuley has been burdened either by the historical past he records or by the narrative mode he has adopted, and indeed adapted (in its stanzaic form) to his own purposes and lyrical talents.

Before leaving McAuley, it should be said that his fine lyrical poetry was influenced early in his career by Rilke, and later by John Clare, Shaw Nielson, and Trakl. As a young poet, he experimented briefly with expressionism, and tried to recover and adapt Greek myth, and, when he later adopts the metrical scheme and name of one of Trakl's poems, he expresses his own sense of a shared poetic awareness. It is this kind of relationship between one poet and another that transcends the problem of emulation or even adaptation. Kindred poetic spirits can and do learn from each other without being dependent the one on the other.

Since McAuley and A. D. Hope, despite the great differences between them, are still frequently compared as traditionalists hostile to modern movements in poetry, it is worth remarking that the most significant difference between them is Hope's frequent recasting of mythology and his discovery of subject matter in an extensive range of reading, which includes psychology, anthropology, the Bible, and many different traditions and languages. His poetry is discursive, sometimes didactic in tone, satirical, comic, and, less frequently, lyrical. He laments the passing of the epistolary and long poem and attempts to revive it in formal, measured verse forms. So far from feeling the burden of the past, he exploits it for his own purposes. His allusiveness can seem to be imitative, but his language is often colloquial and larded with contemporary idiomatic usage.

Two other poets who are masters of lyrical forms but have also experimented with longer poems are David Campbell and Les Murray. David Campbell began his poetic career by renewing the nineteenth-century ballad tradition celebrating country life. Increasingly, however, he seemed to need forms more extended than the short lyric to encompass larger themes. So he constructed sets and sequences which enabled him to reflect on a subject, or examine it from different angles. A wide range of reference to classical mythology, modern art, Aboriginal rock carvings, and Russian poetry enriches the texture of his work, but at its heart is the English lyrical tradition, which he absorbed during his Cambridge years.

In the poetry of Les Murray, the renewal of longer forms brings into a new context his version of the Aboriginal song cycle of the oral tradition. He reflects a strong sense of the continuity of tradition and history. His most remarkable experiment with an extended poem is *The Boys Who Stole the Funeral*—a short story told in a sequence of forty sonnets.[12]

In none of these poets is there evidence of the "cultural cringe" from which, according to some critics, colonial and postcolonial writing still suffers. The essay entitled "The Cultural Cringe" by A. A. Phillips appeared in 1950. Its argument is that "above our writers—and other artists—looms the intimidating mass of Anglo-Saxon achievement."[13] Possibly deservedly, Phillips became the hero of A. D. Hope's version of Pope's *Dunciad—Dunciad Minimus*. Phillips was a nationalist who saw Australian writing as a victim, not a beneficiary, of its cultural heritage, and Hope was a poet with a strong sense of the value of that heritage, and with, at that time, very little interest in Australian subject matter.

In his essay "Tradition and the Individual Talent" to which I alluded earlier, T. S. Eliot discusses Blake, who is cited by Bate as one who, since the death of Pope, "had staggered under the weight of the burden." T. S. Eliot, however, in considering Blake's philosophy, so zealously and tortuously expounded in the prophetic books, concludes that Blake suffered from *not* being able to accept a borrowed philosophy as the foundation of his poetry:

> We have that same respect for Blake's philosophy . . . that we have for an ingenious piece of home-made furniture: we admire the man who has put it together out of the odds and ends about the house. England has produced a fair number of these resourceful Robinson Crusoes but we are not really so far from the Continent, or from our own past, as to be deprived of the advantages of culture if we wish them.[14]

And he goes on to say:

> What his genius required, and what it sadly lacked, was a framework of accepted and traditional ideas which would have prevented him from indulging in a philosophy of his own, and concentrated his attention upon the problems of the poet. (p. 321)

Eliot's argument here is curiously related to *The Waste Land*'s brilliant enactment of the loss of literary traditions and the dissolving structure of modern intellectual life.

At this point, I have one small hypothesis to offer as the start, perhaps, of another discussion.

By leaving Ireland, James Joyce was able to recreate the fragmented memories of European intellectual traditions in the mind of a wandering Dublin Jew. Perhaps the experience of colonial writers and their modern successors was similar. David Campbell began to write bush ballads in Cambridge. Patrick White's years in Europe resulted in an entirely new view of traditional Australian subjects such as pioneering, exploration, Aboriginal contact, and suburban life. A. D. Hope returned from Oxford, escaping "the lush jungle of modern thought/Which is called civilisation over there."[15] There are many other examples.

The path I have been following in this paper began here in Harvard, which offered me space and time to explore and reflect. I was a temporary expatriate and recognized, perhaps more sharply than during student days in Oxford, the benefit of distance. Geoffrey Blainey's "tyranny of distance" was for me transformed into a special kind of liberation.[16]

I shall probably never know what happened to the small group of students I taught, least of all what they might have learned. But I have no doubt about the benefits I continue to enjoy, most especially contacts with scholars from many disciplines, and for these I am profoundly grateful.

Notes

1. William Blake, "Introduction," lines 1–2, "Songs of Experience," *Songs of Innocence and Experience* (London: Oxford University Press, 1972).
2. W. Jackson Bate, *The Burden of the Past and the English Poet* (London: Chatto and Windus, 1970), 134.
3. W. Jackson Bate, (quoting Johnson, Samuel, *Idler and Adventurer*, Yale Edition of the Works of Samuel Johnson, vol. II, ed. W. J. Bate, J. M. Bullitt, L. F. Powell, in *The Adventurer*, no. 95), *The Burden of the Past and the English Poet* (London: Chatto and Windus, 1970), 134.
4. Professor Sir Robert May, *Australia's Heritage of Science and Discovery*, address given at the 5th Admiral Arthur Phillip Commemoration Service, January 25, 1996, in St. Mary-le-Bow Church, Cheapside, City of London, organized by the Britain-Australia Bicentennial Trust under the Chairmanship of Sir Peter Gadsden GBE, AC.
5. Barron Field, "The Kangaroo," in *The Colonial Poets*, ed. G. A. Wilkes (Sydney: Angus & Robertson, 1974), 7–8.
6. Elizabeth Perkins, ed., *The Poetical Works of Charles Harpur* (Sydney: Angus & Robertson, 1984), *xxix*.

7. Bernard Smith, *European Vision and the South Pacific 1768–1850: A Study in the History of Art and Ideas* (Oxford: The Clarendon Press, 1960).
8. Elizabeth Perkins, ed., "A Storm in the Mountains," lines 5–10, in *The Poetical Works of Charles Harpur* (Sydney: Angus & Robertson, 1984), 181.
9. W. Jackson Bate, *The Burden of the Past and the English Poet* (London: Chatto and Windus, 1970), 150.
10. W. Jackson Bate, (quoting Johnson, Samuel, *Idler and Adventurer*, Yale Edition of the Works of Samuel Johnson, vol. II, ed. W. J. Bate, J. M. Bullitt, L. F. Powell, in *The Adventurer*, no. 95), *The Burden of the Past and the English Poet* (London: Chatto and Windus, 1970), 78.
11. James McAuley, "The Quest for the South Land," stanza 6, in *Captain Quiros* (Sydney: Angus & Robertson, 1964), 42.
12. Les Murray, *The Boys Who Stole the Funeral*, 1980.
13. A. A. Phillips, "The Cultural Cringe," in *The Australian Tradition: Studies in a Colonial Culture* (Melbourne: Cheshire Longman, 1958).
14. T. S. Eliot, "William Blake," in *Selected Essays* (London: Faber and Faber, 1949), 321.
15. A. D. Hope, "Australia," stanza 6, line 2; stanza 7, line 4, in *Collected Poems* (Sydney: Angus & Robertson, 1972), 13.
16. Geoffrey Blainey, *The Tyranny of Distance: How Distance Shaped Australia's History* (Melbourne: Sun Books, 1966).

References

Bate, W. Jackson. *The Burden of the Past and the English Poet.* London: Chatto and Windus, 1970.

Blainey, Geoffrey. *The Tyranny of Distance: How Distance Shaped Australia's History.* Melbourne: Sun Books, 1966.

Blake, William. *Songs of Innocence and Experience.* London: Oxford University Press, 1972.

Eliot, T. S. "William Blake." In *Selected Essays.* London: Faber and Faber, 1949.

Field, Barron. "The Kangaroo." In *The Colonial Poets.* Edited by G. A. Wilkes. Sydney: Angus & Robertson, 1974.

Hope, A. D. "Australia." In *Collected Poems.* Sydney: Angus & Robertson, 1972.

May, Professor Sir Robert. "Australia's Heritage of Science and Discovery." Address given at the 5th Admiral Arthur Phillip Commemoration Service. January 25, 1996. London, Britain-Australia Bicentennial Trust.

McAuley, James. "The Quest for the South Land." In *Captain Quiros.* Sydney: Angus & Robertson, 1964.

Murray, Les. *The Boys Who Stole the Funeral*, 1980.

Perkins, Elizabeth, ed. *The Poetical Works of Charles Harpur.* Sydney: Angus & Robertson, 1984.

Phillips, A. A. "The Cultural Cringe." In *The Australian Tradition: Studies in a Colonial Culture.* Melbourne: Cheshire Longman, 1958.

Smith, Bernard. *European Vision and the South Pacific 1768–1850: A Study in the History of Art and Ideas.* Oxford: The Clarendon Press, 1960.

5

The Repeated Rediscovery of America

CHRIS WALLACE-CRABBE, THE AUSTRALIAN CENTRE,
UNIVERSITY OF MELBOURNE

To BE AUSTRALIAN is to keep discovering America, coming at you from unexpected angles, unless you are that kind of teenager who has lived in an imaginary America almost since birth: in that phantasmal, electronic United States which is made up from equal parts of Disneyland, Nike, basketball, McDonald's, Madonna, and baseball caps representing teams from a strange game that the child has never seen played. Publicity precedes praxis, and power—chiefly economic power—looms over all.

But I turn to the larger historical frame of our interactions. In his comic poem of the 1940s, "The True Discovery of Australia," James McAuley took Gulliver's fictive navigation seriously, locating the Lilliputians in Australia and the giant Brobdingnagians in overpowering North America:

XVII
And you will often find, although their heads
Are like a berry on a twig of bones,
They speak as giants of the South Pacific
And treat the islands as their stepping-stones.

XVIII
North-east across the water, Brobdingnag
Casts its momentous shadow on the sea
And fills the sky with thunder, but they smile
And sit on their verandahs taking tea,

XIX
Watching through the pleasant afternoons
Flood fire and cyclone in successive motion
Complete the work the pioneers began
Of shifting all the soil into the ocean.[1]

We should not forget that this was the tough decade in which Prime Minister John Curtin published his "Australia looks to America" article, marking a watershed in Australian foreign policy and in our cultural connections. Brobdingnag—oddly the same size as vulnerable Australia—was to be our military shield in the newly hostile Pacific. It was in the same few war years that the bold, submodernist Angry Penguins made their American discoveries, partly because the prose of Faulkner and of Carson McCullers fed their mildly surreal agenda. It was the Penguins who made contact with two American poets, Karl Shapiro and Harry Roskolenko, who were serving in Australia: they in turn put readers in touch with the poetry of Kenneth Rexroth and Robert Penn Warren, diversifying the usually French tilt of the avant-garde. But these two English-speaking nations of the New World had enjoyed sporadic relations over many decades before World War II and before the years of what Robin Boyd scornfully dubbed "Austerica." It is to the literary expressions of such contact that I especially turn: in particular to the way we southern Lilliputians have perceived the giants of the energetic northeast. At this point I cannot help recalling Alan Davies' influential article, "Small Country Blues," with its reminder of our pigmy population, our anxiety in the face of a world of energy systems. Davies reminds us, rather severely, of the huge gap that exists between geography and culture, between maps and chaps. These two enormous colonies, later democratic nations, can easily be read from their origins as history's deliberate opposites, the intensely religious foundation being well-watered as an expression of God's gratitude, while the bureaucratic settlement of late-Enlightenment years had to confront an island-continent which was largely dry, its soil frequently impoverished, chemically depleted, into the bargain. Of course, this is the trope which A. D. Hope reversed biblically in his endlessly anthologized *paysage moralise*, "Australia," with its half-serious sacralizing of the desert and its unspoiled kinds of wisdom. In his *Inventing Australia,* Richard White has given an excellent account of what the two countries were deemed to have in common in their early colonial days. In a chapter which is cutely entitled "Another America," White picks up some of the links with the older New World going back as far as a newspaper editorial of 1831 which saw the United States as "a model for all countries and New South Wales . . . in particular."[2] More tangible connections came with our almost simultaneous gold rushes at the midpoint of the nineteenth century, since many prospectors, "harbingers of modernity," took part in both. In his recent study, *Goldseeking,* David Goodman has not only examined the forces and phenomena which these two gigantic enterprises had in common but has also pointed back to the most influential goldfields writer, Bret Harte, whose clear, vigorous sentimentality was strongly felt in Australia as well as in North America.[3] Harte's influence was most directly felt by an Australian writer of the next generation, Henry Lawson, who grew up on decayed goldfields and read the diggings in a terse retrospect—which was also frequently sentimental. Henry Handel Richardson, who also wrote of the gold rush in retrospect, belonged to an entirely different, strongly European tradition of fiction and was untouched by Harte or by his fellow Americans. At this point I should swerve aside to an epistemological point about nations and societies. When we are young, or innocent, we entertain caricatures of different cultures (the Frenchman with his beret and baguette, washing down snails and frog legs with a bottle of red wine, for simple example). With maturity, we cast aside these cartoons for their sweeping crudity; we recognize the deep similarity of all human beings and family institutions. In the fullness of time, however, we may come to realize that our first models had a point, not only because they contained a seed of empirical truth but also because we become the cultures we think we are, Ned Kelly and Nelly Melba alive in every suburb. I cannot resist drawing a theoretical parallel here. It is with the way in which many critics of our time cast severe doubt on the capacity of language to mime with conviction anything in the external world, but still express their skepticism in the dullest of academic language. Caricatures, like language itself, are part of our common web of communication and, hence, of meaning-giving. They *signify*. They make sense. They are not to be despised.

Our great nineteenth-century novel, Furphy's *Such is Life*—comically picaresque and democratic, like *Huckleberry Finn*—is a good place to test the waters. Set in the dry grazing country of the Riverina, it nevertheless invokes American writers and mores. Cited or echoed are Benjamin Franklin, Tom Paine (English-born but American by affiliation and revolutionary ardor), Longfellow, Holmes, Mark Twain, and even Whitman. Excised from the final version of the book, however, was a whole novella, *Rigby's Romance,* the theme of which was intensely American, both comically and speculatively. Thus Tom Collins, the self-deconstructing narrator, can practice a ridiculous kind of national identification when he first catches sight of Kate Vanderdecken:

> By the foot, American, thought I, as my politely restricted arc of vision left the party behind—and you'll see by-and-by how infallible this role is. In fact, the foot of the American woman is a badge as distinctive as the moustache of the Australienne. However. there was a good expression in the foot now under notice, it was a generous, loyal, judicious foot, yet replete with idealism and soulfulness; wherefore I became at once prepossessed in favour of its owner.[4]

In the larger picture, what should surprise us is that Furphy has delineated his one representative American male as a committed socialist: so committed, alas, that while he preaches socialism on the banks of the Murray, he fails to notice that Kate Vanderdecken has come to him all the way from the United States; by the time he wakes up to romantic realities, she has gone home again. For Bernard O'Dowd, too, late-nineteenth-century America was the seedbed of radical possibility, and his socialism was fed by his constant reading of Whitman, with whom he was in correspondence (not that it affected his verse forms, alas). Whitman knew that he had a circle of fans in Melbourne and O'Dowd was so ardent a member that his copy of Whitman's poetry was blackened with use and his mates used to hail him with the greeting, "'Day, Bernard. Got your dirty little Walt?"[5]

In their turn the novelists Miles Franklin and Christina Stead were to go and live in the United States, hoping to find the country a fertile ground for their radicalism. And for their narrative realism, I should add. For the first third of our century, Australian culture exhibited a strong anglophilia. The achievement of federation had healed the blisters of our colonial status, and World War I, to which the Americans were striking latecomers, had sealed in blood our Empire loyalties. Moreover, it would not be unfair to say that the American influence was long seen as a cultural blight: its power, manifested both through Hollywood and through the popular music industry could be seen as a capitalist appeal to the lowest common multiple of receptor intelligence. As John Rickard has written,

> The "cultural cringe" gained much of its force from the growing dichotomy between high and popular culture which was itself a creation of the period between the wars . . . Mass entertainment was seen as endangering true cultural values, and a potent snobbery was born. But in Australia the snobbery had an added edge, in that it encouraged a turning to England, the source, as the arbiter of high culture.[6]

For many writers of my own generation, this postwar bias toward a British cultural frame, rather than the American one, was linked to our sense of there being stronger trade union traditions in the Old World, more of a sense of democratic socialism: ideals which have now been cast aside in almost all corners of the Western world. We understood what was meant by *Meanjin's* scornful references to "coca-cola culture." Our left-wing politics were also puritanical in many ways. These literary moves of rediscovery are often located in the mixed sensibilities of what Peter Beilharz characterizes elsewhere as a "state middle class." In contrast to the American model, the readerly stratum of our society has long been located in the public service—journalism, broadcasting, and teaching—remote, on the whole, from the world of capitalist enterprise, and often instinctively hostile to it. This pattern appears to be breaking down: entrepreneurs are now being regarded with some respect, or at least not regarded as feral. To put the matter more crudely, jobs are being squeezed out of the public service and out of teaching: our governments are punishing their old enemies. It is certainly the case that, in modern Australian culture, America has been present in two different ways. There is a continuous ground bass of the electronic arts, its dominance frequently enforced by cartels, as in the mid-century film industry; and there are intermittent melodies coming in over the top, some of them innovative or radical. The tension between these two "readings" of what the United States signifies was never more strikingly visible than during the Vietnam War, in which capitalist America was widely seen as villain, or at least aggressor, while the modes of Australian protest against the conduct of the war were derived from American models: hippy, black, or radical collegiate. Andrew Taylor, who was at Buffalo in 1970 and 1971, recalls that there he "became entangled in a whole scene of involvement in poetry—at that time, naturally, heavily political—which as yet had no real counterpart in Australia."[7] Given the contrast between these two political readings of American texts, it is hardly surprising that most of the self-styled Generation '68 went on after the war to become apolitical or even conservative in their social postures; I think of Tranter, Moorhouse, Adamson, and Forbes in this respect, although Moorhouse has adhered to a degree of sexual radicalism which separates him from the narrowly formalist aesthetic of the male poets. The avant-garde is very often politically conservative.[8] It is in love with aesthetics. Such a radical humanist reader as Fay Zwicky has little time for mere formalism, nor yet for the comic displacement of affect practiced (if that's the appropriate verb) by poets and playwrights of the New York school. She discovered a passionate America, adequate to her needs and romantic in a full sense, within the largenesses of Melville, Whitman, and Mark Twain. For Zwicky, Australian writers are too often timid, displacedly Anglo-Saxon, and hence oddly detached, in comparison with what she dubs "American urgency and excess."[9] Even the solipsism of so much American writing since Emerson can, for her, seem enabling, providing a true basis for contact with, confidence in, other people. Even in Florida she could discover America. Other Australian writers before Zwicky had enjoyed their scenes of discovery. For my peers, colleagues, and mates there were—junior to the prose poles of Faulkner and Hemingway—such novelists as Nabokov, Salinger, and Bellow; such poets as Stevens, Lowell, Marianne Moore, and Louise Bogan. As for Pound, I had been reading him since I was about eighteen, finding him very French and mildly Italian. What I have referred to as the polarity of Hemingway and Faulkner is reflected in our strangely double imagining of American enablers and exemplars. This is fascinatingly betrayed in Joan Kirkby's book *The American Model,* where contributors jump in two interpretative directions. Vincent Buckley represents one impulse in his celebration of "ease of American language,"[10] perceiving a cultural confidence which underlies an *ars celia artem:*

they can at their best produce a poetry which creates immediately the equivalent of sensation, and/or the equivalent of movements within the world of non-linguistic nature: a double emphasis which goes back triumphantly to Whitman. It is the basis of an ease in exposition and of a marked sensuality in physical effect. (p. 159)

Other contributors to the same volume were struck, as I was, by the exotic freedom American writers had to be anything they wanted to be. I had turned to Moore, Stevens, Bishop, and Roethke because they were so astonishingly mandarin, such a source of dictive difference. In my innocence I did not then realize the personal cost which had helped to generate the personal idiolects of some of these badgered souls: alienation as a rhetorical ground. Because texts are not the same as lives, one could easily fail to detect the neurosis, alcohol, drugs (except, a little later, when the Beat writers became ostensibly liberating models), anomie, and self-destructive impulses in these wonderfully exotic writers, although there were intriguing clues of disorder in Salinger's *The Catcher in the Rye*.

The same innocence did not underlie the next generation's fix on Sylvia Plath, where danger baited the hook. Of course, the rise of Plath's dazzling star corresponded with a rapid growth of feminist awareness in Australian culture. Which brings us back to the significant fact that one of the few members of the Generation of '68 who was truly radical in political alignment (apart from Michael Wilding) was Jennifer Maiden, who was also one of the very few female sixty-eighters. The metropolitan culture of the United States, then, is constantly hanging out there, massive in the North Pacific, filling the airwaves with thunder, and available as a source or site: as a ground on which we can discover what it is we need in this or that generation. Being so powerful, it can be just about anything. After all these recognitions, excursions, and invasions, there is some point in concluding with Robert Gray's normative warning to all of us who write:

> I think it is essential that we in Australia should continually assess, by highly-critical standards, the poetry (and here I say *literature*) of the United States—instead of automatically reproducing here each American fashion. We have at present in Australia, amongst many younger writers in particular, an atmosphere of shallow fashion-following: they think their work will have conferred on it some intrinsic value if it is identified with the latest American technique.[11]

This is a bit harsh and magisterial, but its general point is true. Our writers may well learn from John Cheever or Toni Morrison, from Sam Shepard or Jorie Graham or John Ashbery, but only to any purpose after they are released into being their writerly selves in their own place and time: a place and time which still have real existence, whatever the electronic labyrinth may have to retrieve and display. There's no doubt, however, that Australians will keep on taking their random slices off the Great Pumpkin from time to time. Cultural and economic power cannot be gainsaid.

Notes

1. James McAuley, "The True Discovery of Australia," *Collected Poems* (Sydney: Angus & Robertson, 1946), 37–42.
2. Richard White, *Inventing Australia: Images and Identity 1688–1980* (Sydney: Allen & Unwin, 1981).
3. David Goodman, *Goldseeking: Victoria and California in the 1850s* (Sydney: Allen & Unwin, 1994).
4. Joseph Furphy, *Such is Life* (Sydney: Angus & Robertson, 1946), 5–6.
5. Hugh Anderson, *The Poet Militant: Bernard O'Dowd,* (Melbourne: Hill of Content, 1969), 78–79.
6. John Rickard, *Australia: A Cultural History* (London/New York: Longman, 1988), 139.
7. Cited in Joan Kirkby, ed., *The American Model: Influence and Independence in Australian Poetry* (Sydney: Hale & Iremonger, 1982), 60.
8. Stéphane Mallarmé, *Oeuvres Complètes* (Paris: Editions Gallimard, 1945); Terry Eagleton, *The Illusions of Postmodernism* (Cambridge, Mass.: Blackwell Publishers, 1996).
9. Fay Zwicky, *The Lyre in the Pawnshop: Essays on Literature and Survival* (Nedlands: University of Western Australia Press, 1986), 78.
10. Vincent Buckley, "Ease of American Language" in *The American Model: Influence and Independence in Australian Poetry,* ed. Joan Kirkby. (Sydney: Hale & Iremonger, 1982), 137–159.
11. Robert Gray, "Poetry and Living: An Evaluation of the American Poetic Tradition," in *The American Model: Influence and Independence in Australian Poetry,* ed. Joan Kirkby (Sydney: Hale & Iremonger, 1982), 136.

References

Anderson, Hugh. *The Poet Militant: Bernard O'Dowd.* Melbourne: Hill of Content, 1969.

Buckley, Vincent. "Ease of American Language." In *The American Model: Influence and Independence in Australian Poetry.* Edited by Joan Kirkby. Sydney: Hale & Iremonger, 1982.

Curtin, John. "Australia Looks to America." December 27, 1941.

Davies, Alan. "Small Country Blues." *Meanjin* 44, June 2, 1985: 243–252.

Eagleton, Terry. *The Illusions of Postmodernism.* Cambridge, Mass.: Blackwell Publishers, 1996.

Furphy, Joseph. *Such is Life.* Sydney: Angus & Robertson, 1946.

Goodman, David. *Goldseeking: Victoria and California in the 1850s.* Sydney: Allen & Unwin, 1994.

Gray, Robert. "Poetry and Living: An Evaluation of the American Poetic Tradition." In *The American Model: Influence and Independence in Australian Poetry.* Edited by Joan Kirkby. Sydney: Hale & Iremonger, 1982.

Mallarmé, Stéphane. *Oeuvres Complètes.* Paris: Editions Gallimard, 1945.

McAuley, James. "The True Discovery of Australia." In *Collected Poems.* Sydney: Angus & Robertson, 1946.

Rickard, John. *Australia: A Cultural History.* London/New York: Longman, 1988.

White, Richard. *Inventing Australia: Images and Identity 1688–1980.* Sydney: Allen & Unwin, 1981.

Zwicky, Fay. *The Lyre in the Pawnshop: Essays on Literature and Survival.* Nedlands: University of Western Australia Press, 1986.

"Travelling, Despairing, Singing": Two Poetries

PETER STEELE, UNIVERSITY OF MELBOURNE

THE YEAR 1726 was a good year for students of movement in the British Isles. Voltaire, a fugitive from France, came to England; Handel became a British citizen; the musicologist-to-be Charles Burney was born; in Edinburgh, the first circulating library began its wholesome work; and Stephen Hales, for the first time, measured blood pressure. In London, anonymously as was his way, Swift published *Gulliver's Travels;* and his protégé of sorts, George Berkeley, already the formulator of philosophical immaterialism and shortly to be a bishop of the Church of Ireland, wrote a brief, handsome poem, "Verses on the Prospect of Planting Arts and Learning in America." Its culminating verses read:

> *There shall be sung another golden age,*
> *The rise of empire and of arts,*
> *The good and great inspiring epic rage,*
> *The wisest heads and noblest hearts.*

> *Not such as Europe breeds in her decay;*
> *Such as she bred when fresh and young,*
> *When heavenly flame did animate her clay,*
> *By future poets shall be sung.*

> *Westward the course of empire takes its way;*
> *The four first acts already past,*
> *A fifth shall close the drama of the day;*
> *Time's noblest offspring is the last.*[1]

I do not know whether Swift ever read the poem in manuscript—it was not published until after his death—but it is not hard to guess what he would have thought of it. *Gulliver's Travels*, for all its occasional flirtations with utopian dreams, is in the end entirely dismissive of any possibility of their being attained; indeed, if Swift had had the advantage of black-edged paper on which to have the book printed, that would have been an apt choice for at least its last couple of sections. In the event, Berkeley's "Westward the course of empire takes its way" was to find its retort not in Swift but in the concluding line of Louis Simpson's, "To the Western World"; "And grave by grave we civilize the ground." But whether one takes good news or ill to have the last word, it is clear that what mobilizes the imagination in these and countless other American poems is the model of the traveler, and the trope of travel itself. "I find by going where I have to go," Theodore Roethke was to write in a love-poem which is also a life-poem, and that is the motif of any number of American poems, old and new.

The "going" could be various: there are by now entire collections of American poems devoted to the automobile or to rail travel, and if there is not yet one on air-travel I cannot think why. But, of course, in the past if you wanted to get somewhere, more often than not you walked, like the Israelites of the *Book of Exodus* or Eric Newby in *A Short Walk in the Hindu Kush*. As a result, in America as in an array of other countries, the walking poem has had many exponents. Australia, too, whose own "course of empire" took its way westward, has had its share of poems written, as it were, from head to foot. And indeed I take my title from one of these in which Bruce Dawe, considering the ventures and quizzicalities of a normal week, conceives the hope "that finally the heart/would find its way home, now fast, now slow,/but getting there, nosing the bracken, head down, swinging/this way and that, a coat full of burrs,/travelling, despairing, singing."[2] It is a twentieth-century version of *solvitur ambulando,* and it can serve as token for the present modest perambulation of some American, and some Australian, poems.

When I was of a different age and configuration from today's, I learned that if one aimed to march far and fast it was a good idea to begin at a cracking pace: but walking poems may get there by taking things easily, or seeming to do so. Here, for instance, are two by the admirable Billy Collins:

> *Walking Across the Atlantic*

> *I wait for the holiday crowd to clear the beach*
> *before stepping onto the first wave.*

> *Soon I am walking across the Atlantic*
> *thinking about Spain,*
> *checking for waves, waterspouts.*

I feel the water holding up my shifting weight.
Tonight I will sleep on its rocking surface.

But for now I try to imagine what
this must look like to the fish below,
the bottoms of my feet appearing, disappearing.[3]

Etymology

They call Basque an orphan language.
Linguists do not know
what other languages gave it birth.

From the high window of the orphanage
it watches English walking alone to the cemetery
to visit the graves of its parents,
Latin and Anglo-Saxon.[4]

Catching notions about poems is not the same as catching poems, but here are several notions. "Walking Across the Atlantic" may remind us that walking is something one does for oneself, and not simply following where others lead. True, we all began with a tottering aping of the parental stride, but we soon got that knack of self-propulsion whose most full-hearted celebration is found in W. D. Snodgrass's refrain, "Snodgrass is walking through the universe." Self-propulsion can lead to self-absorption, so that Collins' magical walker is thinking, checking, feeling, imagining; but the whole performance makes for spectacle—the fish look up to see a one-man parade. All of these elements are to be found in poems more ambitious than Collins' *jeu.*

"Etymology" can remind us of both the durability and the fragility of language, the thing we always need to say how frail it is. And, in its citation of children and parents, orphan and grave, this poem expresses the fact that every living language blends the ancient and the pristine—no two of us inhabit it in the same way, but we are all confreres or consoeurs in its presence, whatever our dates of birth. When poets take themselves for a walk, these things, too, are likely to emerge, if not as themes, then at least as tinctures in their speech. To invoke examples more widely known than "Etymology," one might think of Walt Whitman's "The Sleepers," or Les Murray's "Walking to the Cattle Place."

Such examples remind us that, if Billy Collins' métier is, as it were, the photograph, many walking poems have the look of film. Here, for instance, is a comparatively early poem by Adrienne Rich, called "A Walk by the Charles":

> Finality broods upon the things that pass:
> Persuaded by this air, the trump of doom
> Might hang unsounded while the autumn gloom
> Darkens the leaf and smokes the river's glass.
> For nothing so susceptible to death
> But on this forenoon seems to hold its breath:
> The silent single oarsmen on the stream
> Are always young, are rowers in a dream.
> The lovers underneath the chestnut tree,
> Though love is over, stand bemused to see
> The season falling where no fall could be.
>
> You oarsmen, when you row beyond the bend,
> Will see the river winding to its end.
> Lovers that hold the chestnut burr in hand
> Will speak at last of death, will understand,
> Foot-deep amid the ruinage of the year,
> What smell it is that stings the gathering air.
>
> From our evasions we are brought at last,
> From all our hopes of constancy, to cast
> One look of recognition at the sky,
> The unimportant leaves that flutter by.
> Why else upon this bank are we so still?
> What lends us anchor but the mutable?
>
> O lovers, let the bridge of your two hands
> Be broken, like the mirrored bridge that bends
> And shivers on the surface of the stream.
> Young oarsmen, who in timeless gesture seem
> Continuous, united with the tide,
> Leave off your bending to the oar, and glide
> Past innocence, beyond these aging bricks
> To where the Charles flows in to join the Styx.[5]

"A Walk by the Charles" is no "Diving into the Wreck" but is as certainly a commanding poem, though different things are under command. The last word is given to the Styx, traditionally the hateful river of the underworld, by whose name even the gods swore at their peril: the stream of Charon and his cargo of the dead. The poem's journey "to where the Charles flows in to join the Styx" is one shadowed by intimations of just such an outcome, beginning as it does with "Finality broods upon the things that pass," a line with adumbrations perhaps of the cultic or the ascetical, but certainly of the classical, one of whose own senses is usually, "the terminal." The Charles is a comparatively small local river, but then so is the Rubicon, and Rich walks "by" her Charles—beside it, but also in some degree to its measure—as by mobile fatality.

The poem's title fortifies this sense when we remember that "a walk," like "course" can be inflected mainly as condition or mainly as deed—a way gone or a way of going—and as such is open to meditations on necessity and freedom. That issue is, I would think, the armature around which the most intense debates of American intellectual life have turned, whether couched in theological, philosophical, political, or psychological terms and each of the turns has found its own imaginative as well as theoretical expression. And while it is not the business of Rich's poem to argufy, I take it that the hearing one gives it is qualified by what might be called the American acoustic: if, behind some of its cadences, one hears the voices of Hardy and of Yeats, one also hears those of Melville and of Dickinson.

It was Melville who said that "meditation and water are wedded for ever," and certainly the Charles itself plays muse to Rich's utterance, as if warranting high speech before disappearing into the lowest of estates. But as Anglo-Saxon poets called the ocean "the whale's road," the Charles is sensed here as a highway of the human, its oarsmen matched with lovers under the chestnut tree. It is as if the poet, taking her path, finds her own fluvial being in rhythm with the smoked and shivering river. It is, she says, motion that gives her, and by implication all of us, pause: "Why else upon this bank are we so still?/What lends us anchor but the mutable?"

Auden commended "a rapture of distress," and we have this here, in a poem whose melodiousness is audible in every line, and whose recurrent melancholy declines to be dispirited. If it is at one level a short course in dis-enchantment—"The lovers underneath the chestnut tree,/Though love is over, stand bemused to see/The season falling where no fall could be"—it is at another one long phrasing of bewitchment, in which palpable chastenings are subsumed in lyric harmonies: "Lovers that hold the chestnut burr in hand/Will speak at last of death, will understand,/Foot-deep amid the ruinage of the year,/What smell it is that stings the gathering air." Elias Canetti said that "Drama is, of all human possibilities of summing-up, the least untruthful,"[6] and the completed drama of "A Walk by the Charles" is one in which manner is at the heart of the matter.

That was in America in the 1950s. In Australia, as the 1980s shaded into the 1990s, Jemal Sharah wrote "Pastoral":

> *We have crossed over the stile, and entered*
> *   this diffident landscape*
> *we saw from the path, as if painted*
> *as neat as a book-plate.*

The oat-grass, blown into plump sheaves,
shines rust, silver and straw;
the verdigris blades of gum leaves
are antiques from old wars.

Let us leave at the fence love and death,
those great human themes:
look where a gum against copper earth
like Kali dances and dreams.

Back at home there is radiant wood
poised to fall into snow,
and apples, cheeks dawn-cold and red,
clustering on the bough;

but we step through the wilderness now
in an austere country:
we have left at the gate all we've learned
and shall tread lightly.[7]

In principle both the past and the future of poetry are reopened every time a poet of some competency begins to write a poem, so there is a limited use at best in speaking of waves or movements—something not always understood either in America or in Australia—but with "Pastoral" as with "A Walk by the Charles" both debts and departures are important. Whitman, near the end of "Passage to India," asks, "Have we not darken'd and dazed ourselves with books long enough?" thus tendentiously adding to the making of books, and we do not lack voices to ask a similar question about so archaic a genre as The Pastoral. Archaic, yes, but also protean: and when one remembers the overtones of "pastoral" or "pastoralist" in Australian speech, overtones which tell against diminishment, one will find a fitness in Sharah's "look where a gum against copper earth/like Kali dances and dreams," Kali goddess of just those "love and death" supposed to have been left at the fence, and Kali the unbiddable and inexorable. To walk into this poem's "diffident landscape" as it seemed from the path is to walk among oat-grass emblematically bright with death's rust, commerce's silver, futility's straw: no wonder that the very gum leaves, so often domesticated by nostalgia, are here verdigris blades from old wars. To get into this poem is to get into trouble.

Classical and neoclassical pastorals had some of this way, as is made clear most succinctly in the "I too was in Arcady" of Death itself. But Sharah's introduction of Kali, counterposed against the radiant wood and the cheeked apples clustering on boughs, and her citation of "an austere country" tells away from those old ways. Canetti's other dictum, "Everywhere, two paces from your daily paths, there is a different air skeptically waiting for you,"[8] is exactly appropriate here: no wonder the poem declares that "we have left at the gate all we've learned," and no wonder the agenda is now to "tread lightly," without the privileges but also without the burdens of proprietorship.

Famously, A. D. Hope's "Australia" declares, "They call her a young country, but they lie," and Jemal Sharah's poem offers access to an Australia not so much ancient as of mythic eternity. This in turn, I would suggest, qualifies one's reception of the decorous form in which the matter is offered; it is less a case of art hiding itself than of art subverting itself. Reading the poem, we are walked not only from a remembered or an anticipated landscape to the real one, but from art's civilities to truth's brutalities. Or, to change the model, it is as if art is the Virgil who can go only so far with the Dantean reader, who is left solitary and exposed at the departure.

There is, of course, an elaborated American rhetoric which celebrates this as poetry's whole policy. It did not begin with Whitman—how could it, since it had been a recurrent motif of just that European tradition which he saw fit to rebuke? Nothing is more characteristically human than to deprecate human complexity; and most anthologies of poetry would be a great deal slimmer without the poems which do exactly that. In the body of American prose and verse which deals with what Roger Gilbert calls "Walks in the World,"[9] from Thoreau to Frank O'Hara, it is common to find the speaker attempting to come to terms with her or his own complexity. The outcome may be anything from Wordsworthian consolation to a prowling moroseness. One poet who often writes *passage* in terms not reducible to either of these is W. S. Merwin. Here is his "Walkers":

> *Then I could walk for a whole day over the stony*
> *ridges along fallen walls and lanes matted with*
> *sloe branches and on through oak woods and around springs*
> *low cliffs mouths of caves and out onto open*
> *hillsides overlooking valleys adrift in the distance*
> *and after the last sheep in their crumbling pastures*
> *fenced with cut brush there would be only the burr of a wren*
> *scolding from rocks or one warbler's phrase repeated*
> *following through the calls of crows and the mossed hush*
> *of ruins palmed in the folds of the crumpled slopes*
> *in deep shade with the secret places of badgers*
> *and no other sound it was the edge of a silence*
> *about to become as though it had never been*
> *for a while before emerging again unbroken*
> *once I looked up a band straight into the small eyes*

> *of a boar watching me and we stared at each other*
> *in that silence before he turned and went on with his*
> *walk and once when I had dried figs in my pocket*
> *I met an old woman who laughed and said this was the way*
> *she had come all her life and between two fingers she*
> *accepted a fig saying Oh you bring me dainties*
> *there was still the man always astray in the dark suit*
> *and string tie who might emerge from a barn and gaze*
> *skyward saying Ah Ah something had happened to him*
> *in the war they said but he never took anything*
> *and there was the gnarled woman from a remote hamlet*
> *hurrying head down never looking at anyone*
> *to a house she owned that had stood empty for decades*
> *there to dust the tables sweep out the rooms cut weeds*
> *in the garden set them smouldering and as quickly*
> *bolt the windows lock the door and be on her way*[10]

Brutus, in *Julius Caesar*, says that "It is the bright day that brings forth the adder/And that craves wary walking," and the Fool, in *King Lear*, cries "Look, here comes a walking fire": Merwin's poetry might be called wary walking in the expectation of meeting walking fires. "Walkers," like most of his poetry for decades now, has no punctuation of any kind, which is among other things a way of signifying that the poems are to be taken as happening in another country, another world, than that of prose; the conclusions they are trying exact incessant watchfulness, and look to illuminations which are as fugitive as they are singular. Antonio Machado says at one point, "Ours is to pass,/to pass while making roads,"[11] and most of Merwin's work has been done in that spirit.

Titles of his poems abound which refer to process as such—"Losing a Language," "Shaving Without a Mirror," "Hearing the Names of the Valleys"—and his ethos is peregrine and tentative, the price of which is sometimes an all-but-Cartesian enclosedness within the cell of the skull. This poem, though, is called not "Walking" but "Walkers," attesting his equally passionate preoccupation with *les autres,* be they human, beastish, or others stranger still. The "burr of a wren/scolding from the rocks," "the mossed hush/of ruins palmed in the folds of the crumpled slopes," the look "up a bank straight into the small eyes/of a boar watching,"—these are points of divination in the poem's topography, and they tell on behalf of a world amenable to salute but impervious to conquest.

Merwin's human fellows, too, are irreducible in their wayfaring. The "old woman who laughed and said this was the way/she had come all her life' is of the same order of being as figures in, say, the early "East of the Sun and West of the Moon," when Merwin was still writing from a more public mythology. The "man always astray in the dark suit . . . saying Ah Ah something had happened to him/in the war they said but he never took anything" has the quasi-heraldic status of a creature from history crossed with myth. And the "gnarled woman from a remote hamlet/hurrying head down never looking at anyone" intent on her own cryptic affairs holds everyone's look as surely as if she emerged from Kafka.

In prose and in verse, sometimes with great bitterness, Merwin has decried the imperial presence of the human species among the others, floral and faunal. In "For a Coming Extinction," addressing the gray whale being sent to "That great god," The End, Merwin says that it is to join its words with those of "Our sacrifices," "The sea cows the Great Auks the gorillas/The irreplaceable hosts," and "Tell him/That it is we who are important": a long way, this, from Berkeley's "Westward the course of empire takes its way." And yet, by the same irony as that in which we use our mortal breath to decry mortality, there is an inescapable element of the imperial in any poem of Merwin's, as of any poem: whatever else they do, they colonize silence. That is the first journey any poem takes, and the last: It walks into silence, around in it, and out of it. And I think that this is what, implicitly, most engages us in the practice of poetry.

Which is not to say that its other engagements are few. A walker in an altogether different country from Merwin's is Peter Porter; and here is "Porter's Retreat."

> Once the difficulty had been
> to cross the Divide, to follow spurs
> which seemed to end in air,
> to swivel about the cobwebs where the creeks
> dipped below their spiders to
> a contrary encircling of your steps—
> to keep on through the undergrowth
> with only stripes of sun above,
> to get beyond these endless-seeming vistas
> and look out on the plain which might contain
> a sea, a minareted island, a mirage,
> whose common epithet was Felix,
> appointed place of all felicity.
>
> There are, of course, bland natures
> back at home, whose only earnest
> is a theory that your expedition
> means to straighten out the land with names,
> to fit a grid of the accounting gods
> on plastic otherness. You'll have to give

a hostage to them—do it now.
Here by Disappointment Bluff, gaze
across the Vale of Sixty to Uncanniness;
beyond the rock-strewn creek
is an escarpment called Incalculable
and the fields are more elided than Elysian—
mark this tree the point of going back
and set it on the map—Porter's Retreat—
the place at which all further progress
ceases to have consequence.

But expeditions never go as planned.
You're given a foretaste of the future:
a set of barbecue emplacements,
Olympic Pool, koala sanctuary,
suggestions for a heliport—
journeys inland have moved Nature
from the coast: this is the people's fort
where families collaborate with the sun
to make home-movies of divinity.
You're far beyond here now,
digging for nurture under balding trees,
only too willing to fold up the map
and start the evening's diary entry—
tomorrow will be another scorcher,
meanwhile this heap of gutted granite
shall be named Mt. Misery
and the muddy tank-full where the river
dips into the underworld will make
a just impression as Lake Longevity.[12]

Can you go to Porter's Retreat? Well, you can and you can't. There is a place of that name about eighty miles due west of Botany Bay, convenient to both Shooters Hill and Black Springs. Its establishing must have cost exertion, and no doubt its inhabitants could construe its name either as consolation or as rebuke. It is certainly far enough from the cities Peter Porter relishes for travel to keep loud its old overtones of "travail." But as Melville once pointed out, true places are not down on any map—the places we identify as personal habitats or horrorscapes. And in that sense "Porter's Retreat" is peculiarly to be found in the title of another of his poems, "Next to Nothing."

It was the practice of Ludwig II of Bavaria to go round and round in his riding school, having specified that he was journeying from (for instance) Munich to Innsbruck—starting at, say, 8:00 p.m. and continuing until 3:00

a.m., with a break for a meal. This perseveration in futility was probably one of the things that caused him to be thought insane, but what might be called the Bavarian Way shows itself in some degree in even the most vivacious of Porter's perambulations, which are many. Movings and thwartings, on terms to be rediscovered from one poem to another, possess many of his beginnings and endings: "Paradis Artificiel" begins, "Barbel-cheeked and hammer-toed,/I'm scrambling up a river bank/in a landscape by Claude"; "Southsea Bubbles" begins, "The box tree in the garden/helped navigators guide/ships to New Farm Wharf,/or else Grandfather lied"; "Home and Hosed" ends, "Soul's straightforwardness is crimped in the fire," and "Hand in Hand," "The species is the soul on trial,/Its pilgrimage a handclasp from despair,/Walking with Hermes to the upper air." It is as if there is always a seat for Beckett at Porter's table.

Our century, often lumbering in its characterization of the obvious, has given birth to many grandiosities of terminology, so that place-names are toponyms and our sense of bodily being in the world, psychogeography. Such peggings-out of our progress or regress fascinate Porter, less, I suspect, because of their satirical potential than because each of them occasions, after all, renewed conjecture as to what it means for us to be moving over the surface of a self-interrogating planet. To an exceptional degree, he understands how often denomination is little more than lexical bravado, and in a poker-faced sort of way he leaves the trace of this understanding wherever he goes—as when, for example, in the present poem, he watches investigators "follow spurs/which seemed to end in air," or concedes that "the fields are more elided than Elysian," or, with formidable understatement, appraises "Porter's Retreat" as "the place at which all further progress/ceases to have consequence." This is a walk in the world, all right, but one in which the air is astringent with skepticism.

Which brings us back, by indirections, both to Bruce Dawe's "travelling, despairing, singing" and to Berkeley's philosophical immaterialism which, with many of his commentators, I take to be at once irrefutable and incredible. Whatever their personal tempers, there is an array of poets, both American and Australian, who when doing that humblest of human things, going for a walk, find that the world is just enough with them for them to be hard put to sing it, or to say it, or to know the difference.

Notes

1. George Berkeley, "Verses on the Prospect of Planting Arts and Learning in America," *The Oxford Book of Travel Verse,* ed. Kevin Crossley-Holland (Oxford: Oxford University Press, 1986), 365.
2. Bruce Dawe, "A Week's Grace," *Sometimes Gladness: Collected Poems, 1954–1978* (Melbourne: Longman Cheshire, 1978), 51.

3. Billy Collins, "Walking Across the Atlantic," *The Apple That Astonished Paris* (Fayetteville: University of Arkansas Press, 1988), 5.

4. Collins, "Etymology," *Apple*, 16.

5. Adrienne Rich, "A Walk by the Charles," *Collected Early Poems, 1950–1970* (New York: W. W. Norton & Co., 1993), 116.

6. Elias Canetti, *The Human Province*, trans. Joachim Neugroschel (New York: Seabury Press, 1978), 13.

7. Jemal Sharah, "Pastoral," *The Oxford Book of Australian Women's Verse*, ed. Susan Lever (Melbourne: Oxford University Press, 1995), 239.

8. Canetti, *Human Province*, 236.

9. Roger Gilbert, *Walks in the World: Representation and Experience in Modern American Poetry* (Princeton, N.J.: Princeton University Press, 1991).

10. W. S. Merwin, "Walkers," *The Vixen: Poems* (New York: Alfred A. Knopf, 1996), 11.

11. Reprinted with permission from *The Dream Below the Sun: Selected Poems of Antonio Machado* ©1981. Published by The Crossing Press: Freedom, CA.

12. Peter Porter, "Porter's Retreat," *Possible Worlds* (Oxford: Oxford University Press, 1989), 50.

References

Berkeley, George. "Verses on the Prospect of Planting Arts and Learning in America." *The Oxford Book of Travel Verse*. Edited by Kevin Crossley-Holland. Oxford: Oxford University Press, 1986.

Canetti, Elias. *The Human Province*. Translated by Joachim Neugroschel. New York: Seabury Press, 1978.

Collins, Billy. "Etymology." *The Apple That Astonished Paris*. Fayetteville: University of Arkansas Press, 1988.

———. "Walking Across the Atlantic." *The Apple That Astonished Paris*. Fayetteville: University of Arkansas Press, 1988.

Dawe, Bruce. "A Week's Grace." *Sometimes Gladness: Collected Poems, 1954–1978*. Melbourne: Longman Cheshire, 1978.

Gilbert, Roger. *Walks in the World: Representation and Experience in Modern American Poetry*. Princeton, N.J.: Princeton University Press, 1991.

Merwin, W. S. "Walkers." *The Vixen: Poems*. New York: Alfred A. Knopf, 1996.

Porter, Peter. "Porter's Retreat." *Possible Worlds*. Oxford: Oxford University Press, 1989.

Rich, Adrienne. "A Walk by the Charles." *Collected Early Poems, 1950–1970*. New York: W. W. Norton & Co., 1993.

Sharah, Jemal. "Pastoral." *The Oxford Book of Australian Women's Verse*. Edited by Susan Lever. Melbourne: Oxford University Press, 1995.

7

The Curve of the Pacific Gets in the Way

KEVIN HART, MONASH UNIVERSITY

I WAS ELEVEN WHEN I SAW MY FIRST IMAGES OF AUSTRALIA, and in retrospect it is clear that great pains had been taken over them. They were set in a lavishly illustrated magazine, one of several piled on a coffee table in Australia House, London. I was sitting with my sister and parents, all of us as starched and sharply pressed as we could be, waiting to be called to an interview. We knew that the next half hour or so was important: our application to migrate to Canada had been turned down, and we had been summarily informed that there was no point in approaching the United States. My father simply didn't have the qualifications needed to migrate anywhere in North America, and we needed to go somewhere because there were to be redundancies at the local gasworks where my father worked. As I flicked through the glossy magazine, I saw colorful pictures of men in whites playing cricket, happy families sunbaking on an endless beach of yellow sand, and enormous airy houses surrounded by large gardens with palm trees. There were photographs of koalas and kangaroos, but to a boy brought up in London's East End, they were no more strange than badgers and cows. My parents were impressed by the picture of employment in warm weather and in particular by the idea of having Christmas lunch on the beach. This theme was developed with great passion by the man from Adelaide who interviewed us. He explained that since it would be far too hot to have a roast chicken, we would have a chicken salad with rings of *pineapple*. To working-class Londoners, the prospect was tantalizing, and my parents wanted to get to this paradise as quickly as possible. It was a nice touch that the man from Adelaide thought so too.

About a year later in 1966 I found myself going to primary school in Brisbane. Life there was much as the glossy magazine had shown it, except that surviving a Queensland summer was like living in a plastic bag for months on end. One day in library period at school I was handed a book that would teach me something about my adopted country. It was a dog-eared copy of John O'Grady's *They're a Weird Mob* (1958), a humorous novel that depicted the problems an Italian migrant was having with his Australian workmates. I may not have known very much about Australians when I started the novel, but I knew nothing at all about Italians, and it was the Italian and not the Australians who seemed weird to me. Over the coming months, though, I started to catch a whiff of Australia's strangeness. It centered on two subjects I encountered in grades six and seven at Corinda Primary School: History and Maps. History turned out to be Australian History. My father, who had a taste for British regnal history, thought this was a bit rich: after all, the land hadn't been settled for even two hundred years, so how could it have a *history?* Brought up myself on history of the ripping yarns style, I tended to agree. I had loved those classes at Thomas Arnold Primary School when the teacher tuned in to the BBC and we listened to tales of Boudicca giving the Romans what for, accounts of the shenanigans of Henry VIII, and stories about those nasty, scheming Jacobites. After such an Arnoldian education, it was hard to get worked up about gold and sheep.

But there was one episode of Australian history that struck me: the discovery of the continent by Captain James Cook. The same story cropped up in Maps. Once a week we had to draw a map of Australia or Queensland and color it in with painful exactitude. We had to scribble with a colored pencil on a piece of blotting paper, then gently rub the blotting paper on the map to give a nice, even hue of yellow (for desert) or green (for plains) that would not cover up the writing, already performed in our best copybook hand: Deception Bay, Mt. Despair, Glasshouse Mountains. Sometimes the assignment was to draw the routes of the country's great explorers in the nineteenth century. In grade seven the teacher was very taken by Burke and Wills. So we drew dotted lines going inland that terminated with a small cross, marking where these intrepid spirits had died in the desert. A couple of times we had to chart the route of the *Endeavour* up the Queensland coast, and what impressed me was the fact that Australia had been *discovered*. No one at Thomas Arnold Primary School had ever said anything about England being discovered; it had always been there. It was an odd feeling, like the one conjured by seeing "Unexplored" written on parts of Papua New Guinea and Central Australia in the old school atlases supplied by the Queensland state government.

I was not very good at drawing maps, but I became entranced with those drawn by others. On summer afternoons I would get home from school, and after several glasses of cordial and a long shower, I would wait for the daily thunderstorm. I sprawled on my bed, gazing at an old atlas that had belonged to my sister in England. After a while the pages of the atlas would fall open to a double-page of the United States. Some states were blue, others red, still others green. The only cities marked were the federal and state capitals, and some of the inevitable big ones like New York and Los

Angeles. I would imagine living in certain states, especially in the south—Alabama, Arkansas, Georgia, Mississippi—and would murmur the names of their capitals to myself, as though the names combined with the color assigned to the states somehow expressed the essence of living there. One birthday I was given a bright new atlas, and for weeks my favorite thing was saying names like Tuscaloosa, Chattanooga, and Charleston over and over. I could feel each name on my tongue, and each one had a taste. Charlotte, inevitably, was apples and cream, and Tallahassee was an explosion of sarsaparilla in the mouth.

So I discovered America, the land I had been forbidden to enter; and then one day I closed the atlas and forgot about my secret land for years. My next discovery occurred when I was in the first or second year of high school, when I was working over the summer holidays as a shop assistant in Myers in Queen Street. At lunchtime I would haunt the Queensland Book Depot in nearby Adelaide Street, mostly dipping in the two or three shelves devoted to mathematics, but sometimes I would drift over to the literature section. There one day I bought a paperback called *Amerika,* and I think I purchased it rather than the other books nearby—*The Castle, The Trial, Metamorphosis*—because of the *k* in the title. What did that mean? It certainly made America seem strange and exotic.

On the train home I began reading the story of Karl Rossmann, and so I started to discover America again. Kafka had no more been to New York than I had, but he knew how the Old World saw the New World, and nowhere more brilliantly did he show this than in his description of the desk owned by Karl Rossmann's benefactor, Uncle Jacob:

> In his room stood an American writing-desk of superior construction, such as his father had coveted for years and tried to pick up cheaply at all kinds of auction sales without ever succeeding, his resources being much too small. This desk, of course, was beyond all comparison with the so-called American writing-desks which turned up at auction sales in Europe. For example, it had a hundred compartments of different sizes, in which the President of the Union himself could have found a fitting place for each of his state documents; there was also a regulator at one side and by turning a handle you could produce the most complicated combinations and permutations of the compartments to please yourself and suit your requirements. Thin panels sank slowly and formed the bottom of a new series at the top of existing drawers promoted from below; even after one turn of the handle the disposition of the whole was quite changed and the transformation took place slowly or at delirious speed according to the rate at which you wound the thing round. It was a very modern invention.[1]

What captivated me in reading this page was not so much the fantasy of modernity as the form of the writing. Years later I would read and admire Kafka's observation to Gustav Janouch: "The form is not the expression of the content but only its power of attraction, the door and the way to the content."[2] The image of Uncle Jacob's writing desk tells us that America *is* form; it is a power of attraction that overwhelms its content. If we want content, we return to the Old World and to Kafka's own desk. Here he is describing it to Oskar Pollak:

> I sat at my fine desk. You don't know it. How could you? You see, it's a respectably minded desk which is meant to educate. Where the writer's knees usually are, it has two horrible wooden spikes. And now pay attention. If you sit down quietly, cautiously at it, and write something respectable, all's well. But if you become excited, look out if your body quivers ever so little, you inescapably feel the spikes in your knees, and how that hurts. I could show you the black-and-blue marks.[3]

Over the years the simple proposition "Australia was discovered" became more and more encrusted with concerns and questions, though the initial shock of living in a place that was discovered has never quite faded. My concerns came in three waves, one in high school, one at university, and one as a teacher. First, I learned that parts of a country later called "Australia" were observed before the land as a whole could be discovered in what was held to be the correct and proper way: by an Englishman. Second, I began to realize that this so-called "discovery" dispossessed the people who already lived in the country, and the consequences for them were and are appalling. And third, it dawned on me that Australia keeps on being discovered. In recent years, however, it isn't a land that is discovered and appropriated, it is a shifting yet always highly selective ensemble of images called "Australia."

I'd like to take my bearings from the title of a panel at the 1996 meeting of the Modern Language Association in Washington, D.C: " 'Home of the Weird': Uncanny, Uncouth, Uncool in Australian Culture." One of the panelists, Nicholas Burns, spoke eloquently of how the American academy is only now discovering something called "Australian literature" and is a little disappointed not to find it stranger than it is. One reason for this disappointment, I'd say, is that there is something a little weird about belated discoveries of new lands. They are discoveries and therefore new, yet they come in a history of European discovery that is nearly complete. What can count as "other" has already been projected in principle and largely filled out in fact. Were these to be the only terms of discussion available to us, Australia would be doubly disabled by its belated discovery by America. On the one hand, it was encountered too late in Western history to be conceived as "other": Australia would be more interesting as something anticipated than found, and I will touch on this in a moment. On the other hand, Australia would have sought cultural identity too late for its quest to be successful. One of the things that has made Australia of interest in America and Europe since World War I is precisely the question of how it will "emerge," "grow," or "mature" into a distinct and distinctive culture. Yet globalism, internationalism, and informationism have reset and redirected the assumption of organic national development that motivates this interest. An older former colony of Britain like the United States might regret losing a cultural unity (even if it was imaginary) in increasing regional, racial, and social fragmentation; a younger one like Australia has never achieved this kind of unity in the first place. We have aimed at it and done little, by way of public symbols, to get there. When Australia becomes a republic, as it surely will before very much longer, the change will occur in a world that no longer regards an affirmation of national independence as a charged or charmed event. There will, of course, be talk of what has been symbolically achieved, but the event will have come too late to do much by way of social unification or imaginative independence.

How fast Australia will have to run with globalization or how significantly it will recoil from it into cultural nationalism are not issues that I want to raise here. What intrigues me is the image that Nicholas Burns presents of America gazing at Australia. It is not only a matter of academic curiosity. John Ashbery captures what I have in mind in several lines of his "Poem at the New Year":

> I wonder about Australia. Is it anything like Canada?
> Do pigeons flutter? Is there a strangeness there, to complete
> the one in me? Or must I relearn my filing system?[4]

For several decades Americans have conceived Australia either with nostalgia (a frontier land, not unlike how America used to be, "like Canada") or as teasingly exotic ("a strangeness there"). The land down under becomes a representation of a selective American past or, at a pinch, a shimmering image of a country that falls beyond their experience but whose alienness is not seriously un-American: one's filing system is fundamentally okay, only a few cards need to be added.

I suspect there may be a parallel for literary and cultural criticism. An American critic can gaze at Australian literature and see an early phase in the formation of a national canon. It must seem strange to see a national poetry that still debates whether it begins as far back as Charles Harpur or as recently as Kenneth Slessor. Indeed, Americans do more than gaze. An Australian canon is partly fashioned by decisions made in the United States, by literary agents and publishers, by anthologists and conference conveners, by professors selecting texts for courses, and by members of professional groups like the AAALS and the MLA. It has never been a matter of Australian writers picking the right American authors and then being influenced by them, as some members of the Generation of '68 used to advocate. The task, rather, would be more dialectical. We must see how America expresses itself through its others, as well as in itself—that is, in its moments when it wishes not to recognize alterity in order to affirm itself. We must see how Australian writers work in a space marked by America as "other" but an "other" it can recognize and affirm. One can aim to occupy this space and arrive there quite comfortably (Peter Carey and David Malouf are two different examples), or one can miss it by trying too hard (John Tranter, for instance, seems too American to be of deep interest to the Americans); one can stumble into it, to the astonishment of the Australian critics (B. Wongar enjoys more critical esteem in the United States than at home); and one can keep one's head down and simply ignore it. Be all that as it may, it can be hard to tell whether Australian literature is being discovered or invented by Americans.

Not that the distinction between discovery and invention is always so clear back home. For Australians, like Americans, are sometimes disappointed to find that the great south land is not as weird as it might have been, and America is sometimes involved in this picture of things. Who really discovered Australia? Surprisingly, the question still has a bit of kick. James McAuley asked it tongue-in-cheek forty odd years ago in his poem "The True Discovery of Australia," and after dismissing the usual candidates—Janszoon and Dampier—and completely bypassing Cook, he proposed Lemuel Gulliver as our first father. McAuley was thinking of the passage in *Gulliver's Travels* when the good ship *Antelope* is driven by "a violent Storm to the North-west of *Van Diemen's* Land" and the hapless crew find themselves "in the Latitude of 30 Degrees 2 Minutes South."[5] Anyone with an atlas can see that Gulliver sets foot on dry land somewhere near Lake Torrens in South Australia. This offers McAuley the chance to recast Australia as Lilliput, the land of little people with big ideas about themselves.

In "The True Discovery of Australia," McAuley quotes a document supposedly found at the Mitchell Library. It is a letter in which Gulliver describes Australians to Lord Peterborough in 1729:

> *And you will often find, although their heads*
> *Are like a berry on a twig of bones,*
> *They speak as Giants of the South Pacific*
> *And treat the islands as their stepping-stones.*

> *North-east across the water, Brobdingnag*
> *Casts its momentous shadow on the sea*

And fills the sky with thunder; but they smile
And sit on their verandahs taking tea,

Watching through the pleasant afternoons
Flood fire and cyclone in successive motion
Complete the work the pioneers began
Of shifting all the soil into the ocean.[6]

Utterly complacent, McAuley's Australians gaze mindlessly across the Pacific and take no cognizance of the United States bearing down on us in all its sublimity. By the time we reach the 1960s, though, all eyes are looking in that direction. Indeed, "America" comes to be figured as savior, both in conservative politics—"All the way with LBJ," as Harold Holt put it—and in the new poetry. The America valued by the younger Australian poets grouped around *New Poetry* or *The Ear in a Wheatfield* was not the one praised by Government Ministers. Rather, it was the brave new world projected by Donald Allen's *New American Poetry*, an anthology that gained a certain noteriety by being banned in Australia because of its indecency but almost certainly in part because of its contestatory politics.

The new enthusiasm for America can be heard in that quintessential sixties poet, John Forbes. In his paean "To the Bobbydazzlers," Forbes addresses "American poets" as those who "saved me" in 1970. It is worth noting in passing that "American poets" for Forbes means "North American poets." Although it was fashionable to like Pablo Neruda in the sixties, the Generation of '68 as a whole showed little interest in South American poetry. "Internationalism" was a rallying call, but it rallied people to New York and San Francisco, not Buenos Aires or Rio de Janeiro. So when Forbes gazes across the Pacific it is up to the north, and not to California, but to the East Coast. Unlike McAuley's Australians blithely taking tea on their verandahs, he looks east with admiration, desire, and is touched by a quite different sense of the sublime:

American poets!
you have saved
America from
its reputation
if not its fate
& you saved me
too, in 1970
when I first
breathed freely
in Ted Berrigan's
Sonnets, *escaping*

the talented
earache of Modern
Poetry.
  Sitting
on the beach I
look toward you
but the curve
of the Pacific
gets in the way
& I see stars
instead, knocked
out by your poems
American poets
the Great Dead
are smiling
in your faces.
I salute their
luminous hum![7]

In their own ways, both McAuley and Forbes believe in the "Great Dead" up there enjoying the music of the spheres, but Forbes's forefathers are infinitely more benign than McAuley's. Dryden, Pope, and Swift are made to lead each Lilliputian to sit in Kafka's desk, that "respectably minded desk which is meant to educate," with its wooden spikes, rather than Uncle Jacob's superior American writing desk. Doubtless also the two Australians differ over how the tradition of greatness is communicated. For McAuley, the tradition begins in England and is passed to Australia—but at the wrong moment, when Romanticism had become a literary orthodoxy. Modernism can all too easily take root in this poor soil. Seeing this, one must correct the tradition by turning the gaze of Australians to Neoclassicism. For Forbes, though, the tradition has already moved west to America, and it is precisely our inability directly to see the New World—"the curve of the pacific"—that generates the sublime. The poet is "knocked out" by Ted Berrigan, John Ashbery, and Frank O'Hara, and sees stars; and the American poets are themselves those stars.

For McAuley the allure of an exotic past that never was becomes a way of satirizing a contemporary Australia. His Australia is more uncouth and uncool than weird or uncanny; in fact, he is keen to root out the weird and uncanny he finds in the imported surrealism of the Angry Penguins group, represented by the Australian poet Ern Malley:

For lucid Ern, ye penguins, weep no more:
Henceforth he is the genius of the shore.

If, unawares, you stumble into sense,
His arm shall save, and your own impudence.[8]

In contrast, the map of Australian poetry as drawn by McAuley is seen by Forbes as "the talented/earache of Modern/Poetry" from which the American poets have saved him. Inevitably, McAuley pokes fun at Max Harris and the others for being gulled by Ern Malley, whose complete works he and Harold Stewart composed one marvellous afternoon. It is hard to know what is the most weird: the fact that Australia's greatest surrealist poet never existed; the fact that at the time a nonexistent poet was a better poet than his creators; or the fact that McAuley writes badly when imitating Swift and Pope and rather well when writing surrealist verse. At any rate, the appeal to a fictional origin in Gulliver is used to realign Australian literature with the correct canon, one in which "The Age of Pope" has a privileged status.

The image of McAuley as a displaced Opposition satirist was never very convincing, not even, in the end, to himself, although the idea of another Australia did not leave him. It must be uncanny to be shadowed by a past that never happened. What if Australia had been discovered by Captain Quiros? The question prompted McAuley's longest poem. We have already entered a possible world where Australia was Lilliput, and Swift and Pope survived in order to keep Grub Street in its place. Now we enter another possible world where Australia is Catholic: a visionary country, Australia del Espíritu Santo. But since that is not our earth, those of us unable to turn possibility into actuality have only one choice: to travel within ourselves and discover another Australia there. The opening words of McAuley's lyric "Terra Australis" tell us precisely what we have to do: "Voyage within you." In order to find the other Australia, we must pass from the exotic to the esoteric, from the visible to the invisible.

For McAuley it would be impossible for the true Australia to be revealed in a film. Interestingly enough, the same idea is strongly urged in my favorite Australian movie, *The Interior.* There is a story that needs to be told about the making of this remarkable work: the only film, I think, that comes close to capturing what is truly weird about Australia. In order to make *The Interior,* the director left Melbourne and traveled inland. He stopped at one of the towns on the plains and stayed in a hotel. As it happens, we have a preproduction note he made on his first night deep inland:

Not a soul in this district knows who I am or what I mean to do here. Odd to think that of all the plainsfolk lying asleep (in sprawling houses of white weatherboard with red iron roofs and great arid gardens dominated by pepper-trees and kurrajongs and rows of tamarisks) not one has seen the view of the plains that I am soon to disclose.[9]

As is well known, the plainsmen recognize only their own culture, dismissing the whole of the coastal region as "Other Australia."

One day a number of powerful landowners, patrons of culture on the plains, came to town; and in the very hotel where the filmmaker was staying they conducted long, boozy interviews for prestigious positions in their households. It is common in inner Australia for all sorts of artists and researchers to be employed in the great houses: illusionists and family genealogists, historians of horse racing and collectors of mandalas, inventors of inconclusive board games and designers of impractical costumes. The filmmaker was interviewed, and he spoke of how he wished to make a film whose last scenes would be set on the plains; it would "show even the textures of grassblades in obscure hollows and of mossy rockfaces on bleak outcrops on a plain that any of them recognise although none had seen more than mere fragments," and it would involve a young woman of the plains—pehaps a daughter of his patron (pp. 59–60). After listening to this pitch, one of the landowners slams down his glass; the other patrons retire, leaving the filmmaker to hear, or overhear, the angry landowner's reflections on his project.

Again, I'll simply quote from the director's notes, made after the interview which in its measure turned out to be successful:

> He found much of what I had said outrageous. I knew, surely, that no film had ever been made with the plains as its setting. My proposal suggested that I had overlooked the most obvious qualities of the plains. How did I expect to find so easily what so many others had never found—a visible equivalent of the plains, as though they were mere surfaces reflecting sunlight? There was also the question of his daughter. Did I think that by persuading her to stand against a vista of a few paddocks and to look towards a camera I would *discover* [my emphasis] about her what I would never in fact learn if I followed her for years with my own eyes? (pp. 61–62)

It turns out that one cannot make a film of Australia because the land redistributes the values usually grouped by way of the visible and the invisible. The first difficulty is that in Australia the difference between the visible and the invisible never converges with the gap between the material and the intelligible. "Australia" has never designated a concept, let alone an ideal, in the way that "America" has. And this is one reason why, on the central plains, one cannot always draw a line between fiction and philosophy. By the same token, one cannot simply represent the material world and call it Australia, even though the project has been frequently attempted on the coast. In the words of a photographer who worked with the director of *The Interior,* the visible is "an island lapped by the boundless ocean of the invisible," and this island is set deep within our inner darkness (p. 113).

In a land like this, one is bound to find the occasional weirdo. The director of *The Interior* tells us that "They affect no shabbiness in their dress and no uncouthness in their manners" (p. 103). My favorite is the man "who travels every year at the beginning of spring with a servant on a weeks-long journey across the plains and back again, never parting the dark curtains around him in the rear compartment of his car" (pp. 103–104). This is eccentric behavior not because of the man's disdain for sensory impressions but because he parades his supreme inwardness year in and year out. *The Interior* does not show us a beautiful country, not even a land that is beautiful in its harshness. It discloses a country apprehended only by individuals on the verge of solipsism, a land that forbids representation. The narrative that discusses the film that cannot be made of the interior is of course Gerald Murnane's *The Plains*. In this extraordinary novella, Murnane has been taken to lament "an Australian literature that has never been written."[10] In other words, "If only we had been more weird!" I wonder who says it the more convincingly, Australians or Americans?

Notes

1. Franz Kafka, *Amerika,* trans. Willa and Edwin Muir, pref. Klaus Mann, afterword Max Brod (New York: Schocken Books, 1946), 41.

2. Gustav Janouch, *Conversations with Kafka,* trans. Goronwy Rees, introd. Hugh Haughton (London: Quartet Books, 1985), 158.

3. Franz Kafka, *Letters to Friends, Family, and Editors,* trans. Richard and Clara Winston (New York: Schocken Books, 1977), 3.

4. John Ashbery, *Hotel Lautréamont* (New York: Alfred A. Knopf, 1992), 83.

5. Jonathan Swift, *Gulliver's Travels,* introd. Harold Williams, in *The Prose Writings of Jonathan Swift,* ed. Herbert Davis (Oxford: Basil Blackwell, 1941), 4.

6. James McAuley, "The True Discovery of Australia," in *Collected Poems 1936–1970* (Sydney: Angus & Robertson, 1971).

7. John Forbes, "To the Bobbydazzlers," in *New and Selected Poems* (Sydney: Angus & Robertson, 1992).

8. "Ern Malley" is the name of a poet of modernist tendencies whose entire works were jointly written by Harold Stewart and James McAuley. His poetry was published by Max Harris in his journal *Angry Penguins*. After publication of the poems, Stewart and McAuley revealed that "Ern Malley" was a hoax.

9. Gerald Murnane, *The Plains* (Melbourne: Nostrillia Press, 1982), 10–11.

10. From the dustjacket of Murnane, *The Plains.*

References

Ashbery, John. *Hotel Lautréamont.* New York: Alfred A. Knopf, 1992.

Forbes, John. *New and Selected Poems.* Sydney: Angus & Robertson, 1992.

CHAPTER

8

....

Double Vision: Antipodean or Not?

JAN SENBERGS

I WOULD LIKE TO MAKE some comments about the art world; how it seems from a painter's viewpoint both in the United States and in Australia—some personal observations of a painter from the Antipodes, if you like.

As always, whenever I come to the states, one of the continual pleasures is to be able to see some of the great art collections in this country. It's that natural instinct of any painter when traveling to get up close to the brush marks and to check out those well-known images that are fixed in your mind, to see how they differ from the reproductions in the books you have at home.

The great pleasure of looking at paintings.

As an Australian painter, what intrigues me is to see how the two stories of American and Australian art have developed. How similar they are in some ways and yet how differently arrived at they are to the present day. I am leaving aside for the moment the contribution of indigenous art of both countries and also the extensive European collections, particularly here in America.

Let me just scan briefly over the two histories: here in America, we start out with those fastidious and early limners; then we skip into the grand landscapes of the nineteenth century with artists such as Thomas Cole and Frederick Church among others; then we see the regional viewpoint with acknowledgments to early modernism; then we encounter the increasing School of Paris influences. Later, arriving in the 1940s, we see clear attempts to seek a more distinctive modern American vision, and a conscious effort to discard those Parisian affectations; then we move on to the self-assured and high-lit time of Pollock, de Kooning, Newman, Still, Rothko, and many others; and finally we arrive at the present day, where it all becomes exactly the same as anywhere else in the world—or does it?

Now let's glance at the Australian counterpart where we can start with those early schematic topographer painters of Sydney Cove; then we skip to the European landscapists in a foreign terrain; then we move on to the glorious and light-filled bush painters such as Roberts, Streeton, McCubbin, and others; then we see the polite attempts at modernism, looking to Paris but via London; then in the 1940s we find the "bush Bloomsbury" group at Heide by the Yarra River in Melbourne where a maverick but modernist spark was lit; and later from the 1950s on, we look broadly toward the world, wanting to be up to date in Kansas City; and finally today we look just the same as in New York or anywhere else in the world—or is it different?

Now that's a real broad brush sweep of both histories that I've just made. A broom-size sweep, in fact. But what I'd like to angle in on briefly here is first, how in different ways, both American and Australian artists, particularly in the 1940s, arrived at their version of a more independent modern art view, away from the strong ties of European art history. And secondly, how valid and important is it to articulate a regional view in art considering how global the art world looks today?

To give an example of that earlier period of American modernism and the Paris connection, I think of the time when I was at Harvard teaching in 1989–1990, when during one of the term breaks, we drove down to Pennsylvania. Among other things I wanted to see Frank Lloyd Wright's Fallingwater house as well as some of the territory of that wonderful 1920s Scottish-American painter called John Kane. I wanted to see the Alleghenies that he painted and that road along the Monongahela River that leads into Pittsburgh with all those now silent and rusty but mighty steel mill structures.

After checking out the paintings of John Kane in Pittsburgh, I wandered into the Carnegie Institute Art Gallery and walked into a room full of paintings by Kandinsky, Mondrian, Paul Klee, Miro, and others—but when I looked closer at the labels next to the paintings, I saw to my surprise that they all had American names. They were American artists of the 1930s who were painting just like those European pioneers of modernism. It occurred to me there how differently and how directly the American artists of that time had absorbed their modernist attitudes from Europe in comparison with the indirect sources of the Australian attempts at modernism. It seemed to me that the American artists in that room at the Carnegie Institute had almost learned their modernist lessons too well. They seemed to have sat almost too close at their master's elbow.

They knew their Kandinsky too well.

Arshile Gorky, for example, also knew his Picasso so well for so many years before finally breaking away late in his life to make his own distinctive mark as an American artist.

It wasn't until the mid to late 1940s, as we all know, before a younger generation of American artists such as Pollock, de Kooning, Newman, Still, and others challenged the omnipotence of those recently arrived and haughty European masters in New York—and finally made their own considerable impact as pioneers of a new American sensibility in modern art.

What became evident to me was that that kind of sequence of knowingness could not have happened in Australia. The Australian artists of that time (except for a few expatriates) were far removed from the aesthetic centers of Paris and Europe, and before the 1940s, the few enthusiasts of modernism in a very conservative artistic landscape tried their hand at a generally polite and English version of modernism.

They got their Cezanne from London but they did not know Paris like the Americans.

Similarly, it wasn't until the 1940s, when more individual artists in Australia started to look a bit wider—and it was probably around the circle of art patrons John and Sunday Reed on the outskirts of Melbourne, at their bush Bloomsbury-like salon at a homestead called Heide—that some of the more adventurous and refreshing attempts at an Australian making-do type of modernism was instigated, with artists such as Sidney Nolan, John Perceval, Albert Tucker, and Arthur Boyd.

Unlike their American counterparts who were on a path to an extended abstraction, this group of Australians retained an expressive figurative aspect, based on European expressionist tendencies, the wonderment of naive and child art, local adaptations of Breughel and Bosch even, but with an abiding attachment to the Australian landscape. Also, unlike the American iconoclasts of the 1940s, with their direct experience of the European modernist canon, these Australian artists' sources were very second hand. Magazines, books, postcards, and other news from the centers were their main sources of stimulation.

However, this lack of worldly sophistication, I believe, was a blessing in disguise—it allowed for a development of what I would call an improvised maverick modernism. It enabled these artists to develop their personal and Antipodean idiosyncrasies, and it produced for a short while some of the most adventurous and innovative paintings done in Australia. They were innocently confident, quirky, and bold—they were paintings that only young artists could do.

I know it's easier to romance with hindsight and distance, but that period in the 1940s in both countries had a certain touch of the heroic about it that does not exist today. Meanwhile, the American artists gained momentum and confidence and then with a second generation of artists went on as we know into the 1960s to really establish New York as the center of contemporary art. Down in the Antipodes, it became more difficult to sustain that initial and exciting Australian vision. Some continued to make interesting paintings in that vein, but, because of Australia's geographical isolation, by the 1950s it became necessary for inquiring artists to look at the world more—to measure themselves against a broader artistic backdrop.

Yet the curious thing is, despite all kinds of world trends in recent times and claims for a cool and cerebral approach to art in some contemporary quarters, there are still quite a number of important and serious artists in Australia who wrestle with their landscape in various ways, wanting to acknowledge a sense of place. This involvement with a personal landscape is still a strong element in Australian contemporary art—and in recent years it has been bolstered significantly by a vivid and portable contemporary Aboriginal art presence.

I think any alternative fluctuations in the art world today are important, because in recent times when one looks at the various Art Biennials and International Survey exhibitions around the world, they seem to be looking more similar to each other no matter where in the world they may be—and the artists in these exhibitions at times look less independent and more like demonstrators of the various current modes exhibited there despite their claims to newness.

Generally speaking, I think that most of the artistic innovations of the twentieth century were basically tackled and done by the mid-1920s. The first two or three decades were a period of genuine iconoclasm and discovery—thereafter, with the exception of some outstanding individual artists, it has been mainly streamlining and making variations in successive and periodical mainstreams of Western art. So, now in our post-postmodern period so many of the original concepts are dressed up in new clothes and technological sheen and paraded stridently with an ever-increasing curatorial hype but intellectual conformity.

Novelty art is once again dominant in contemporary art circles, and I don't mean interesting, funky, home-grown art such as some Californian or Chicago art, but what I would call serious novelty art, such as the endless variations of wall and floor installations, TV monitors with earnest video messages, and other serious assembling, usually accompanied by extended catalogue texts, often pontificating in the most cryptic manner about the supposed intellectual significance of the endeavor, and critics and writers tending more to reviewing each other's catalogue texts rather than the work.

Now it needs to be said that there is nothing invalid or lacking in invention about this area of art making—as Clement Greenberg once said, "One cannot condemn tendencies in art, one can only condemn works of art." It's just that these tendencies have been around now for some time, and continue to claim the so-called cutting-edge status, that one has to question and say—well, we've been there and done that now for over thirty years, are we still amused?

As a result, painting and drawing are once again under threat as viable and relevant art forms in the 1990s. It's a cyclical thing; painting has periodically been under this kind of questioning ever since the invention of the camera. In recent times, however, there seems to be this increasingly dumb fascination with the "new technology" as an art form. It's understandable that new methods and new tools are interesting and any way of making art is valid, but as ever, it's not the tools or methods that count no matter how impressive—it's the hand and mind behind it. It's an age-old thing, the fascination and absorption with new techniques as if they can make you a better artist. But there is a tendency in some sections of the art world to think that, for example, installation art or certain aspects of postconceptual art and theory, simply by their nature, are regarded as an advanced art form and therefore are assumed to be more valid and are able to signify current intellectual issues more effectively than painting, for instance.

To me, a desperate mark on a street wall can often carry more meaning and profundity than a highly regarded white-walled gallery space lined with video monitors, flickering repetitive images and texts—insisting on the seriousness of life and art.

However, in recent years there has been a reevaluation of contemporary art. After the excessive 1980s where anything went and a lot was accepted, there is now in the 1990s a more detached observation of what's being made and what is given the accolades, as well as a reassessment of some of the previous heroes of the art world. It's a time of a general *aesthetic audit* of the last fifty years, and like any audit, it makes people nervous. As a general thing, such an examination of recent claims is no bad thing—it sorts out the "sprinters from the stayers" but it also understandably shakes up the confidence of the collectors, so as a result they alternatively dive for the safety of history—at auction houses for stamped and approved works no matter how minor. It brings out the pedants and spoil-sports of the art world, who seek intellectual regimentation in art. In this climate, I'm on the side of excess.

Still, things changed noticeably as modernism in art in recent times got tired of repeating its variations around the world. Postmodernism took its analytical place. It seemed the way to go—a logical examination of recent art. Some quarters of the art world were even insisting that art could be judged of its quality by its intention—that in demonstrating a particular cause or theory it could gain validity as an artwork. Looking back and quoting with irony was the message.

But that knowing detachment soon began to circle inward and became more the intellectual property of the art world theorists rather than the practitioners. For all its virtues of second-looking at history, the postmodernist phase in art was mainly a frontal embellishment to a vacant imagination.

If we look at the contemporary art world in terms of where it's at or its general position, I would say that we are now in a time of what I think is a late twentieth-century *mannerist* period in art. This is assuming that the first decades were the period of its modernistic renaissance. Today is a period of a worldly sophistication in the visual arts—superficially diverse, but often intellectually conforming. It is not unlike how those 1930s artists looked in the Carnegie Institute in their day. What made the later 1940s generation of American and also Australian artists more interesting was their feeling and need to break away from those revered yet constricting modernist examples that they understood and add something new and exciting to their chapters of art history.

If I could put it this way, I think we are in an art environment curiously equivalent to that of the 1930s and 1940s—a kind of artistic cusp—but of course on a much broader and global scale. I like to believe that there are in the United States, in Australia, and in other parts of the world, interesting and maverick artists hovering around and challenging *today's* revered and established ways of looking at contemporary art—showing us once again yet another world view from their particular patch—just as those earlier artists did.

That's what I find interesting in contemporary art.

Note

1. Clement Greenberg, *Art and Culture: Critical Essays* (Boston: Beacon Press, 1965). From essay on Wyndham Lewis against abstract art (1957).

PART III

History

9

········

Not As the Song of Other Lands

GEOFFREY BLAINEY, UNIVERSITY OF MELBOURNE

I OFFER YOU SIX VERSES, not to sing but to chew. I wish to outline six kinds of Australian nationalism. These six categories are distinct in spirit. They can also overlay. At times they seem likely to merge and at times they seem likely to draw apart.

Many debates of importance in Australia are flavored by nationalist attitudes. In nearly every debate, one group believes that it has a near-monopoly of nationalism or is the true guardian of nationalism. But perhaps nationalism is too complex, too shifting, and too many-sided to be pegged out and neatly claimed. Moreover, in the last three decades, nationalism in Australia has changed in unpredicted ways.

ECONOMIC NATIONALISM

Nationalism usually means a sense of belonging, and often an articulate sense of belonging. It also means an emphasis on the nation-state. Using these two definitions, economic nationalism was probably the earliest form of nationalism to be conspicuous in Australia.

Economic nationalism increased once the Australian colonies gained self-government and the right to impose tariffs on imports. From the 1850s they could impose duties on imports from Britain so long as those duties were no higher than the duties imposed on goods from elsewhere. By 1870 Victoria led in this kind of nationalism. Duties were placed on a host of imports, even those from New South Wales. Anyone outside Victoria was a foreigner.

When in 1901 the Commonwealth of Australia was created, it formed in sheer area one of the world's largest common markets, and soon it was protectionist. Not only were Australian factories increasingly protected against foreign imports but so, too, were the coastal ships protected against foreign-owned ships. The sugarcane industry along the coast of northern New South Wales and Queensland was the first primary industry to be protected. It was protected against foreign sugar, especially from Mauritius. The protection of Australian sugar was seen as a way to populate and thereby to defend a vital part of sparsely settled tropical Australia.

"Develop the North" was for long one of the slogans of economic nationalism. Those who chant this slogan have grown hoarse. "Shackle the North" is almost today's comparable slogan, not so much because economic nationalism has *drastically* declined but largely because new kinds of nationalism—especially a black nationalism and a green nationalism—are in the ascendant.

Some of this old-time protection was conferred on Australian industries by sleight of hand. Some other Australian industry or the average Australian consumer was often paying for it or subsidizing it. But these other Australian interests could not so easily appeal to nationalism. Nationalism—this is a generalization—thrives on simplicity. In complex economic matters, the nationalist argument seems to fire the big guns. It can even capture a political party. Two of the strongest political movements in Australia began life as free traders or antiprotectionists. These were the NSW Labor Party, which in 1891 became the first Labor Party to succeed, and then early in this century the Country Party—now the National Party. They could not derail the protectionist and nationalist train they had opposed, so they jumped aboard.

By 1910 economic nationalism as an ideology and a sentiment was powerful in Australia. It presided with special flair over the packaging of Australian goods. Mimmo Cozzolino in his book *Symbols of Australia*—really a catalog history of the Australian label—displays scores of examples.[1] Thus Nathan Ale of South Australia used a big label reading "Australia: The Land of Promise." McCracken's Bitter Ale displayed the motto "Advance Australia," and kangaroos and emus abounded on labels such as the brand called Billy Tea—a popular product that really popularized the words of "Waltzing Matilda." Children of that generation might well have been far more influenced by the message from Billy Tea than by the paintings of the Heidelberg School and the prose and poetry of Henry Lawson. In studying history we tend to skate over the power of the ephemeral.

In Australia the traditional version of economic nationalism with its protectionist flavor enjoyed a wonderful innings until the late 1960s. Since then it has been in retreat, though not on every front. The retreat will possibly be reversed. Even in East Asia, whose economic success we claim to be emulating, the banner of economic nationalism flies high.

RED, WHITE, AND BLUE NATIONALISM

It is essentially a subspecies of British nationalism but distinctive and often powerful. I call it "red, white, and blue" nationalism. Today, it is sometimes mocked, and Prime Minister Keating for a time was foremost in this fun-loving sport. It is now usually viewed by the serious media as simply main-stream British nationalism. But in Australia, for many decades, it was believed to be some steps removed from British nationalism. This kind of nationalism assumed that Britain was the greatest empire in the world and the fountain of civilization, but it assumed that Australia, on those British foundations, had built a new and superior edifice.

As time went on, there was more rivalry between the species and the sub-species. The spread of the word *pommy* (a derogatory term for an English immigrant), coined just before World War I, was a sign of the rivalry. Prime Minister Billy Hughes, busying himself at the Paris Peace Conference in 1919 by deserting from the British delegation and running alone in an attempt to chase away the Japanese, was another sign of the contrast.

Many of the early republicans in Australia were really red, white, and blue nationalists who could see the advantages of separation while remaining closely linked to Britain in defense, culture, and commerce. The fathers of Australian federation were overwhelmingly red, white, and blue national-ists. The creation of the Commonwealth of Australia in 1901 possibly origi-nated as much from their desire to strengthen links with Britain, notably in defense, as from what we would now identify as Australian nationalism.

Many of the Catholic Irish in Australia—and they became the main source of quotable and articulate nationalism—reacted against red, white, and blue nationalism. Their love of Australia was probably no more intense than that of the typical red, white, and blues: they just expressed themselves more positively. Moreover, their Irish homeland, compared with England, was so depressed emotionally and economically that they had less incentive to return home. Here is a simple and eloquent declaration written in Victoria in 1881 by Mrs. Mary Allen of The Ten Mile. "Our little William and my brother George we buried in the Australian soil. I love this land of which our family is part. Where else could we have such freedom and such opportunity." She had left County Clare a mere twenty-one years ago.[2]

Red, white, and blue nationalism might have declined more rapidly but for the Boer War and the two world wars. The wars strengthened the old emotional bonds. Since 1970 the influence of this kind of nationalism has diminished. Some of the reasons are self-evident: Japan was replacing Britain as the main trading partner, the United States replaced Britain as the main military ally, Britain joined the European Community, and Britons ceased to crowd the migrant ships and migrant planes coming to Australia.

The recent surge of republicanism in Australia reflects some of these underlying changes to Australia's old relationships. Much of the opposition to republicanism today stems from the red, white, and blue nationalists. Incidentally, this kind of nationalism has been bolstered in an odd way by the anti-British strand in the official version of multiculturalism in vogue in the last ten or so years of the Hawke and Keating governments.

The two strands of nationalism I have outlined so far—the economic and the red, white, and blue—have lost much of their influence. Red, white, and blue nationalism is subscribed to by a smaller proportion of the population but will revive strongly when the republican debates really begin. Economic nationalism is temporarily in decline during this period of world history where globalization is so pronounced. Economic nationalism in Australia and in many other Western countries is likely to revive in the next fifteen years, both for better and for worse.

ATHLETIC NATIONALISM

In most nations one would not dream of setting up a category called athletic nationalism. In Australia and almost certainly in New Zealand, it is a vital category.

Let me fill in the background as I see it. The chip on many Australians' shoulders a century ago was the memory of the convict past. That was why South Australians held their heads so high and have done so ever since. When Australia began to play England in sports—and cricket and professional rowing were the only real international contests in the nineteenth century—an Australian victory was greeted here with jubilation, being hailed by many Australians as the sign of how a new land, climate, and culture could improve what was secretly feared to have been discarded British stock. It was Professor John Plamenatz, an Oxford professor born in Montenegro, who wrote, "nationalism is a reaction of peoples who feel culturally at a disadvantage."[3] I do not think he had Australia in mind, but his words of 1975 are still relevant.

The role of sport in Australian nationalism was accentuated because Australia did so well at it—we were really a forerunner of the East Germany of the 1970s. In contrast to East Germany, the performance-enhancing drugs used by Australians in that earlier era consisted of a high amount of leisure, impressive prosperity, a friendly outdoor climate, and cheap land and plentiful water for sports. By the start of this century, Australia was perhaps the first country in the world to be so obsessed by spectator sport.[4]

In 1915 the Anzac (Australian and New Zealand Army Corps) tradition was quickly grafted onto athletic nationalism. The success at Gallipoli was important to Australian feelings largely because war was still seen as the ultimate in sporting contests. War was the test of national fitness, which to some extent the Olympic Games now provide. At Gallipoli in 1915, the Australians believed they were playing in a world Match of the Day for the first time. In the end Australia officially recorded the result as an impressive draw resulting from an away fixture. In the first month, however, the landing on the beach and cliffs of Gallipoli was seen as a triumph over the Turks. We like to think that Australians are unusual in fashioning their national legends out of defeats and disasters, but Gallipoli initially became a legend at a time when it was seen as a decided success.

Today war is increasingly seen as no longer a sport. Significantly, the four-day battle of Isurava and the other battles along the Kokoda Track in New Guinea in 1942, and the repelling of the Japanese soldiers who crossed the Owen Stanley mountains and advanced close to Port Moresby, are the phases of World War II possibly accorded the status of legend in Australia.[5] Kokoda still conveys—with the aid of filmmakers—the aura of a mighty athletic contest. It can easily be dressed up to appear like the final minutes of a football match slogged out in near-darkness on a muddy sloping ground. Here were events in which the technology of death did not seem to be all-conquering.

Athletic nationalism in Australia is alive and well, as Sydney in the year 2000 will presumably reveal. At its peak it has more capacity than any other kind of nationalism to unite the nation for a few weeks.

SHOWCASE NATIONALISM

This is a lesser kind of nationalism but worthy of comment. To be a show-case, to be a social laboratory for the world to marvel at, has been a source of pride or self-respect to Australians of various generations.

Thus Australia was a pioneer of democracy and especially of the secret ballot, which was christened the Victorian or Australian ballot in other lands. Both Australia and New Zealand, pioneers of social reform, were vast human laboratories inspected by excited or dismayed visitors about the start of this century. The first labor government in the world emerged in Australia—indeed in Queensland. The attempt to develop tropical Australia solely with white labor in the first years of this century was an experiment watched closely in Europe and North America. Likewise, multiculturalism and the pursuit of racial and cultural diversity are now hailed by some Australians as object lessons for the world.

Alfred Deakin's favorite Australian poet was the Toowoomba man, George Essex Evans, who displayed a version of showcase nationalism when he wrote "An Australian Symphony":

> *Not as the song of other lands*
> *Her song shall be,*
> *Where dim Her purple shore-line stands*
> *Above the sea!*[6]

In including showcase nationalism, I was influenced by Plamenatz's idea that nationalism is the haunt of those who feel at a cultural disadvantage. Nationalism is also the platform of those who feel advantaged and feel a deep need to proclaim it.

THE NATIONALISM OF PLACE

I have half a mind to describe the next category as wattle nationalism, but that might make a variety of nationalism, which is more alive than ever, seem slightly archaic.

Most migrants coming here from Western Europe did not find it easy to feel at home. The climate, light, vegetation, and the upside-down-seasons could be disconcerting. But in settling down here they were helped by those Australians whose painting, poetry, and prose groped for and shaped what is now a powerful strand of nationalism. These artists of the second half of the nineteenth century extolled symbols of place: the poet Kendall selected the bellbird; curiously the glorious, more typical magpie has never been enthroned, except at Collingwood and Port Adelaide. Adam Lindsay Gordon chose the wattle. He and "Banjo" Paterson also chose the bush horseman, thus combining athletic nationalism with the nationalism of place.

In the second half of the 1880s, the Heidelberg School of painters selected the fierce blue sky and distant blue ranges and summer grass. More than a decade later, Dorothea Mackellar selected a sunburned country. Almost at the same time, in 1903, the Southern Cross was selected as a special nationalist symbol and placed on the Australian flag. The Southern Cross is a manifestly Christian symbol as well as unique to nations of the southern hemisphere. Interestingly, both the wattle and the Southern Cross have slipped as national symbols.

Slowly this affection for the land, this sense of place, grew. Aborigines had always possessed it, so far as we know. Artists and writers were foremost in painting a pleasing varnish on a rough land. Knowledge of native plants and animals was a vital wing of this kind of nationalism. The mining town of Broken Hill, a stronghold of this knowledge of natural history, was a home of the infant Green movement long before the blue gum reached Fitzroy's cramped front gardens.

During the last third of the century, the new Green movement increased this sense of place in Australia. It also grafted a strong international strand onto what was primarily a nationalist movement. It is fair to say that in Australia the Dark Greens tend to be the internationalists. This articulate minority holds the Green seats in those parliaments where proportional representation prevails. These Dark Greens are driven more by the world's fragile ecology, the growing global population, nuclear threats, the greenhouse fears, and the ozone fears. I think the Light Greens—and most Australians are Light Greens—are slightly more nationalist than internationalist, though there is ebb and flow from year to year.

The Light Green movement, embodying a quiet nationalist feeling, has a long and influential history in Australia; and the popular use, the almost ineradicable use, of the word *Green* camouflages that history. A color borrowed from cool Europe and North America is not very appropriate in mainland Australia; but it is here to stay. I should modify that sentence. No strand of nationalism is here to stay, unchanged.

The Green label shows how much a nationalist movement has been lassoed by internationalists. Rolf Boldrewood, probably the most widely read Australian novelist in his heyday, would be astonished. He had gone to England about 1860 as a young man, familiar with the Victorian grasslands, and was taken aback by the sight of the pretty Hampshire landscape: "The greenness of the pastures was at first sight oppressive," he recalled.[7] He was Dorothea Mackellar's spiritual father.

BLACK NATIONALISM

This is the sixth and final strand I single out here. It has already been touched on with illumination by Rhys Jones, John Mulvaney, and Les Hiatt in Part 1.

Everyone living in Australia in the last twenty years has seen the remarkable spread of this kind of nationalism, and it is not confined simply to Aborigines. If it were confined to them, to two percent of the population, it would be weaker politically. Black nationalism, once invisible, can be seen in the history books, films, parliamentary debates, and the high court.

Black nationalism consists of a justifiable pride in the long Aboriginal history—the Torres Strait Islanders, with their relatively short history, are admitted more for political reasons. Black nationalism generally includes a belief that the Aborigines were unusually spiritual. It often includes a belief, probably now at its peak, that Aboriginal life before 1788 was not too far from utopia. Nearly always it includes a belief that the Aborigines were the archetypal Dark Greens, living in harmony with nature and with one another. This is the picture you might pick up from the letters columns of *The Age* and the *Sydney Morning Herald* and many news items on the Australian Broadcasting Corporation as well as from certain schools of historians. Similarly, red, white, and blue nationalism in its heyday gloried in a heightened sense of white Australian virtues while looking down on Aborigines and their civilization.

In the last twenty years, there has been an astonishing rewriting of large slices of Australian history, and the place of Aborigines has become central. It is rare in the modern world for such a rewriting of a nation's history to take place so quickly. The main exceptions are when a political revolution takes place or when a nation is defeated in war. Even Japan, though defeated decisively in war, has probably evaded a rewriting of such magnitude as we are experiencing in Australia. After such a quick move from one extreme to another, Australia will experience a period of settling down.

The ascent of the Green movement and black nationalism—two powerful strands in present-day Australian nationalism—are in part the result of what I call a swing of the ideological seesaw inside the Western world. When Western civilization and its lode star, Applied Science, fall somewhat from favor, the values at the other end of the seesaw rise in compensation. When Nature and those believed to be living close to Nature rise in esteem, our science-based civilization tends to fall in esteem.[8]

Nationalism is a complicated topic: it contains many strands. The strands frequently alter in strength and influence. Indeed, I now realize that my original title, "What shall we do with a drunken sailor?" is not entirely irrelevant. In the ship of nationalism there are various categories of sailors, both sober and drunk; and in the coming century there will be enlistments and desertions.

Notes

1. Mimmo Cozzolino, *Symbols of Australia* (Ringwood: Penguin Books, 1980).
2. Brian Lloyd, *Tales of the Ten Mile: Ballybeg to the Bush* (Melbourne: Histech Publications, 1995), 168.
3. John Plamenatz, "Two Types of Nationalism," in *Nationalism: The Nature and Evolution of an Idea,* ed. Eugene Kamenka (Canberra: Australian National University Press, 1975), 27.
4. On sporting heroes, see Geoffrey Blainey, "Heroes of the Arena," in *Monuments for an Age without Heroes,* ed. Claudio Veliz (Boston: Boston University Press, 1996), esp. 79–80.
5. While writing this speech, I received a letter from the 2/14th Battalion Association arguing that the Battle for Isurava was "the battle that saved Australia from invasion."
6. G. E. Evans cited in *The Dictionary of Australian Quotations,* ed. Stephen Murray-Smith (Richmond: Heinemann, 1984), 76–77.
7. Rolf Boldrewood, in *Australians Abroad: An Anthology,* ed. C. Higham and M. Wilding (Melbourne: F. W. Cheshire, 1967), 18.
8. Geoffrey Blainey, *The Great Seesaw: A New View of the Western World, 1750–2000* (South Melbourne: Macmillan, 1988), 313–314.

References

Blainey, Geoffrey. "Heroes of the Arena." In *Monuments for an Age without Heroes.* Edited by Claudio Veliz. Boston: Boston University Press, 1996.

———. *The Great Seesaw: A New View of the Western World, 1750–2000.* South Melbourne: Macmillan, 1988.

Boldrewood, Rolf. *Australians Abroad: An Anthology.* Edited by C. Higham and M. Wilding. Melbourne: F. W. Cheshire, 1967.

Cozzolino, Mimmo. *Symbols of Australia*. Ringwood: Penguin Books, 1980.

Evans, G. E. *The Dictionary of Australian Quotations*. Edited by Stephen Murray-Smith. Richmond: Heinemann, 1984.

Lloyd, Brian. *Tales of the Ten Mile: Ballybeg to the Bush*. Melbourne: Histech Publications, 1995.

Plamenatz, John. "Two Types of Nationalism." In *Nationalism: The Nature and Evolution of an Idea*. Edited by Eugene Kamenka. Canberra: Australian National University Press, 1975.

10

Australian Women in America, from Miles Franklin to Jill Ker Conway

JILL ROE, MACQUARIE UNIVERSITY

*"I used to say I had only to present myself and
the Americans did all the rest."
[Miles Franklin to Bruce Sutherland,
March 18, 1954]*

AS ONLY THE SECOND WOMAN to be appointed to the Chair of Australian
Studies at Harvard, and the first in the field of Women's Studies, I became
interested in the story of Australian women in America, and conversely of
American women in Australia. This paper explores some interactions, from
the 1890s to the 1960s.[1]

I begin, as I often do, with the Australian writer and feminist Miles
Franklin (1879–1954). As will be seen, her experience serves as a touchstone of interactions to be sketched over a century or so, from the 1890s to
the Great War, when Australian and American women were, like their male
counterparts, "radical cousins"; through war and depression, when the relationship changed and America offered paths to professionalism for a
minority; on to another war and the onset of a closer but later edgy "family" relationship, when Eleanor Roosevelt visited Australia and marriage
dominated women's lives everywhere; through to the sisterly sixties, when
interaction again became intense, and increasingly equal. Or did it? Some
recent evidence suggests uncertainties in an era of globalization, maybe
even something of a standoff; and while personal relations remain as warm
and welcoming as in Miles Franklin's day—certainly in my own experience—it now seems to be mostly a matter of what, in another context,
Canberra political scientist Marian Sawer has called "sisters in suits."[2]

MILES FRANKLIN

In a letter to a newfound American friend, the literary scholar Bruce Sutherland, written March 18, 1954, some six months before her death, Miles Franklin recalled arriving in California almost fifty years earlier, in April 1906, and her trip cross-country that same year to Chicago, where she paused and stayed on to work for the National Women's Trade Union League of America (NWTUL) until 1915. It is one of her best letters. It reads like yesterday, so vivid are its recollections of "the sweet peas and opulence of Redlands California," of the beauty of Salt Lake City and surrounding mountains, and of the Rockies and its rapids, where her riding skills and freak success as a shooter impressed the locals. Other memories came flooding back as she wrote—I should say typed, as she became a good typist in Chicago—of farmhouses in Michigan, paddleboats on the Missouri, the joys of train travel in America, and the wild grapes of Connecticut, conveying well the excitement and exhilaration of those first encounters with America. "What a country, & all a going concern!" she exclaims. As for the people, "I had only to present myself and the Americans did all the rest." Their efforts en route to Chicago apparently included an offer to join a circus and a proposal of marriage from a vaudeville strongman. Evidently, with her open face and agile mind, and not yet twenty-six years old, Miles made quite an impact.[3]

Among hundreds of extant letters between Miles Franklin and her American friends, at least one more refers to those first encounters with America. Miles sailed from Sydney on the SS *Ventura* on April 7, 1906, arriving in San Francisco a fortnight or so later, soon after the great earthquake (April 18, 1906). Writing to Margaret Dreier Robins in 1930, she recalled that Carrie Whelan of Oakland "chartered a tug and came out and got me off the ship down the harbour." No wonder she thought fondly of her American friends and admired their energy and boldness! Of Robins herself, Miles wrote in an article on American working women published in the *Sydney Morning Herald* in 1909, that "[i]n a country where brilliant women abound," Robins was "one of the ablest alive." Apropos the abilities of American women, it was commonplace at the time to regard American women as socially advanced even though still unenfranchised, and Miles was shocked when she went to Britain at the "unpardonable dowdiness" of British women, and the domestic discomfort there.[4]

We know from several sources that Franklin's spirits fluctuated quite markedly during her American years and that even the first impact was not all delights. She suffered a nervous collapse soon after arrival in California and another in Chicago, following the death of her sister in 1907. Nor was the way forward immediately plain. Jack London proved amiable but unhelpful when it came to finding publishers; and to her grandmother's dismay, she was working as a barmaid, not a writer, through the Rockies.

However, for reasons to be noticed shortly, she fell among friends in Chicago, and stayed on as a working woman until troubles in the League and the Great War caused her to leave for London, and as it turned out, for good, late 1915. However, in the course of her work, Franklin came to know America well. Her travels included Boston, where in October 1914 she met up with the Goldstein sisters of Melbourne and studied Christian Science. (Which, incidentally, in a sense smoothed the way for me. When I arrived in Boston on September 1, 1994, knowing no one and dazed from the flight, my first walk was along Mass. Ave., and it was a boon to come upon the First Church of Christ Scientist—more mellow now than on the c. 1914 postcard in the Franklin Papers in the Mitchell Library, but immediately recognizable.)[5]

The 1954 letter to Sutherland was not an occasion for criticism, though other correspondence shows Franklin was far from uncritical of America, for example, of labor conditions and "dollar imperialism." She merely regretted that she had lacked "the qualities to acquire and be on the make" which led to success there. For Franklin, aged 74 and in failing health, America had been a mighty experience, gladly acknowledged (though not much mentioned later, as younger writer Marjorie Barnard once noted with some irritation; but this was probably to avoid the envy and irritation that are common responses to travelers' tales in Australia, as elsewhere). She still loved "the beautiful land and its people—forever and into eternity if there be identity there."[6]

It was Bruce Sutherland who first drew attention to Miles Franklin's American years. Thanks to Verna Coleman's *Miles Franklin in America: Her (Unknown) Brilliant Career* (1981), this dimension is now quite well understood (though not yet its implications). Not much more need be said of Franklin hereafter. Other women would choose America, and work there, including more married women, as Miles was not. Some, like her, would return home, to varying fates. Others stayed on, and, as expatriates who either retained or renounced Australian citizenship, depending largely on U.S. residency and other requirements, made significant contributions to American life and culture, with regular visits to Australia an increasing option. Meanwhile, more American women would make their way to Australia, and the impression that American women were more advanced strengthened. Did a new version of the "cultural cringe" develop, is a question now asked.[7]

Franklin was by no means the first Australian woman to choose America. South Australian–bred Harriet Clisby (1830–1931), physician and feminist, a Swedenborgian who left Australia for London in the 1860s in search of medical qualifications, obtained them in New York, and settled in Boston about 1871. Clisby never returned to Australia; but she is recorded as saying, "I love Australia. I have always loved it."[8]

RADICAL COUSINS

Recent scholarship has reminded us that middle-class Australian women have been keen travelers for a century or more and that there was always an international dimension to the Australian women's movement. International networks pertaining to temperance and the suffrage first formed in the 1890s, and the woman delegate became a familiar type. One destination was America. The distinguished South Australian Catherine Helen Spence (1825–1910) was an early bird. She went to the Chicago Expo in 1893, representing a variety of South Australian reform organizations. Leading Sydney temperance suffragist Mary Windeyer (1836–1912) organized a New South Wales presence there also, and her daughter Margaret was a New South Wales Commissioner, said to be the only Lady Commissioner at the Fair. The World's Woman's Christian Temperance Union conferences also offered an opportunity (the first in Fanueil Hall, Boston, in 1891); and no doubt some delegates made the pilgrimage to founder Frances Willard's home in Illinois. In 1902 a number of antipodean women's organizations sent Victorian suffragist Vida Goldstein (1869–1949)—"Our Delegate"—to a suffrage conference in Washington, where she was elected Secretary of the First International Woman Suffrage Committee, and the International Woman Suffrage Alliance came into being. Later, in 1909 residents Alice Henry and Miles Franklin were "unofficial" delegates at the Second Biennial Convention of the National Women's Trade Union League in Chicago.[9]

The delegates did not appear in any deferential spirit. This was the era of "radical cousins."[10] For a brief moment before the Great War, being the only nationally enfranchised women in the world (along with New Zealanders) and having a strong temperance movement, the self-esteem and national pride of Australian women was high. Thus Spence spent nearly a year in North America after the Expo lecturing on "effective voting," Goldstein appeared before Congress Committees, and when experienced Melbourne journalist Alice Henry arrived in Chicago in 1906, she quickly became a guru to the emerging women's trade union movement, having behind her the Victorian experience of wage and factory legislation. Such things interested the Progressives. It will hardly surprise to hear that it was Goldstein who encouraged Miles Franklin to travel via America, and that Alice Henry welcomed her to Chicago and became her coworker there. Behind them stood the supportive figure of Miles's mother, native-born country-woman Susannah Franklin (1850–1938). It seems Susannah Franklin, too, thought of Americans as "radical cousins," though Miles's political mentor Rose Scott (1847–1925) could not approve her departure.[11]

Another dimension is added when we consider American women in Australia in the era of "radical cousins." Probably there were few. The most important was undoubtedly Jessie Ackermann (1857?–1951), a Woman's

Christian Temperance Union (WCTU) missionary, though mention should also be made of Texas-born journalist Jennie Scott Griffiths (1875–1951) who moved from Hawaii to work the radical press in Queensland 1914–1920. Ackermann revitalized the woman's temperance movement in Australia in the early 1890s and organized it on a federal basis. In one photograph she appears in a gospel van in the outback. Australian temperance women loved Ackermann, and she amply repaid them with the minor classic written after a second visit in 1912, *Australia from a Woman's Point of View,* a work that I believe influenced the writing of Australian women's history in the 1970s, for example, by Beverley Kingston. The WCTU may have been an expression of American cultural imperialism, as argued by Kingston's colleague Ian Tyrrell, but it was also a great strengthener of women's shared aspirations. Nor was it all one way. Tyrrell has identified several successful Australian lecturers on the wider temperance stage, such as twice-married Bessie Harrison Lee Cowie, who died in California in 1950 at age 90.[12]

A whole paper could be written on the radical religious, from the spiritualist trance lecturers such as New Yorker Emma Hardinge Britten in Sydney in the 1870s to the unfortunate Mrs. (or was she?) Mattie Lincicombe of Oregon in Melbourne in 1902, a missioner for Mary Baker Eddy's teachings, which increasingly attracted Australian women of a certain class, notably Vida Goldstein, who joined in Boston in 1902; also the Reverend Veenie Cooper-Mathieson, originally associated with the New Thought movement and last heard of conducting prayer meetings in floating garments in her garden on the banks of the Derwent in 1930s Hobart.[13]

The Great War of 1914–1918 brought the era of "radical cousins" to an end. Most likely there would always be exuberance, as when the Sydneyite Olive King (1885–1958) climbed Mt. Popocatepetl in Mexico in 1910, and in the amazing story of champion swimmer Annette Kellerman (1886–1975), "the Australian mermaid," whose long career in aquatic vaudeville in America was preceded by being arrested on a Boston beach for wearing a one-piece swimsuit about the same time. But the young Jessie Lillington (Street, about whom I'll say more later) was a transitional figure, working in New York in 1915 at Waverley House, a reception house for young women arrested as prostitutes. Dulcie Deamer, Queen of Sydney Bohemia in the 1920s, was briefly there too. It could be hard for Australians before America joined the war in 1917, as Franklin had found. Melbourne doctor Hilda Esson, in New York with her dramatist husband Louis in 1916, did not care for it and left for London as soon as possible. As I have indicated elsewhere, whereas the Great War was a serious setback for women in Australia, it was a great leap forward for American women, with enfranchisement in 1920 and significant postwar welfare initiatives, but in an increasingly isolationist context.[14]

When Lola Ridge (Rosa Webster, 1883–1941), a modernist poet of the 1930s and 1940s, left for New York is unknown. Reportedly born in Dublin, Ireland, and New Zealand-bred, the only Australian trace seems to be a couple of references in the Mitchell Library catalogue. However, there are several references in Nan Bowman Albinski's invaluable listings of sources for Australian Studies in North American Libraries, and Harvard's Widener Library catalogue discloses five collections of poetry published in New York in the interwar years. (There is also a little publishing correspondence among Houghton Library holdings.) The earliest American collection *The Ghetto and Other Poems* (1918), which includes poems previously appearing in such places as the *New Republic,* is dedicated to "the American people." Is she important? Or even in any real sense Australian?[15]

All I can suggest at this juncture is that there were not many openings for modernist poets in Australia in the interwar years. Indeed, it seems the most ferocious indictment of an alleged torpor in Australian cultural life in the interwar years came from women who later found their feet and their voices in America, *viz.* Shirley Hazzard (born 1931) in her Boyer lectures of 1984, *Growing Up in Australia,* and Christina Stead (1902–1983)—than whom, of course, there is none more ferocious, even on American women, as in *Letty Fox: Her Luck* (1946):

> The men marry us, feed us and our children; give us allowances, buy life insurance, and leave us their money, even hand us alimony! But all for one reason, and one reason alone. To buy us off! They don't want us running the world; they are willing to pay a lot so they can run it themselves.

Likewise Stead ascribed the advanced social status of American women to the Protestant ethic:

> What luck you have, you American women! Men who pay for everything and don't ask for accounts. Yes, it's Protestantism. The men believe they've done their wives an insult and injury by sleeping with them. They must pay forever!

As de facto wife of a radical American who could never bring himself to divorce, Stead doubtless knew what she was talking about. But hers is a later story. Although she met Bill Blake in London in 1928, it was not until the late 1930s that they went to America, where she spent the war years and set her most anti-Australian male work, *The Man Who Loved Children* (1940). Letters of the period make clear it was the thought of her father that kept her from Australia.[16]

PATHS TO PROFESSIONALISM

The contradictions of citizenship—a marked disjunction between the advanced political and backward social status of Australian women—came into focus in the interwar years, and the women's movement took an internationalist, largely imperial, turn. Some of the young, however, chose America. As with my friend and 1960s expatriate, the Yale-based Russian scholar Katerina Clark, who when asked what she was doing for the women's cause wittily replied that she was getting on with her work, some forty years earlier a few young women set off to seek qualifications unobtainable in Australia and unusual in the United Kingdom, noticeably in the social sciences. This was the case with the first State Psychologists [*sic*], New South Wales teacher Lorna Hodgkinson (1887–1951), and Ethel Stoneman of Perth (1890–1973). In 1920 Hodgkinson obtained paid leave from the NSW Education Department to obtain a D.Ed. at Harvard on the treatment of "mental retardates" in state education systems, returning in 1922 to a very brief tenure as the first state psychologist in NSW. (She was forced out after less than a year and set up the Sunshine Home at Gore Hill, Sydney, soon after.)[17]

A similar story may be told of Ethel Stoneman, who went to Stanford in 1916 to study intelligence testing and abnormal psychology, returned to Perth, and in 1926 persuaded a Labor government to establish a State Psychological Clinic. Stoneman's clinic was closed in 1930, due it is said in the *Australian Dictionary of Biography,* to sexual discrimination, professional rivalries, and ideological antipathy—a cocktail pressed on more than one returning woman of this period and later, it may be added. Stoneman went into private practice and later removed to Melbourne. However, in hope of trained support staff, she had encouraged her West Australian students to go to America; and the story of social work in Australia entered a new chapter. One such was Norma Parker (born 1906), later Professor Norma Parker, an outstanding figure in the history of social work in Australia who obtained her qualifications at the Catholic University in Washington in the late 1920s and went on to set up the first almoner's department at St. Vincent's Hospital, Darlinghurst. On the way home on the boat, she met the redoubtable Kate Ogilvie, returning from two months' inquiry into hospital administration in the United States funded by Rachel Forster Hospital, Sydney, where she was founding almoner in 1934.[18]

Equally distinguished economist Persia Campbell (1898–1974), daughter of country schoolteachers and an outstanding history graduate of the University of Sydney, went first to the London School of Economics (LSE), then Bryn Mawr, and, after eight years back in Sydney engaged in important intellectual work on topics such as race and immigration, obtained a Rockefeller fellowship to study agricultural policy in America in 1930. She married, taught at Columbia, and was a founder of the American consumer movement. I'm afraid Miles Franklin was quite catty about Campbell in

London in 1922—said she so took the fancy of that philanderer Bertrand Russell that he got her a job at Bryn Mawr—but Campbell is one of the few Australian women to appear in American dictionaries of biography, due to her work as an advisor to government and the United Nations. She also helped set up consumer organizations in Sydney in the 1960s.[19]

There is one conspicuous gap in this account of professional pathways in the interwar years. No women anthropologists show up in the literature. This seems surprising at first, since academic anthropology in Australia dates from the 1920s, and most of the first women in the field were native-born, except for Phyllis Kaberry (1910–1977). Kaberry, author of the pioneering *Aboriginal Women: Sacred and Profane* (1939), was born in California, Sydney-educated, and her Ph.D. (1938) was from the LSE. No doubt the imperial origins and impetus of Australian anthropology and the overbearing character of the founding professors more than adequately explains the gap. But the American influence was there all the same. *Coming of Age in Samoa* appeared in 1928, and *Growing Up in New Guinea* appeared in 1930. The author Margaret Mead visited Sydney in 1933; and it is suggested that she became a role model and mentor for Kaberry.[20]

Here we have a psychologist, a social worker, an economist, an anthropologist indirectly. To this list may be added artists. As with scholars, the exodus of artists in the interwar years was mainly to Europe, but at least one made her way to, and her mark in, America—Melbourne professor's daughter, Mary Cecil Allen (1893–1962). Cecil Allen's abilities so impressed a visiting American that she employed Allen as a gallery tour guide in Europe. Mary Cecil Allen left Melbourne in 1926 and in 1931 organized the first New York exhibition of Australian art at the Roerich Museum gallery. She lectured and painted, and it is said her pictures sold well in the United States; but they proved too radical for Melbourne when she returned, on the first of several trips, in 1935. Maybe like others before, Goldstein for instance, and Franklin too, she was thought too pro-American. Her remains are in Provincetown, Massachusetts, where she lived after 1950.[21]

Margel Hinder (born New York, 1906–1995) seems fair exchange for such losses. A sculptor trained in Buffalo, New York, and at the Boston Museum School of Art (1926–28), Hinder married painter Frank Hinder in America. They returned to Sydney in 1934, where they settled, and she sculpted and taught for over forty years. The Hinders were a main line to all that was abstract and internationalist in art, and a strong partnership. This suggests a modification of Pesman's promising hypothesis about the Australian culture in the interwar years that "if the nationalist strand in Australian culture and social life was masculine and masculinist, it may be that the cosmopolitan components were women's contribution."[22]

There can be little doubt as to the most forceful American woman in Australia in this period. A professional woman, Chicago-born and MIT-trained, the brilliant architectural renderer Marion Mahony Griffin (1871–1961) spent almost twenty-five years in Australia from 1914 to 1938, and, like Persia Campbell, appears in the relevant American biographical dictionaries. Having helped her husband, Prairie School architect-planner Walter Burley Griffin, prepare the prize-winning design for Canberra, Australia's new federal capital, in 1911, she was mainstay of the partnership during their Australian years, and was with Griffin when he died unexpectedly in India in 1937. She told him she had had a wonderful life with him. And so she had, though the marriage was not without its tensions. Marion Griffin—Mrs. Griffin as she was always called—met with a mixed reception in Australia, where women architects were, and still are, uncommon. Men, on the whole, disliked her. But she was welcome in Sydney Bohemia, where her decorative abilities were appreciated, and the serious women of the anthroposophical circle at the Griffins' ideal suburb Castlecrag on Sydney's Lower North Shore in the 1930s plainly adored her. From photographs it is clear Marion Mahony Griffin epitomized the view that American women were far freer than Australian women. When the widowed Griffin left for Chicago in 1938, copious tears were shed at Circular Quay.[23]

A comprehensive account of the interaction of Australian and American women in the interwar years would take into account popular culture, not only stars such as Hobart-born Merle Oberon (1911–1973) and later, Sydneyite Shirley Ann Richards (born 1918), but also the wannabes of film and the transcribers of radio programs. Likewise, something should be said of American families who were in Australia for commercial purposes—one example will be given shortly—and women travelers, such as Barnard College graduate and executive secretary to Boston businessman Edward A. Filene in the 1930s, Lillian Schoedler (1891–1963).[24]

A FAMILY AT WAR?

It is a cliché to say that the Japanese assault on Pearl Harbor on December 7, 1941, and the fall of Singapore two months later changed everything; but it's true enough, even for women. As that great literary partnership M. Barnard Eldershaw put it in *Tomorrow and Tomorrow and Tomorrow* (1947, 1983), "the imperial dream died." How Marion Griffin would have rejoiced at that! What she and Walter objected to most in Australia was its imperial veneer; her unpublished *magnum opus* is entitled "The Magic of America." Her more politically aware friend Miles Franklin knew that the adjustment would be painful, but she, too, welcomed America's entry into the war. Just before the fall of Singapore, Franklin wrote to the family of publicist C. Hartley Grattan in New York:

> Well . . . Japan has decided to gamble on Asiatic conquest. If America does not decide to forgive her for her double and treble talk, she will get that lesson which she nor the world will not forget, but, ah, what will it cost us.[25]

And then the Americans came, about a million of them, between 1942–1945. It was not the invasion expected, but it was an invasion of a kind, almost all were men, but there were some women in the support services, seldom mentioned but occasionally present in photographs or in deposits such as the papers of Betsy Quinlan, an American Red Cross worker.[26]

Recent feminist scholarship has emphasized sexual liberation as the real meaning of World War II for Australian women. Certainly there is abundant evidence of the appeal of the Americans, for example Molly Mann and Bethia Foott's rather breathless Brisbane memoir, *We Drove the Americans* (1944), which also suggests it was nice to have a uniform of one's own.[27]

In an assessment of *The Fatal Days* (1947), a novel by her friend Henrietta Drake-Brockman about American soldiers in the provincial city of Ballarat, Miles Franklin attempted to introduce a note of realism, as follows:

> The narrative concerns the billeting of the United States soldiers in homes on different financial levels in Ballarat, and there are interiors of the Australian way of life. It shows the domestic side of the arrival—which existed in wholesome swaths despite the stews of King's Cross, Sydney, and the ports, where the cry "the Fleet's in!" sent those young mothers of the race described in waterside pubs as fleet lice, flocking like gulls to the harvest; a side so played up in fiction, so bulky in police reports and social welfare card-catalogues, that sometimes fears arise that ordinary family life is ceasing to be.[28]

However, the mixed metaphors of gulls flocking to the harvest suggest unease, and the fact is that by far the largest number of Australian women to choose America did so during and after World War II. About 12,000 is the generally accepted estimate of the number of "war brides" leaving for America from 1942 to 1948, the majority between 1944 and 1946. There is a nice account of a "bride ship" out of Brisbane in 1945 by Alexandra Hasluck in her autobiography, *Portrait in a Mirror* (c. 1982). Aboard were some 900 brides, all "extremely pretty"; but what lay ahead, Hasluck wondered.[29]

Hasluck was traveling to join her husband, Paul, head of the Australian diplomatic mission to the United Nations in New York in 1946. By the 1940s, the interchange seems increasingly a matter of married women, and increasingly of women who came or stayed in America due to residency and other requirements, as with composer and *New York Herald-Tribune* music critic

Peggy Glanville-Hicks (1912–1990), who took out U.S. citizenship for grant application purposes. It was the issue of war brides' status and entitlements which prompted Jessie Street, the most prominent Australian feminist of the 1940s, to write to Eleanor Roosevelt (1884–1964) in 1942.[30]

Roosevelt herself visited Australia in 1943 during a tour of the South Pacific as Special Delegate of the American Red Cross (August 17 to September 23, 1943). The First Lady flew to Canberra from Auckland on September 3, departing Brisbane for New Caledonia ten days later, having visited Melbourne, Sydney, Rockhampton, and Cairns. She was well, indeed almost royally, received, though with a newly elected Labor government, conservatives watched anxiously for signs of a weakening of allegiance to Britain, and it was claimed that the visit highlighted differences rather than similarities between the two societies, as with reactions to Roosevelt's security guards. Australian prime ministers' wives were immeasurably lower key. (In fact, Roosevelt herself found the guards and other restrictions oppressive: "[t]hey treat me like a frail flower & won't let me approach any danger," she wrote in her diary, noting also "this royalty business is painful but I don't know how to avoid it.")[31]

It would be wrong, nonetheless, to project a variant of the royal tour, especially since allegiance to the British Crown was in fact strengthened by its brave behavior during World War II. Rather, Roosevelt stressed she had come "to see our boys"; and she was welcomed as the world's leading democratic woman. "In the eyes of most of us," said W. M. Hughes at an official luncheon in Canberra on September 4, 1943, "she is the ideal woman, bred and conditioned in an environment of democracy." Her other expressed purpose was to see as much as she could of women's war work. On the spot, she also sought to ease tensions between local and American Red Cross workers, who took over care of U.S. troops in 1943. Arguably the outcome was a respectful ambivalence, which increased during the Cold War and through to Vietnam as the wider relationship with America moved from adventure and opportunity to alliance, and the profile of women everywhere went down as they stayed home replenishing the stock.[32]

Nonetheless, the alliance bought more Australian women into the public sphere, and to America. Mary Alice Evatt (1898–1973), an American manufacturing chemist's daughter, accompanied her husband, Labor's H. V. Evatt, to Washington in 1942 and, it is said, helped raise American consciousness of Australia at a crucial time. The same and more was true of journalist and close friend of Maie Casey, Pat Jarrett (1911–1990), the subject of a recent biography by Audrey Tate. Even Christina Stead had toned down during the war, writing to Thistle Harris from New York on April 6, 1942 that she had not taken out American citizenship, and indeed saw no reason why she should, "with the relations between the USA and Australia so very close and I should say unbreakable."[33]

In the long run, the effect of the Pacific war surely was to strengthen and diversify contacts, so that it was not only a matter of intellectuals and artists, such as Sydney/New York sculptor Anne Wienholt (born Leura, NSW, c. 1920) and the previously mentioned Peggy Glanville-Hicks, on the one hand, and on the other, the largely anonymous war brides. It was a pivotal moment when Jessie Street (1889–1970), who first went to New York in 1915 in aid of young women arrested as prostitutes, returned as the only woman in the Australian delegation to the San Francisco conference, which established the United Nations, where she helped found and later served on the Status of Women Commission. Another significant moment, and the first of its kind so far as I know, was when that great Aboriginal Australian Margaret Tucker (1904–1997) went with an Australian delegation to Moral Rearmament's headquarters on Mackinac Island, Michigan, in about 1959. "America gave me so much" she wrote in her autobiography, *If Everyone Cared* (1977).[34]

To go much further is to risk a purely anecdotal approach. One thinks again of Alexandra Hasluck, the young wife and mother in the New York suburbs who nonetheless took precedence at many a New York dinner table as a United Nations wife from first-in-the-alphabet Australia; of writer Shirley Hazzard at the United Nations in the 1950s; of an increasing number of journalists since the late Lilian Roxon and her *Rock Encyclopedia* (1969); and of Bettina Gorton, the American wife of John Grey Gorton, Prime Minister of Australia from 1969 to 1971, who retained her citizenship. Fitting for mention, too, are Dorothy Davis, Director of Welfare Services in the New South Wales division of the Red Cross in the 1950s, who obtained a masters degree in social science administration at the University of Chicago in 1957; and Wilma R. Hunt, professor, feminist, and environmentalist, the daughter of a picture theater manager from Kempsey who graduated in dentistry at Sydney in 1951 and went to Boston soon after, where she married and works to the present. In 1977, Hunt published *The Health of Women at Work* and visited Australia, making contact with the women's movement. In 1978–1981, she was a senior administrator in the Environmental Protection Agency, Washington, DC, serving at the top levels of the Carter administration.[35]

Quite soon along this trajectory to radical sisterhood and the 1960s, one comes to "the road from Coorain"; which I was astonished to see advertized in America in 1995 as a successor to *My Brilliant Career.* Maybe I should not have been. After all, Franklin's Thornford (near Goulburn, in the southern highlands of New South Wales) and Conway's "Coorain" (an Aboriginal word meaning "windy place," some seventy-five miles east of Hillston, in the Western Division of New South Wales) are equally remote as far as Americans are concerned; and even by Australian standards they are not that far apart. And just as Margaret Fink's firmly focused film version of *My Brilliant Career* (1979) made Miles Franklin's name in North America, so there is no gainsaying a widely expressed respect for Ker Conway's achievement there. Of course, from an Australian point of view there are contrasts to be noted too; but it does seem that some of the points thrown up by the preceding perspective find expression in the two stories, for example those pertaining to marital status and citizenship. And while Miles Franklin often lamented that Australian writers got nowhere until they were dead (and what good was that), she could hardly have disapproved of Ker Conway's success as a writer. From the moment she returned home for good in 1932, Franklin vigorously promoted the view that Australia would be the new literary frontier. "Australia is a coming fictional fashion, make no mistake," she wrote hopefully to Hartley Grattan in 1933.[36]

By the early 1960s, when Jill Ker found an American lover and went to Harvard, the patriarchal pressures and gerontocratic features of Australian cultural systems that so oppressed clever women were weakening, and opportunities everywhere seemed to improve. As well, interchanges would become more frequent and sojourns shorter, as air travel became the only way to go. Post 1960s, especially post-women's liberation when reservations were expressed from time to time, it all seemed more equal again.[37]

Is it full circle then? Perhaps, regrettably, not really; but there is now a much closer and more diverse acquaintance. Jill Ker was unusual in choosing America in the early sixties, but, as we have seen, there were precedents. Many more women have followed since—to the point where, in a context of increasing emigration by skilled Australians, some have worried about a senior woman brain drain, especially to America. Moreover, a widening interaction seems true of every category one cares to think of, though Australian women still seem to do best in America when it comes to new things like directing films.[38]

Meanwhile, Americans are still a small minority in multicultural Australia, but there are more American women in Australia than ever before, including academic sociologists like Dr. Hester Eisenstein in the 1980s, who has examined significant differences between Australian and American women such as attitudes to the state, with consequently enhanced understandings. Even so, intellectual interchange and knowledge levels still seem highly unequal. Although a considerable contribution by expatriate women may be documented in both societies, as in the cases of Persia Campbell and Marion Mahony Griffin, how far things at a popular level have really changed since 1947, when Alexandra Hasluck's black maid Hattie found it hard to believe they were returning to Australia. "You don't *wan'* live in America?" she asked incredulously. And while there have been more frequent and equal interchanges between Australian women and America since the 1960s, and the radical dimension has been restored, relations between Australian women and America may not necessarily come much closer, due to wider trends. It seems unlikely, for example, that further

Americanization will be good for Australian women workers and, as suggested at the beginning of this paper, feminism seems more and more a matter of "sisters in suits." As well, from within feminism a new and critical note may be heard, to the effect that the American women's movement is too individualistic and media-oriented.[39]

Nonetheless, and by way of conclusion, it seems clear that the general perception of America as a land of opportunity has held true for at least some Australian women of preceding generations, in terms of adventure, career, expanded horizons, or all three, and that American women have found increasing scope for their talents and energy in Australia. However, the stories told so far have been of high-profile women. Of less conspicuous interchanges, such as those of the war brides, very little is as yet known. Also, more needs to be said about mediating circumstances in Australia, where the status of women has fluctuated quite markedly across the twentieth century.

The story of interaction between Australian and American women is an ongoing one. I will end on an exhortatory note. In view of the many and productive interchanges between Australian women and America in earlier times, and the uncertainties which seem to beset us today, it seems all the more important that lines of academic communication remain clear and are strengthened. The Harvard Chair is well placed to see that they are, especially if, as I would hope, a graduate dimension is added to its armory. What a good way that could be to extend our knowledge of topics such as mine.

Notes

1. Unlike travel to Europe, Australian women's encounters with America have yet to be quantified; re American women in Australia, census data indicates a fewness of American women nationals resident in period, and as compared with American men, though numbers increased from 663 in 1933 (25%) to 3,165 in 1961 (38%). (Commonwealth of Australia *Census* 1961, vol. VIII, 56, Table 28.)
2. Marian Sawer, *Sisters in Suits: Women and Public Policy in Australia* (Sydney: Allen & Unwin, 1990).
3. Jill Roe, ed., *My Congenials: Miles Franklin and Friends in Letters, 1879–1954,* vol. 2 (Sydney: Angus & Robertson, 1993), 341–342.
4. Ibid., vol. 1, 241, 70; *Sydney Morning Herald,* December 15, 1909, 5.
5. Verna Coleman, *Miles Franklin in America: Her (Unknown) Brilliant Career* (Sydney: Angus & Robertson, 1981), 73–75; Roe, *My Congenials,* vol. 1, 49; Franklin Papers, Mitchell Library, Sydney, MSS 364/3 and 364/111; Jill Roe, "'Testimonies from the Field': The Coming of Christian Science to Australia, c. 1890–1910" (*Journal of Religious History,* forthcoming).
6. Marjorie Barnard, *Miles Franklin* (New York: Twayne Publishers Inc., 1967), 89; Peter Pierce, "'Turn Gladly Home': The Figure of the Revenant in Australian Literary Culture," *Island Magazine* 38 (1989).

7. Bruce Sutherland, "Stella Miles Franklin's American Years," *Meanjin* 24, no. 4 (1965). For the phrase "cultural cringe," see A. A. Phillips, *The Australian Tradition: Studies in a Colonial Culture* (Melbourne: Cheshire, 1958).

8. *Australian Dictionary of Biography*, vol. 3 "Clisby, Harriet" (Kathleen Thomson), *ADB* vol. 3, (Melbourne: Melbourne University Press), 1969.

9. Ros Pesman, *Duty Free: Australian Women Abroad* (Melbourne: Oxford University Press, 1996), esp. 69–76, 112; Jill Roe, "Leading the World: The Internationalism of the Australian Women's Movement since the 1890s," in *Women of Attitude: 100 Years of Political Action,* ed. Marion Stell (Canberra: National Museum of Australia, 1995), 10–12; Heather Radi, ed., *200 Australian Women* (Sydney: Redress Press, 1988), 24, 33; *Australian Dictionary of Biography,* s.v. "Windeyer, Mary" (Heather Radi) *ADB* vol. 12 (Melbourne: Melbourne University Press, 1990); I. Tyrrell, *Woman's World, Woman's Empire: The Woman's Christian Temperance Movement in International Perspective, 1880–1930* (Chapel Hill and London: University of North Carolina Press, 1993), 44; Janette Bomford, *That Dangerous and Persuasive Woman: Vida Goldstein* (Melbourne: Melbourne University Press, 1993), 33–38; *Sydney Morning Herald,* December 5, 1909, 5.

10. Joseph Jones, *Radical Cousins: Nineteenth Century American & Australian Writers* (Queensland: University of Queensland Press, 1976).

11. Diane Kirkby, *Alice Henry: The Power of Pen and Voice: The Life of an Australian-American Labor Reformer* (Cambridge: Cambridge University Press, 1991) and *Australian Worker,* September 1915, 9; and for a biographical study of Scott's feminism, Judith A. Allen, *Rose Scott: Vision and Revision in Feminism* (Melbourne: Oxford University Press, 1994).

12. Tyrrell, *Woman's World,* 371, 292; Jessie Ackermann, *Australia from a Woman's Point of View* (London: Cassell, 1913; reprinted Cassell Australia, 1981); Beverley Kingston, ed., *The World Moves Slowly: A Documentary History of Australian Women* (Camperdown, N.S.W.: Cassell, Australia, 1977); Jupp, *The Australian People,* 268 ; and Roe, *My Congenials,* vol. 2, 381 (Griffiths).

13. Jill Roe, *Beyond Belief: Theosophy in Australia, 1879–1939* (N.S.W.: New South Wales University Press, 1986), 39 and "Dayspring: The New Age in Australia, from the 1890s to Nimbin" (*Australian Cultural History,* forthcoming); Alison Alexander, *A Mortal Flame: Marie Bjelke-Petersen, Australian Romance Writer* (Hobart: Blubber Head Press, 1994), 181.

14. Pesman, *Duty Free,* 92; *Australian Dictionary of Biography,* s.v. "Kellermann, Annette" (G. P. Walsh) *ADB* vol. 9, MUP 1983; Heather Radi, ed., *Jessie Street: Documents and Essays* (Sydney: Redress Press, 1990), 1; *Australian Dictionary of Biography,* s.v. "Deamer, Mary" (1890–1972) (Martha Rutledge) *ADB* vol. 8, MUP 1981 ; Peter Fitzpatrick, *Pioneer Players: The Lives of Louis and Hilda Esson* (Melbourne: Cambridge University Press, 1995), 134–140; Jill Roe, "Chivalry and Social Policy in the Antipodes," *[Australian] Historical Studies* 88 (April 1987): 397–398.

15. A. G. Stephens Papers, Mitchell Library, Sydney, MSS 4937 Box 10, item 1, also *Lone Hand,* December 1908, and *Verses by Lola Ridge,* typescript, n.d.; Nan

Bowman Albinski, *Directory of Resources for Australian Studies in North America*, National Centre for Australian Studies, Monash University, and Australia and New Zealand Studies Center, Penn. State, 1992. Cataloged titles in Widener are *The Ghetto and Other Poems* (New York: Huebsch, 1918); *Sun-up, and Other Poems* (New York: Huebsch, 1920); *Red Flag* (New York: Viking, 1927); *Firehead* (New York: Payson & Clarke, 1929); *Dance of Fire* (New York: Smith & Haas, 1935). I thank Desley Deacon for subsequent confirmation of the importance of Ridge in the history of modernism in the United States.

16. Both quotations appear in Stephen Murray-Smith, ed., *The Dictionary of Australian Quotations* (Richmond, Vic.: Heinemann Australia, 1984); Hazel Rowley, *Christina Stead: A Biography* (Port Melbourne, Vic.: Heinemann Australia, 1993); R. G. Geering, ed., *A Web of Friendship: Selected Letters: Christina Stead (1928–1973)* (Sydney: Angus & Robertson, 1992), 93.

17. *Australian Dictionary of Biography*, s.v. "Hodgkinson, Lorna" (Alison M. Turtle) *ADB* vol. 14, MUP 1996, and "Stoneman, Ethel" *ADB* vol. 12, MUP 1990.

18. R. J. Lawrence, *Norma Parker's Record of Service*, typescript, 1969 (Mitchell Library, Sydney); *Kate Ogilvie: Social Work Educator: An Appreciation by Her Colleagues*, Department of Social Work, University of Sydney, n.d. I thank Kerry Regan for help with social work biography.

19. Barbara Sicherman et al., eds., *Notable America Women, The Modern Period: A Biographical Dictionary Prepared under the Auspices of Radcliffe College* (Cambridge, Mass: Harvard University Press, 1980); *Australian Dictionary of Biography*, s.v. "Campbell, Persia" (Heather Rodi) *ADB* vol. 13, MUP 1993; and Roe, *My Congenials*, vol. 1, 159.

20. Christine Cheater, "From Sydney Schoolgirl to African Queen Mother: Tracing the Career of Phyllis Mary Kaberry," in *First in Their Field: Woman and Australian Anthropology*, ed. Julie Marcus (Melbourne: Melbourne University Press, 1993).

21. *Australian Dictionary of Biography*, s.v. "Allen, Mary Cecil" (Frances A. M. L. Derham) *ABD* vol. 7, MUP 1979; Andrea Lloyd, "The Mary Cecil" Allen Story," *Meanjin* 55, no. 3 (1996); Albinski, *Dictionary of Resources*.

22. Alan McCulloch, *Encyclopedia of Australian Art*, vol. 1 (Hawthorn, Vic.: Hutchinson Australia, 1984), 580; Pesman, *Duty Free*, 176.

23. *Notable American Women*, s.v. "Marion Mahony Griffin"; Anna Rubbo, "Marion Mahony Griffin: A Portrait," in *Walter Burley Griffin: A Re-View* (Monash University Gallery, 1988); Jill Roe, "The Magical World of Marion Mahony Griffin: Castlecrag in the Interwar Years," in *Minorities: Cultural Diversity in Sydney*, ed. Shirley Fitzgerald and Garry Wotherspoon (State Library of New South Wales Press, 1995).

24. *International Film Encyclopedia* (London: Macmillan, 1980), 971; Schoedler's Papers are in the Schlesinger Library, Radcliffe College.

25. Roe, *My Congenials*, vol. 2, 65; on Grattan, see Laurie Hergenhan, *No Casual Traveller: Hartley Grattan and Australia* (Queensland: University of Queensland Press, 1995).

26. Joan Beaumont, ed., *Australia's War* (St. Leonards, N.S.W.: Allen & Unwin, 1996); Betsy Lane Quinlan Papers, Dept. of Cultural Resources, Raleigh, North Carolina.

27. Marilyn Lake, "Female Desires: The Meaning of World War II," *Australian Historical Studies* 24 (October 1990); Molly Mann and Bethia Foott, *We Drove the Americans* (Sydney: Angus & Robertson, 1944). The most recent study is Anthony J. Barker and Lisa Jackson, *Fleeting Attraction: A Social History of American Servicemen in Western Australia during the Second World War* (Western Australia: University of Western Australia Press, 1996).

28. Miles Franklin, *Laughter, Not for a Cage* (Sydney: Angus & Robertson, 1956), 208.

29. E. Daniel and Annette Potts, *Yanks Down Under, 1941–1945: The American Impact in Australia* (Melbourne: Oxford University Press, 1985), 362, 372–373, 330; Annette Potts, *For the Love of a Soldier: Australian War Brides and Their GIs* (Crow's Nest, N.S.W.: ABC Enterprises, 1987); Alexandra Hasluck, *Portrait in a Mirror: An Autobiography* (Melbourne: Oxford University Press, n.d. [c. 1982]), 170.

30. Wendy Beckett, *Peggy Glanville-Hicks* (Sydney: Angus & Robertson, 1992), 63; E. Daniel and Annette Potts, *Yanks Down Under,* 332.

31. Eleanor Roosevelt Trip Files, Pacific Theater, 1943, 190.4: Correspondence, Itineraries, Speeches, and Articles, Diary (entry cited Sept. 10), Eleanor Roosevelt Papers, Franklin D. Roosevelt Library, Hyde Park, N.Y.; E. Daniel and Annette Potts, *Yanks Down Under,* 300; for the contrast, see Diane Langmore, *Prime Ministers' Wives* (Ringwood, Vic.: McPhee Gribble/Penguin Books, 1992), re Elizabeth Chifley.

32. Eleanor Roosevelt Papers, Speeches and Article file, Diary (entry Sept. 5th); and Bound Press Cuttings (*Daily Telegraph,* September 8, 1943, re summary of work by Australian women's organizations prepared by Jessie Street, Ruby Rich, and Mona Ravenscroft).

33. *Australian Dictionary of Biography,* s.v. " Evatt, Mary Alice" (Barbara Dale) *ADB* vol. 14, MUP 1996; Audrey Tate, *Fair Comment: The Life of Pat Jarrett, 1911–1990* (Melbourne: Melbourne University Press, 1996); Geering, *Web of Friendship,* 93.

34. Anne Wienholt, "Playing Scrabble Against Yourself," *Westerly* 4 (1987); Radi, *200 Australian Women,* s.v. "Jessie Street"; D. Horton, ed. *Encyclopedia of Aboriginal Australia,* ed. (Canberra: Aboriginal Studies Press, 1994).

35. Hunt Papers, Schlesinger Library, Radcliffe College; pers. comm., May 15, 1997.

36. Jil Ker Conway, *The Road from Coorain: An Australian Memoir* (London: Heinemann, 1989), 23, 49; Conway entry, Andrea Lofthouse (comp.) *Who's Who of Australian Women* (Sydney: Methuen Australia, 1982), 116–117; Roe, *My Congenials,* vol. 1, after p. 270.

37. I thank Dr. Sue Wills for the recollection of reservations expressed during the women's lib years.

38. "More Australians Leaving Australia for Good," *Sydney Morning Herald,* January 21, 1994.

39. Hester Eisenstein, *Gender Shock: Practising Feminism in Two Continents* (N. Sydney: Allen & Unwin, 1991).

References

A. G. Stephens Papers. Mitchell Library. Sydney.

Ackermann, Jessie. *Australia from a Woman's Point of View.* London: Cassell, 1913; Reprinted Cassell Australia, 1981.

Albinski, Nan Bowman. *Directory of Resources for Australian Studies in North America.* National Centre for Australian Studies, Monash University, and Australia and New Zealand Studies Center, Penn. State, 1992.

Alexander, Alison. *A Mortal Flame: Marie Bjelke-Petersen, Australian Romance Writer.* Hobart: Blubber Head Press, 1994.

Allen, Judith A. *Rose Scott: Vision and Revision in Feminism.* Melbourne: Oxford University Press, 1994.

Australian Dictionary of Biography. Melbourne: Melbourne University Press, vols. 1–14 (1963–1996).

Barker, Anthony J., and Lisa Jackson. *Fleeting Attraction: A Social History of American Servicemen in Western Australia during the Second World War.* Western Australia: University of Western Australia Press, 1996.

Barnard, Marjorie. *Miles Franklin.* New York: Twayne Publishers Inc., 1967.

Beaumont, Joan, ed. *Australia's War.* St. Leonards, N.S.W.: Allen & Unwin, 1995.

Beckett, Wendy. *Peggy Glanville-Hicks.* Sydney: Angus & Robertson, 1992.

Bomford, Janette. *That Dangerous and Persuasive Woman: Vida Goldstein.* Melbourne: Melbourne University Press, 1993.

Cheater, Christine. "From Sydney Schoolgirl to African Queen Mother: Tracing the Career of Phyllis Mary Kaberry." In *First in Their Field: Woman and Australian Anthropology.* Edited by Julie Marcus. Melbourne: Melbourne University Press, 1993.

Coleman, Verna. *Miles Franklin in America: Her (Unknown) Brilliant Career.* Sydney: Angus & Robertson, 1981.

Commonwealth of Australia. *Census.* Vol. 8, 1961.

Conway, Jill Ker. *The Road from Coorain: An Australian Memoir.* London: Heinemann, 1989.

Department of Social Work. *Kate Ogilvie: Social Work Educator: An Appreciation by Her Colleagues.* Dept. of Social Work. University of Sydney, n.d.

Eisenstein, Hester. *Gender Shock: Practising Feminism in Two Continents.* N. Sydney: Allen & Unwin, 1991.

Eleanor Roosevelt Papers, Franklin D. Roosevelt Library, Hyde Park, N.Y.

Fitzpatrick, Peter. *Pioneer Players: The Lives of Louis and Hilda Esson.* Melbourne: Cambridge University Press, 1995.

Franklin Papers. Mitchell Library, Sydney.

Franklin, Miles. *Laughter, Not for a Cage.* Sydney: Angus & Robertson, 1956.

Geering, R. G., ed. *A Web of Friendship: Selected Letters: Christina Stead (1928–1973).* Sydney: Angus & Robertson, 1992.

Hasluck, Alexandra. *Portrait in a Mirror: An Autobiography.* Melbourne: Oxford University Press, n.d. (c. 1982).

Hergenhan, Laurie. *No Casual Traveller: Hartley Grattan and Australia*. Queensland: University of Queensland Press, 1995.

Horton, D., ed. *Encyclopedia of Aboriginal Australia*. Canberra: Aboriginal Studies Press, 1994.

Hunt Papers. Schlesinger Library. Radcliffe College.

International Film Encyclopedia. London: Macmillan, 1980.

Jones, Joseph. *Radical Cousins: Nineteenth Century American & Australian Writers*. Queensland: University of Queensland Press, 1976.

Jupp, J., ed. *The Australian People*. Sydney: Angus & Robertson, 1988.

Kingston, Beverley, ed. *The World Moves Slowly: A Documentary History of Australian Women*. Camperdown, N.S.W.: Cassell Australia, 1977.

Kirkby, Diane. *Alice Henry: The Power of Pen and Voice: The Life of an Australian-American Labor Reformer*. Cambridge: Cambridge University Press, 1991.

Lake, Marilyn. "Female Desires: The Meaning of World War II." *Australian Historical Studies* 24 (October 1990).

Langmore, Diane. *Prime Ministers' Wives*. Ringwood, Vic.: McPhee Gribble/Penguin Books, 1992).

Lawrence, R. J. *Norma Parker's Record of Service*. Typescript, 1969. Mitchell Library. Sydney.

Lloyd, Andrea. "The Mary Cecil Allen Story." *Meanjin* 55, no. 3 (1996).

Lofthouse, Andrea, comp. *Who's Who of Australian Women*. Australia: Methuen, 1982.

Mann, Molly, and Bethia Foott. *We Drove the Americans*. Sydney: Angus & Robertson, 1944.

McCulloch, Alan. *Encyclopedia of Australian Art*. Vol. 1. Hawthorn, Vic.: Hutchinson, 1984.

Murray-Smith, Stephen, ed. *The Dictionary of Australian Quotations*. Richmond, Vic.: Heinemann Australia, 1984.

Pesman, Ros. *Duty Free: Australian Women Abroad*. Melbourne: Oxford University Press, 1996.

Phillips, A. A. *The Australian Tradition: Studies in a Colonial Culture*. Melbourne: Cheshire, 1958.

Pierce, Peter. "'Turn Gladly Home': The Figure of the Revenant in Australian Literary Culture." *Island Magazine* 38 (1989).

Potts, Daniel E., and Annette. *For the Love of a Soldier: Australian War Brides and Their GIs*. New South Wales: Crow's Nest, 1987.

———. *Yanks Down Under, 1941–1945: The American Impact on Australia*. Melbourne: Oxford University Press, 1985.

Quinlan, Betsy Lane. Papers, Dept. of Cultural Resources, Raleigh, North Carolina.

Radi, Heather, ed. *200 Australian Women*. Sydney: Redress Press, 1988.

———. *Jessie Street: Documents and Essays*. Sydney: Redress Press, 1990.

Roe, Jill. *Beyond Belief: Theosophy in Australia 1879–1939*. N.S.W.: New South Wales University Press, 1986.

————. "Chivalry and Social Policy in the Antipodes." *[Australian] Historical Studies* 88 (April 1987): 397–398.

————. "Dayspring: The New Age in Australia, from the 1890s to Nimbin." *Australian Cultural History,* forthcoming.

————. "Leading the World: The Internationalism of the Australian Women's Movement since the 1890s." In *Women of Attitude: 100 Years of Political Action.* Edited by Marion Stell. Canberra: National Museum of Australia, 1995.

————. "The Magical World of Marion Mahony Griffin: Castlecrag in the Interwar Years." In *Minorities: Cultural Diversity in Sydney.* Edited by Shirley Fitzgerald and Garry Wotherspoon. N.S.W.: State Library of New South Wales Press, 1995.

————. "'Testimonies from the Field': The Coming of Christian Science to Australia, 1890–1910." *Journal of Religious History,* forthcoming.

————, ed. *My Congenials: Miles Franklin and Friends in Letters, 1879–1954.* Vols. 1 and 2. Sydney: Angus & Robertson, 1993.

Rowley, Hazel. *Christina Stead: A Biography.* Port Melbourne, Vic.: Heinemann Australia, 1993.

Rubbo, Anna. "Marion Mahony Griffin: A Portrait." In *Walter Burley Griffin: A Re-View.* Monash University Gallery, 1988.

Sawer, Marian. *Sisters in Suits: Women and Public Policy in Australia.* Sydney: Allen & Unwin, 1990.

Sicherman, Barbara, et al., ed. *Notable America Women, The Modern Period: A Biographical Dictionary Prepared under the Auspices of Radcliffe College.* Cambridge, Mass.: Harvard University Press, 1980.

Sutherland, Bruce. "Stella Miles Franklin's American Years." *Meanjin* 24, no. 4 (1965).

Tate, Audrey. *Fair Comment: The Life of Pat Jarrett, 1911–1990.* Melbourne: Melbourne University Press, 1996.

Tyrrell, I. *Woman's World, Woman's Empire: The Woman's Christian Temperance Movement in International Perspective, 1880–1930.* Chapel Hill and London: University of North Carolina Press, 1993.

Wienholt, Anne. "Playing Scrabble Against Yourself." *Westerly* 4 (1987).

11

Driving to Austerica: The Americanization of the Postwar Australian City

GRAEME DAVISON, MONASH UNIVERSITY

LONG BEFORE THE STUDY of comparative urban history began, trans-Pacific travelers had noticed a strong family resemblance between the cities of North America and Australia. It became common to liken the cities of the antipodes to their North American counterparts and to expect that their histories would follow similar paths. Just as the American West had its little Parises and Warsaws, so upstart frontier towns in Australia and New Zealand often saw themselves as future Chicagos, New Yorks, and San Franciscos.[1]

Since America was considered a success story, the expectation that Australia would follow in its path was a pleasing one. It was perhaps not until the 1960s, when the bonds of the British influence began to slacken and American economic, political, and cultural influences grew stronger, that the connection was submitted to a more searching scrutiny. In 1965 the American architect Arthur Odell, addressing a group of his Australian colleagues, remarked: "In our two countries, we are faced with markedly similar social and technical problems. The height of materialistic aspiration for the average citizen seems to be ownership of a detached suburban house and two or more automobiles."[2] Odell came as a messenger of The Great Society, bearing word not only of American achievements in freeway and urban design but of the War on Poverty, highway beautification schemes, and programs of urban renewal. He was one of many American industrialists, highway designers, motel proprietors, project home builders, and urban designers whose expertise helped to remake the cities of postwar Australia.

Americans who visit Australia today are likely to experience a constant sense of déjà vu. Along every highway they will see the familiar landmarks— not only the ubiquitous McDonald's big M and the face of Colonel Sanders, but ranch and Cape Cod houses, service stations, supermarkets, motels, and drive-ins that seem almost indistinguishable from their American counterparts. These resemblances are more than a matter of cultural convergence; they are the tangible evidence of how American technical know-how, style, business organization, and investment remade the postwar Australian city.

The most lively contemporary Australian critic of Americanization was the architect Robin Boyd. Boyd was a son of one of Australia's most distinguished artistic families—it included the painter Arthur Boyd and the novelist Martin Boyd—and he brought to his defense of an Australian modernism a wit and patrician certainty of judgment that often awed more timid contemporaries. In 1957, shortly after his return from Boston, Boyd coined the word "Austerica" to describe the cut-price imitative style of Americanization that had become such a feature of the postwar Australian landscape.

Austerica [Boyd wrote] is on no map. It is, as an Austerican advertisement would say, not a place but a way of life. It is found in any country, including parts of America, where an austerity version of the American dream overtakes the indigenous culture. As its name also implies, it is slightly hysterical and it flourishes best of all in Australia, which is already half overtaken by the hysteria. Austerica's chief industry is the imitation of the froth on the top of the American soda-fountain drink. Its religion is "glamor" and the devotees are psychologically displaced persons who picture heaven as the pool terrace of a Las Vegas hotel. Its high priests are expense account men who judge the USA on a two-weeks hop between various Hilton and Statler hotels and return home intoxicated with conceptions of American willingness to labor (judged by the attitude of martini-waiters), the average American's standard of living (judged by a week-end at the managing director's house on Long Island), and American godliness (judged by a copy of "Guideposts . . . an inspirational publication," which is left by the bedside for every one of the hotel guests of Mr. Conrad Hilton).[3]

In coining the word "Austerica," Boyd performed not a double, but a triple word play. It was not just a hybrid American-Australianism, but a frenetic (i.e., hysterical) pursuit of what was cheapest and nastiest in American culture (i.e., the austerity version). Boyd recognized that Australia's exposure to American influences was not really avoidable (it was, he said, "inevitable that Australia should be drawn deep into the aura of American influence in the second half of the American century."), but he held Australians accountable for the undiscriminating way in which they absorbed the trashiest and most dated examples of American culture—the glitzy surface rather than the functional substance.

Boyd could claim to have some personal insight into this distinction. In 1956–1957 he had studied American architecture as a Fulbright Fellow at Massachusetts Institute of Technology. There he became a friend of Walter Gropius and other members of the generation of European émigrés whose influence was so important to the development of postwar American architecture.[4] He was not, therefore, averse to American influences as such, though he was critical of the process by which, it seemed, American culture deteriorated as it spread westward. "The main trouble [in Australia]," he wrote to Gropius, "is the popular tendency to model everything on West Coast—never East Coast—Americana."[5] His vantage point was similar to that of American critics of suburbia, such as Lewis Mumford, and his old London acquaintance Reyner Banham, who saw in European communitarianism an antidote to the excesses of unbridled capitalism.[6] *The Australian Ugliness,* the book in which his essay later appeared, has echoes of *The Ugly American,* the 1958 book by William Lederer and Eugene Burdick.

Boyd's critique of Austerica, like much else in Australian social criticism, derived in part from American self-criticism. The political scientist Alan Davies was among the first to notice, in a 1967 essay, how avidly Australian intellectuals had followed American pop sociology's discovery of the suburbs in the mid-fifties.[7] In l963 a young Chris Wallace-Crabbe had denounced the cultural uniformity of suburban Melbourne ("an extreme and unmollified example of modern mass society") in tones reminiscent of Lewis Mumford's attack on the uniformity and barrenness of American suburbia.[8] Davies, too, had done his share of borrowing: His sketch of the Australian suburbanite's "deep circumambient apathy" toward politics echoed the diagnoses of William F. Whyte's *The Organisation Man* and David Riesman's *The Lonely Crowd.* When Carlton and Paddington intellectuals ventured into the Australian suburbs, what they found, perhaps unsurprisingly, was what American sociologists and critics had found before them. In this respect Boyd's Austerica reflects a convergence of both social norms and critical perceptions.

What readers were most likely to take from Boyd's *The Australian Ugliness* was the immediate sense of recognition that came from Boyd's devastatingly accurate eye for detail, accentuated by his satirical pen-and-ink illustrations. His loathing for the tawdriness of Austerican style was exceeded only by the relish with which he seized on the choicest examples. Like Barry Humphries, the stage satirist of Australian suburbia with whose work he has strong affinities, Boyd operated largely on an aesthetic level. A critic of Australian superficiality, he is himself, in the last resort, a critic of exterior surfaces only—of chrome grilles, rainbow paint schemes, white-walled tires and glaring neon—just as Humphries was largely a critic of interior ones— frosted glass, chenille bedspreads, and burgundy Axminster carpets. While

Austerica Illustrated: Robin Boyd's satirical line drawing for the Australian Ugliness (1960). Reproduced with permision of Mrs. Patricia Davies.

Austerica Illustrated: Robin Boyd's satirical line drawing for the Australian Ugliness (1960). Reproduced with permission of Mrs. Patricia Davies.

he is able to hold up a clear mirror to Austerica, Boyd's insight into the processes by which American influence was disseminated and absorbed was limited. His muscular prose is full of verbs—invade, submerge, dominate—without identifiable subjects. Like other aesthetes, he knew what he didn't like, and he could lead his readers to dislike it too. But, beyond his own personal example, regular rallying cries to his fellow architects, and calls for the education of public taste, he was unable to suggest how the advance of Austerica should be stemmed.

Yet in one important respect, Boyd was right: Austerica was not just a place, or even a style, but a way of life.[9] While Boyd's vigilant eye fell mainly on the material manifestations of Austerica, he occasionally hinted at how the process took place. The American odysseys of the "expense account men;" the conclaves of jabbering journalists who took their ideas secondhand from *Life* or *The New Yorker;* the 1958 visit to Miami of Mr. Bruce Small, the bicycle millionaire and creator of Surfer's Paradise—these were emblematic of processes of social interaction and cultural transmission which Boyd alluded to, but nowhere clearly examined.

Boyd's neologism soon entered the Australian language, sometimes taking on broader connotations than Boyd himself had given it. In 1966 the left-wing nationalist journal *Meanjin* commissioned a series of articles under the general title "Godzone," taking stock of contemporary developments in Australian social and cultural life. Like Boyd's Austerica, the title "Godzone" suggested that Australia was steadily drifting into the cultural and ideological orbit of the United States (God's Own Country), and acquiring secondhand, as it were, some of America's sense of providential good fortune. Left-wing nationalist contributors to the debate were the most hostile to this trend, seeing American cultural and economic penetration of Australia as a prelude to its effective incorporation as a fifty-first state of the United States. "We are happily—or phlegmatically—exchanging one neo-colonial situation for another," wrote Geoffrey Serle, Robin Boyd's future biographer, in an article entitled "Austerica Unlimited." "Australia has abandoned the prospect of independent nationhood; we are going to become just slightly different sorts of Americans."[10]

It was left to more conservative contributors to unpick the economic, technological, cultural, and political threads of American influence. Bruce Miller wondered "whether it is 'Americanism' that is upon us, or simply modern technology."[11] It was by no means clear, added Geoffrey Blainey, that American influence in one phase of Australian life automatically carried over into another. Higher levels of American company ownership, for example, did not necessarily mean that Australia was more controlled from Wall Street. Small nations had limited choices, but so far from being a submissive client of the United States, "Australia," Blainey suggested, was "more independent than at any time in its history."[12]

Boyd's critique of Austerica rested on an oversimplified model of cultural transmission. America is large, powerful, irresistible; Australians, accustomed to the role of a colony, are supine, dependent, unsophisticated. The process of Americanization seems to occur by a kind of immersion, or osmosis, as the smaller body assumes the characteristics of the larger. Examined close-up, however, Americanization is a complex, if unequal, process of cultural exchange in which the two societies were engaged in mutually defining their identities and interests. It is a social, as well as a cultural, process, for it can be understood in terms of specific individual and institutional interactions, visits, conferences, trade delegations, professional affiliations, patent agreements, political treaties, and the like.[13] The flow of high culture, represented by Boyd's contacts with Gropius, was paralleled by a flow of practical know-how through visiting Australian businessmen, engineers, doctors, and politicians. Boyd believed that this process was a lopsided and superficial one, in which the influence was all in one direction and the inferior adopted an uncritical attitude toward the superior. As a polemical device, his concentration on Austerican style was brilliantly effective, but, as his own career and contacts suggest, critics of Americanization were often hand-in-glove with the Americanizers.

One way of being more precise about these issues is to limit the historical context in which they are studied; I focus here on the transformation of the Australian urban landscape in the 1950s and early 1960s, especially in Melbourne, then the fastest-growing and most industrialized city in the country.

From the windows of my office in Monash University's Menzies Building, about fifteen kilometers from Melbourne's center, I look out on one of the most extensive regions of low-density suburbs in the world—a vista of cream brick walls and terra cotta roofs that stretches as far as the eye can see. Founded in 1961, Monash became the country's first drive-in university. Our students now park on the abandoned site of one Australia's first drive-in theaters. A mile or so to the north is the extension of the South-Eastern Freeway, Melbourne's first, and nearby is the Pinewood shopping center (1957), built by the biggest of Australia's project builders, A. V. Jennings. From the top floor of the Menzies Building you can glimpse the sawtooth roofs of General Motors Holdens Dandenong plant. Drive back along Dandenong Road toward the city and you pass Melbourne's first motel before you come to Chadstone, its first regional drive-in shopping center. This is Austerica's heartland: a world made possible by the car but shaped, unmistakably, by American style, organization, and know-how.

Only now, as the era that created it comes to an end, can we begin to see it for what it is—the characteristic Australian landscape of our times. I first glimpsed its approach one afternoon in about 1952 as I was walking home from primary school along Buckley Street Essendon with my friend Maurice Johnson. We liked to spot cars and our favorites were the sleek new

American sedans that were beginning to displace the old, square, prewar, often English-made, saloons. Maurice was the first to notice the brand-new cream Chevrolet utility, or pick-up truck, with the wide chrome grille that was making its way down the street, but I was the one who cried out as I observed, with astonishment, my own father at the wheel. For years, it had seemed, the family had debated what new car we would get to replace our old 1928 Essex Super Six. Would it be a British Bedford (Dad, the son of English immigrants, had a lingering loyalty to the Old Country) or would it be one of the new Holdens, "Australia's Own Car," made by a subsidiary of GM? But the Bedford was too small, and as yet Holden didn't make a utility truck, so Dad, with the encouragement of his accommodating bank manager, had taken the plunge and purchased the magnificent Chev.

I find it hard, now, to think of those years without "the ute," as we called it. It was not only the workhorse of the family business—Dad was a plumber working on the spec-built timber houses that were going up along Melbourne's northern frontier—but, with a canvas canopy and one of the old Essex's horsehair-filled seats in the back, it doubled as the family car. With a caravan (trailer) hitched behind, it took us on holiday to Phillip Island, Jeparit, and Lakes Entrance. It took my junior cricket team to away matches. It carted furniture and garden rubbish. It widened our horizons, diversified our choices, consolidated our sense of family togetherness.

When we got the Chev, only one Melburnian in eight, or roughly one household in three, owned a car. By 1953 it was one in five, and by 1962 one in three. In 1950 only fifteen percent of Melburnians drove to work; by 1964 almost half did so; by 1970 it was almost two-thirds.[14] Over these years the landscape, especially the suburban landscape, was comprehensively remodeled to accommodate the car. America invented, and Australia imported, a repertoire of novel urban forms—the high-speed road, the roadside diner, the garage and carport, the cash-wash, the parking meter, the motel, the drive-in theater, the service station, the automobile-based shopping center, and the mobile home.

As the American historian Kenneth Jackson shows in his admirable book *Crabgrass Frontier: The Suburbanization of the United States,* many of these novel institutions were born during America's first automobile age in the 1920s and 1930s. The first self-proclaimed "motel" had appeared in San Luis Obispo, California, in 1926; the first drive-in theater in Camden, New Jersey, in 1933; the first drive-in shopping center in Kansas City in 1923; the first drive-in restaurant in Dallas, Texas, in 1921.[15] But only in the postwar era did the drive-in principle become ubiquitous, first in North America, and later throughout the rest of the world. The Australian reception of four of these developments—the motel, the drive-in cinema, the shopping center, and the high-speed road—is illustrative of the broader process of cultural transmission we call "Americanization."

THE MOTEL

In 1950, when wartime petrol rationing had just been abolished, a Sydney company announced plans to build "modern roadside accommodation on American lines" up the east coast from Melbourne to Brisbane. "'Motels' are very popular in the United States, and if run on the same lines, and not hedged about with too many Government restrictions, should be just as popular here," a motoring magazine forecast.[16] In the postwar period the American motel had been re-born. The first motels, established on the outskirts of big cities in the 1920s and 1930s, had a sleazy image. The establishment of the Holiday Inn chain in 1952 began the process of rehabilitation, and it was the respectable family tourist motel, rather than a venue for what Americans called the "hot pillow trade," that the first Australian motel operators aimed to introduce.[17] They capitalized on "the growing discontent" with ordinary hotels which, as one contemporary complained, were "really only drinking houses." "I feel that motels, built on American lines, will gradually cater for the traveling public to the near exclusion of the present so-called hotels."[18] By 1954 there were still fewer than a dozen motels in Australia, all privately owned. But the American correspondents of Australian magazines were already describing the latest developments in the motel business in the confident expectation that "as the business becomes

Oakleigh Motel, Melbourne's first, was opened early in 1957, close to the spot on the Princes Highway where the 1956 Olympic marathoners turned back towards the Melbourne Cricket Ground. Photo courtesy of the Oakleigh Motel.

more competitive, motel keepers are sure to dip in to the tried and true American bag of tricks." Some motel operators underlined the American connection by choosing names like "The Niagara," "The Californian," "The Atlantic," "The Bel Air," or simply "The American."[19]

An American motel expert, W. L. Edmundson, who visited Australia in 1955, believed that Australian motels might become a model for the rest of the world "because all the mistakes of the American motel industry would be avoided." Edmundson shrewdly identified the points on which motels beat hotels and anticipated the tastes of an affluent, leisured society. "Americans like motels because of the informal, pleasant atmosphere, without elevators, hotel foyers and parking difficulties. Motels provide good friendly service and there is no tipping."[20] If anything, Australians excelled even Americans in their informality, their preference for self-catering, and their dislike of tipping. The typical Australian motel of the 1950s was a low-slung ensemble of single-story or box-like rooms, grouped around a court-yard and entered by a small reception office and breakfast room. All rooms were equipped with electric jugs, toasters, irons, and sometimes a stove. Unlike the grand hotels of an earlier generation which had created an aura of the exotic and the opulent, the motel impressed by its familiarity, by being simply a home, albeit an up-to-date home, away from home.[21]

The Oakleigh Motel, Melbourne's first, was opened in 1957 on the Princes Highway at the city's eastern gateway, just opposite the spot where, a year before, the Olympic marathon runners had turned back toward the MCG. It was the brainchild of Cyril Lewis, "formerly well-known in the car-selling game," who had toured the United States, inspecting and living in motels all the way, as he gathered ideas for a motel that he boasted was "equal to America's best." Lewis had secured some high-level political support: the Victorian premier Henry Bolte had even written on his behalf to the Australian Treasurer Arthur Fadden in support of a loan. (Fadden refused.)[22] "Australia shows America" was the headline of one of Lewis's advertisements. "Your car in your bedroom" read another, perhaps inviting the idea that the Australian's love affair with the car was to be physically consummated. Modernity, luxury, comfort, convenience, and individuality—the values associated with the car itself—were also built into the motel. But it was in the modernity of its private spaces rather than the opulence of its public spaces that the qualities of the motel were most clearly revealed: "Every room is air-conditioned; every room has its own shower recess and toilet; every room is tastefully furnished with the most modern fittings, and every room is sound-proofed for slumber comfort."[23]

In the eyes of its most stringent critic, the typical Australian motel was a textbook example of the "Australian Ugliness." "In its approach to the public, in social and aesthetic values, in style, the motel often turned out to be a substantial offspring of the merry-go-round or the juke-box," said Boyd.

He poured contempt on "the raw colors, the checker-board painting of fibro panels, the jaunty skillion roof and the angled props to the eaves, the autumnal stone veneering and the rest of the catchpenny style."[24]

In 1960, the year he published *The Australian Ugliness,* Boyd had met a thirty-year-old businessman, David Yencken. Yencken, the son of an Australian-born British diplomat, had grown up in Europe, read history at Cambridge, and had recently returned to Australia by way of the United States, where he observed the new fashion for motels. He decided there might be a place for a new kind of motel, better designed and more attuned to the Australian environment. At first he encountered considerable skepticism. "They won't be appreciated or treated properly," he was warned. "Australians are born thieves." In 1957, in partnership with the architect John Mockridge, he built the Mitchell Valley Motel in Bairnsdale, and in 1960 in partnership with Boyd, he built the Black Dolphin at Merimbula. With its simple uncluttered lines, use of unpainted rough-sawn timber, and splendid views of bush and sea, the Black Dolphin showed how an environmentally sensitive modernism might Australianize the new functional forms of the motor age. In his advertisements in the fortnightly magazine, *Nation,* Yencken cleverly appealed to an intelligentsia newly awakened—largely thanks to Boyd—to the aesthetic sins of Austerica. "At the Black Dolphin you will not find—Palm trees—Pretentious menus—A war of primary colours—Second-rate imported wines—The latest American gimmicks," a typical advertisement read. "Even our architect, Mr. Robin Boyd, assures us that we are not featurists."[25]

THE DRIVE-IN CINEMA

Like the motel, the drive-in theater was heralded long before its arrival in Australia. As early as 1950, Australians were reading that American drive-ins were growing at a rate of almost a thousand a year. "The drive-in," it was reported, "appeals to a different audience from that of the indoor theaters. Many of its customers are elderly people, cripples, and "shut-ins." They also attract people who dislike dressing for the movies, and couples who bring their children and thus save the cost of a baby-sitter."[26] The first Australian drive-in at Burwood, on Melbourne's suburban frontier, opened in July 1954, just two years before the arrival of television, and a second at Ringwood had opened by Christmas. Fourteen months later, the city had two others; Sydney, Ballarat, and Albury were planning drive-ins, and Perth had also opened its first.[27]

Visiting the drive-in became a popular family outing. Like the motel room, the parked car was a new kind of domestic space, a mobile extension of the family living room. Burwood drive-in claimed to have improved upon the American prototype by offering a superior standard of service, similar to that of an old-fashioned cinema. As the motorist drove through the entrance gates, he was shown to his parking space by an attendant waving a torch, like a cinema usher, and as he stopped, another attendant handed him a loudspeaker to hang inside the car. A switch on the top of the speaker enabled the driver to call an attendant for hot refreshments, hot water bottles for the shivering children, or to clean the fogged-up windscreen. Raw steaks, hamburgers, and hotdogs could be purchased at a central cafe and barbecued while the family warmed themselves by coke braziers. Below the screen was a special children's playground with swings and toys and a doorkeeper dressed as a frog who welcomed the pajama-clad youngsters with free sweets as they entered. Ringwood added new attractions—a swimming pool, merry-go-round, open-air dance floor, and miniature golf course.[28]

The golden age of the drive-in was short-lived. The competition of television soon forced proprietors to cut the level of services and seek a more specialized audience. By the 1960s, most young families preferred the superior comfort and privacy of the family room and the television screen. Only as they acquired cars of their own, and a need for entertainment of a kind not supplied by the small screen, did the younger members of the family again resort to the drive-in. Soon the playgrounds and family barbecues were shut down, cartoons and musicals gave way to rock-and-roll and horror movies, and, as car ownership spread among the young, the family movie house became what we colloquially knew as the "passion-pit."

DRIVE-IN SHOPPING

In the 1950s, when only a minority of city dwellers used cars on a daily basis, the application of the "drive-in" principle was largely confined to experimental uses in well-to-do car-owning suburbs. The most decisive shift toward automobilized shopping came with the decision of the Myer Emporium in 1957 to develop what is still the nation's largest drive-in shopping center at Chadstone.[29]

Chadstone was the creation of Kenneth and Baillieu Myer, the sons of the company's founder, Sidney Myer. The Myers had maintained close family and business connections with the United States since the early 1920s when Sidney had lived for a time in California; his sons were educated partly in the United States, and after their discharge from the Australian Navy at the end of World War II, both had worked and traveled extensively in America.[30] Baillieu, the younger son, had worked for Macy's both in Manhattan and in suburban White Plains and had visited the company's influential Garden Plaza development in New Jersey and Northland in Detroit.[31] Kenneth had been educated partly at Princeton and had visited the United States to observe retailing trends in 1949 and 1953. He was especially influenced by his observations of motorized shopping on the West

Coast and on his return alerted his fellow directors to their possible application in a rapidly automobilizing Australia. "Gentlemen, I am convinced of the future development of retail business in areas other than the centre of capital cities. We should be turning our minds to the possibilities of regional centres of the kind making their appearance in America."[32] Some encouragement had been given to the development of regional shopping centers by the 1954 Melbourne Planning Scheme, a point which Myer, who was influential in town planning circles, would have been quick to grasp. (He was a prominent member of the Town and Country Planning Association and a founder of the City Development Association, a pressure group of civic-minded businessmen, again based on American models.) The Myer brothers purchased a large parcel of land on Burwood Highway but were unable to persuade their fellow directors to back their plan for a regional shopping center; the land was later sold to a rival retailer, G. J. Coles, and became the site of Australia's first Kmart.

Two years later the board was won over and Myers resolved to build its first drive-in shopping center in Melbourne's rapidly growing eastern suburbs. It hired the Larry Smith Organization of Seattle to carry out preliminary research and planning. (Smith and Victor Gruen were co-authors of an influential American textbook, *Shoppingtowns USA*.)[33] The location was determined only after a survey of metropolitan traffic patterns and residential development had demonstrated that the largest potential patronage lay in an area centered on the intersection of Warrigal and Dandenong roads, about 20 kilometers from the central business district, in the center of the city's main eastern development corridor. The new center would lie at the center of the city's most rapidly growing area, with more than 400,000 people resident within a five-mile radius, and sixty-six percent of households owning a car.[34] Chadstone, according to the journalist Graham Perkin, who covered its opening in 1960, embodied "a new shopping logic. It is not an original logic because it has been adapted from an American pattern, but it is refreshingly new in Australian conditions."[35] Like other drive-ins, the drive-in shopping center represented a new economy of shopping time: "one stop and shop."

Myer created Chadstone for a customer who had still barely appeared on the Australian urban scene, the motoring housewife. "Since women do most of the shopping Chadstone is planned and geared for women's needs," a contemporary observed. "Mrs. Suburbia can drive into the centre after the morning peak hour with her under-age school children and the family dog," Parking spaces were angled at forty-five degrees, in order, so it was said, "that women will be able to park easily. There will be no embarrassing manoeuvres into small spaces."[36] Child-care facilities, a supervised children's playground, a delivery service from store to car, and a motoring school advertising lessons for would-be women drivers were some of the other facilities Chadstone offered its new female clientele.

Like the first drive-in theaters, Chadstone sought to reinforce, and perhaps exploit, contemporary family and community values. Town planners in the 1940s had sought to promote the creation of community centers in the new suburbs, and Chadstone incorporated an auditorium for theatrical productions, reception rooms, a radio studio, and a ten-pin bowling alley—another American innovation. It is hard to know whether these community facilities were designed as bait for the shoppers or as a gesture of civic idealism. By the late 1960s, it had become clear that, with the exception of the bowling alley, they were not paying their way, and like the Strawberry Room, they have gradually been absorbed into the retail complex. When Myer opened further drive-in shopping centers at Northland, Southland (1964), and Eastland (1970), such facilities were conspicuous by their absence.

THE FREEWAY

If "autopia" had a symbol, it was surely the dream highway, or freeway. Here the city was most dramatically reshaped in accordance with the needs of automobility. These sweeping ribbons of carriageway, with their overpasses, clover leafs, underpasses, and exchanges, crowded with motor cars, each self-directed yet moving in swift tidal flows, exemplified the new social and political order brought into being by the car. The freeway was at once a symbol of freedom and of order, of the individual's desire to go where and when one wished, without dependence on the services of others or the imposition of timetables, speed restrictions, or delays; and of the capacity of a technological society to anticipate, plan, and channel those desires into orderly patterns of traffic movement.

The freeway did for the city what Henry Ford's production line and the principles of scientific management had done for industry. Industrial management called for a rigorous analysis of the component phases of production, the precise measurement of the volumes, timing, and effort involved in each, and their reprogramming into a smooth logical sequence. The freeway was the outcome of a similar process in which traffic flows were first measured and analyzed, their volumes and sequences plotted and predicted, and complex systems of roads, traffic signals, parking lots, and policing devised to cater for them.[37]

While the motel, the drive-in theater, and, to a lesser extent, the drive-in shopping center, were products of individual enterprise, the remaking of the urban highway system that connected them required a more profound and extensive change in social and political organization. Here America was not only an inventor of specific technological devices, such as the freeway or the parking meter, but of more profoundly influential paradigms of research, styles of analysis, and forms of political organization. It was the knowledge systems as well as the techniques, the politics as well as the practicalities, of road design that American road and traffic experts brought to Australia in the 1950s and 1960s.

Australian planners and road engineers had long looked to the United States as a model of highway design and administration. In 1924 the chairman of the Victorian Country Roads Board, William Calder, returned from an overseas visit convinced that the American road system was "one of the outstanding wonders of modern transportation."[38] In 1937 Calder's successor as chairman of the CRB, William McCormack, inspected American highways on both the West and East coasts and visited the U.S. Bureau of Roads in Washington. "Design," McCormack wrote on his return, quoting his American advisors, "must keep as the main objective directional, free-flowing lines that give velocity and rhythm, and no obstruction to traffic."[39] From the late 1940s Australian motoring magazines often published illustrated articles describing the joys of freeway driving. In 1949 *The Radiator,* the journal of the Royal Automobile Club of Victoria (RACV), was arguing that "the development of the great highways of the United States should give our road authorities food for thought. Highway development there is in the direction of greater widths, more under and over passes, easier curves and less steep grades to increase sighting distance."[40] The pictures accompanying these articles were often more expressive than the text—high aerial shots of sweeping multilaned highways weave across the page, merging and dividing, leaping over and diving under each other, like strands of white ribbon strewn casually across the countryside.

Australian businessmen returned from the United States full of praise for the Californian highway system. In 1951 the electrical goods manufacturer Keith Healing reported that "California's highway and road maintenance are splendid . . . America as a whole realizes that her automobiles are an asset and does all that is humanly possible to keep the traffic flowing so that car production need not be restricted."[41] Premier Henry Bolte, returning from one of his regular "Promote Victoria" tours, admitted that he was "impressed with the USA where people thought big and tackled big jobs in a big way. There is a lesson for everybody to be learned by visiting the USA, particularly in problems associated with traffic."[42]

The flow of information from homecoming Australians was reinforced by a reverse flow of American highway and planning experts visiting Australia. In 1953 Kenneth Myer, the creator of Chadstone, sponsored a visit by Charles Bennett, Chief Planner of Los Angeles and an enthusiastic freeway advocate. The Myer brothers had met Bennett through a family friend, now mayor of Los Angeles. The personable, smooth-talking, cigar-smoking visitor was every Australian's image of the can-do Yankee expert, and he persuaded many younger businessmen, including the Myers, of the need to adopt American solutions to traffic congestion such as parking meters and off-street parking stations. In the following year the RACV and the City Development Association jointly sponsored a longer visit by D. Grant Mickle, a traffic engineer from the Automotive Safety Foundation in Washington and a former consultant to the city of Los Angeles. Mickle, a quietly spoken, conservatively dressed pipe smoker, was a more reassuring, and perhaps more influential, figure than Bennett. The press, which covered his visit extensively, portrayed him as a kind of friendly boffin, a "Mr. Fix-it" for the city's failing traffic system.[43] He prepared a report on Melbourne's traffic problem, then at its chaotic worst, which called for the creation of a federal Department of Roads on the American model, the upgrading of technical training and research, and comprehensive street and traffic management plans, including the creation of a metropolitan traffic authority.[44] While tactfully refusing to say that Melbourne's extensive tramway system should be scrapped, he stressed that "all large American cities that were beating traffic tangles were getting rid of trams."[45]

Convinced of the intimate link between highway provision and their emerging retail strategy, in 1956 the Myer brothers established a scholarship to send an Australian engineer to the traffic engineering course held each year at Yale University. The graduates from the Yale course include some of the most influential figures in Australian transport policy over the next thirty years.[46] Joe Delaney, later head of the Commonwealth Bureau of Roads, believed, as most of his colleagues did, that "America's present was Australia's future. I think the American experience of traffic, and volumes of traffic, [was] far advanced in one sense. I remember thinking: we'd better have a look and see what the Americans do. If we haven't learned from it, we'll come back, but we won't make the same mistakes as the Americans." [47]

Traffic engineering, like market research, scientific management, project building, or any of the other new American forms of expertise that were transforming the Australian urban environment in the postwar era, derived from a common model of which the Ford assembly plant was the prototype. According to this model, human activity was broken down into its constituent units, measured, analyzed then reconstituted, temporally and spatially, into stepwise sequences of activity in the form of production lines, sales floors, marketing campaigns, highway interchanges, housing assembly plans, and fast-food outlets. The objective of the design, whether it was a production flowchart or a freeway interchange, was to reduce uncertainty, friction, effort, dead time, and wasted space; to streamline decision making and to increase the volume and accelerate the flow of transactions, movements, and decisions.[48] The supermarket, the motel, and the drive-in theater were applications of much the same logic.

But learning even an apparently technical subject like traffic engineering is also a social process. Students in the Yale course recalled the influence of charismatic teachers, like Wilbur Smith, chief consultant to the American road lobby, whose southern drawl and casual teaching style had a particular appeal to Australian engineers. "He was a very personable character," Joe Delaney recalled. "I couldn't help liking the guy . . . He was a farm boy originally, and he had this basic, hard, down-the-line, no bull-shit [way], and sufficient of the theory to be able to apply it, and to come up with solutions which were politically balanced." During their year in the United States, the young engineers also traveled the country observing traffic and highway developments, writing back with elated reports of their mile-a-minute journeys along the New Jersey Turnpike.[49] American experts continued to arrive in Melbourne through the late 1950s and early 1960s. In 1956 Ralph Dovey acted as consultant to the city of Melbourne, and later, the principal consultant to the American road lobby and Yale instructor, Wilbur Smith, was appointed as consultant to the 1966–1968 Melbourne Transportation Study, an ambitious inquiry which projected the city's transport needs into the mid-1980s, as well as several other Australian traffic studies.[50] It was on the basis of this study, carried out largely by Yale graduates according to Yale methodology, that recommendations were formulated to build a network of 307 miles of metropolitan freeways costing over two billion dollars.

This ambitious road plan called for massive resumption of property in the central city and middle-distance suburbs and would have changed the ecology of Melbourne beyond recognition. It would also have called for levels of public expenditure on transportation unparalleled since the 1880s landboom. In the event, the freeways were not built. By the early 1970s, public protests, especially in the inner city, the oil price shock of 1974, and the refusal of the newly elected Whitlam (federal) government to finance the scheme obliged the Hamer (state) government to prune it radically.[51] The story of that struggle lies beyond the scope of this paper, but the scars it inflicted on the American-educated traffic engineers are still raw and strongly influence their view of the preceding decade, when their prestige was still high and their influence almost unfettered. Some are unrepentant freeway advocates and see the frustration of their plans as having delivered the city a hybrid and unworkable transport system. Others now interpret the 1968 plan as a misjudged ambit claim, a grand scheme that was expected to deliver only a fraction of what it asked for. Others again, having reflected since on the example of European and Canadian, as well as American, traffic planning, and the survival of the city with a much less extensive highway system, attempt to sift the valuable kernel of analytical skills that they derived from the Yale experience from the specific engineering solutions that they then associated with it. No longer freeway advocates, they nevertheless believe that the analytical skills, the know-how, that they acquired in America are of enduring value and influence.[52]

CONCLUSION

Theirs is a very different verdict on the American experience from Robin Boyd's. Americanization, they imply, went deeper than mere style: it influenced the engine as well as the fins, the plan of the house as well as the color scheme, the soda as well as the froth on top. It was a process in which Australians were willing and sometimes discerning agents. Those who first introduced American ideas, such as the motel, the drive-in theater and shopping center, for example, often aspired to adapt them to local conditions, to learn from America's mistakes, only to see them eventually assimilate to the American, and increasingly international, pattern. In his role as architect, Robin Boyd had himself attempted to do this by demonstrating that the basic building blocks of suburbia—houses, shopping centers, motels, and even fast-food outlets—could be redeemed by good design. A key role in Americanizing Australian suburbs was played by Australian business and professional men, such as Kenneth Myer, who acted as cultural brokers in promoting American ideas both within their own companies, industries, and professions and to the rest of the society. In doing so, they were doubtless acting in what they saw as the interests of themselves and their companies, convinced that American ways were simply bound to succeed. But they were also the bearers of a distinctively American notion of civic duty which led them to remake public institutions and services along similar lines. As well as Chadstone and the parking meter, the Myer family also brought Melbourne the Myer Music Bowl, modeled on the Hollywood Bowl, and the Myer Foundation, its first major philanthropic trust.

If we examine the range of American innovations in urban life which came in the 1950s, they display a distinct family resemblance. Underlying them all is the Fordist logic of functional analysis, survey and measurement, subdivision of function, and flow technology. As that logic was applied to one area of Australian business or public management, it cleared the way for its application to others; like the logic of economic rationalism, thirty years later, it had a powerful internal dynamic. Whether it is the development of the project house, market research and supermarket design, traffic research and highway design, scientific management and factory layout, the American imprint was unmistakable.[53] Some features of this paradigm would be applied elsewhere, and some would be superseded. In the 1950s, however, it was the United States which had applied it most rigorously, and it was only through direct American influence that it could have influenced Australian urban development as profoundly as it did.

In the 1960s most Australians hoped that America's today would be Australia's tomorrow. Contemporaries anticipated that rising prosperity and growing suburbanization would produce societies, on both sides of the Pacific, that were more homogeneous, cohesive and—to that extent—more bland and boring. A generation later the terms of cultural exchange between Australia and the United States have abruptly changed. Now, it seems, observers of the Australian city are more likely to *fear,* than to hope, that America's present may be Australia's future. In the United States, the suburb—once the classic site of class convergence—has become synonymous with social polarization. As the white middle class flee the inner cities for the suburbs, creating new belts of affluence and political conservatism on the urban periphery, the gulf between rich and poor, black and white, grows wider.[54]

These new suburbs are a response to distinctively American problems of race, crime, and fiscal imbalance. Yet in Australia, too, there are echoes of that more dismal urban scenario. From my office I now look beyond the empty carparks of the Nissan car assembly plant toward Springvale, now one of the largest concentrations of unemployment in the city. It is also, not quite coincidentally, one of the largest concentrations of Indo-Chinese immigrants. As Bob Gregory and Boyd Hunter have recently shown, the gap between Australia's rich and poor, and between its rich and poor suburbs, is also widening. There are suburbs now, where a majority of households have no employed breadwinner. In reaching for language to describe these disturbing new realities, it is to the United States that our social scientists almost instinctively turn. Is Australia developing an "underclass"? Gregory and Hunter ask. Are our poor suburbs becoming "ghettoes"?[55]

Like the theories of class convergence which an earlier generation of social scientists borrowed uncritically from their American peers, such language may do as much to obscure, as to illuminate, Australian realities.[56] But their appearance reinforces the suspicion that it is not just the "jabbering journalists" and the "expense account men," but the intellectuals, including Robin Boyd—including even ourselves—who have often taken the wheel in the drive toward Austerica.

Notes

This paper draws on the Postwar Melbourne Project, a collaborative venture funded by the Australian Research Council. I wish to acknowledge the contribution of my research assistant, Sheryl Yelland, and use of material in unpublished essays on Chadstone by two of my former students, Fiona Pettigrew and Giles Bartram.

1. David Hamer, *New Towns in the New World: Images and Perceptions of the Nineteenth Century Urban Frontier* (New York: Columbia University Press, 1990); Adna Weber, *The Growth of Cities in the Nineteenth Century: A Study in Statistics* (Ithaca: Cornell University Press, 1963, [1899]), 1, 138–142, 472.

2. Arthur Odell, "The Architect, Civic Development, and Society," *Architecture in Australia* 54, no. 2 (June 1965): 72–75.

3. Robin Boyd, *The Australian Ugliness* (Melbourne: Penguin, 1960), 78–79; first published in the *Age,* September 21, 1957.

4. Geoffrey Serle, *Robin Boyd: A Life* (Melbourne: Melbourne University Press, 1995), 159–176.

5. Robin Boyd, "The Boyd/Gropius Letters," *Transition* 38 (1992): 121.

6. Serle, *Robin Boyd*, 59–60, 127, and compare Lewis Mumford, *The Culture of Cities* (London: Secker and Warburg, 1946), *The Highway and the City* (New York: Harcourt, Brace and World, 1963), and Reyner Banham, "The Machine Aesthetic," *Architectural Review* (April 1955) reprinted in *Design by Choice,* ed. Penny Sparke (London: Academy Editions, 1981), 44–122; "Speed the Citizen," *Architectural Review* 136 (August 1964): 103–108; *Theory and Design for the First Machine Age* (London: Architectural Press, 1960); *Los Angeles: The Architecture of Four Ecologies* (London: Allen Lane, 1967).

7. A. F. Davies, *Essays in Political Sociology* (Melbourne: Cheshire, 1972), 36.

8. Chris Wallace-Crabbe, "Melbourne," *Current Affairs Bulletin* 32, no. 11 (October 1963): 168.

9. Note Richard White's observations on the parallels between the American and Australian ways of life in *Inventing Australia* (Sydney: Allen & Unwin, 1981), chap. 10.

10. Geoffrey Serle, "Austerica Unlimited," *Meanjin* (September 1967): 240. Serle was characteristically the most pessimistic of the commentators, although also interestingly he was willing to acknowledge the radical, positive, and untrashy aspects of America.

11. Geoffrey Serle, "Other Places," *Meanjin* (June 1967): 121. Compare with Richard White's warning against conflating Americanization with "the totality of post-industrial cultural change: modernisation, standardisation, privatization, commoditication, internationalisation, commercialization or whatever neologisation is appropriate." Richard White, "'A Backwater Awash': The Australian Experience of Americanization," *Theory, Culture, and Society* 3 (1983): 110.

12. Geoffrey Blainey, "The New Australia: A Legend of the Lake," *Meanjin* (December 1967): 368.

13. Philip Bell and Roger Bell, *Implicated: The United States in Australia* (Melbourne: Oxford University Press, 1993), esp. chap. 6.

14. Ian Manning, *The Open Street: Public Transport, Motor Cars, and Politics in Australian Cities* (Sydney: Transit Australia Publishing, 1991).

15. Kenneth Jackson, *Crabgrass Frontier: The Suburbanization of the United States* (New York: Oxford University Press, 1985), chap. 14.

16. *Radiator,* September 20, 1950.

17. Jackson, *Crabgrass Frontier,* 253–255; John Jakle, Keith Sculle, and Jefferson Rogers, *The Motel in America* (Baltimore: Johns Hopkins University Press, 1996), 18–56.

18. *Royalauto,* October 1, 1954, 11.

19. From listing in *Motor Manual,* February 1, 1960, 56.

20. *Australian Motor Manual,* May 16, 1955, 8–9.

21. *Australian Women's Weekly,* December 14, 1955, 20.

22. Cyril Lewis to Henry Bolte, January 16, 1956, Bolte to Arthur Fadden, March 8, 1956, Fadden to Bolte, March 22, 1956, in "Motels," *VPRS* 1163/1174.

23. *Royalauto Journal,* January 1957, 36–37, and August 1957.

24. Boyd, *The Australian Ugliness,* 76–77.

25. Personal communication from David Yencken, April 1, 1995; Serle, *Robin Boyd,* 193–196; *Nation,* July 28, 1962, 17.

26. *Radiator,* January 18, 1950, 13.

27. John Richardson, "Movies under the Stars: Drive-ins and Modernity," *Continuum: An Australian Journal of the Media* 1, no. 1 (1987): 111–115.

28. *Australian Motor Manual,* July 15, 1955, 16–17; *Royalauto,* December 1954, 27.

29. Peter Spearritt, "Suburban Cathedrals: The Rise of the Drive-in Shopping Centre," in *The Cream Brick Frontier: Histories of Australian Suburbia,* no. 19, ed. Graeme Davison, Tony Dingle, and Seamus O'Hanlon (Melbourne: Monash Publications in History, 1995), 88–107; Beverley Kingston, *Basket, Bag, and Trolley: The History of Shopping in Australia* (Melbourne: Oxford University Press, 1995), chap. 6.

30. Ambrose Pratt, *Sidney Myer: A Biography* (Melbourne: Quartet Books, 1978), 104–112; Alan Marshall, *The Gay Provider: The Myer Story* (Melbourne: Cheshire, 1961), 28–36.

31. Interview with S. B. Myer, November 22, 1995.

32. *Herald,* October 3, 1960.

33. Lisabeth Cohen, "From Town Center to Shopping Center: The Reconfiguration of Community Marketplaces in Postwar America," *American Historical Review* 101, no. 4 (October 1996): 1056–1060.

34. George McCahon, *A Regional Shopping Centre at Chadstone: Progress Report to Mr. A. H. Tolley, December 1958* (Coles-Myer Archives); R. J. Johnson and P. J. Rimmer, "The Competitive Position of a Planned Shopping Centre," *Australian Geographer* 10, no. 3 (1966): 160–168; "A Survey of Chadstone Shopping Habits," *Australian Planning Institute Journal* 4, no. 3 (July 1966): 75–77.

35. *Age,* October 3, 1960.

36. Ibid., February 20, 1959.

37. I draw here upon the valuable discussion in John D. Fairfield, "The Scientific Management of Urban Space: Professional City Planning and the Legacy of Progressive Reform," *Journal of Urban History* 20, no. 2 (February 1994): 179–204.

38. William Calder, R*eport on His Investigations of Road Problems in Europe and America during 1924* (Melbourne: Government Printer, 1925), 2.

39. U.S Bureau of Public Roads as quoted in W. T. B. McCormack, *Report on His Investigation of Road Problems in the United States and Canada in 1937* (Melbourne: Government Printer, 1937), 38.

40. *Radiator,* February 16, 1949, 7; also see ibid., June 14, 1950, 4.

41. Ibid., September 19, 1951, 4.

42. *Royalauto,* October 1956, 12–13.

43. *Sun,* October 8, 19, 30, 1954; *Wheels,* January 1955, 34.

44. D. Grant Mickle, *Melbourne's Traffic Problem,* City Development Association, Melbourne, October 1954.

45. *Sun,* October 8, 1954.

46. *Bureau of Highway Traffic: Yale University, Biennial Report and Roster of Graduates, 1963–1964* (New Haven, Ct., 1964), 15–33.

47. Interview with Joe Delaney, June 1994.

48. *Royalauto,* February 1957. The influence of American models on the development of the house building industry can be charted in the history of A. V. Jennings, Australia's largest project builders and developers; see Don Garden, *Builders to the Nation: The A. V. Jennings Story* (Melbourne: Melbourne University Press, 1992), 91, 159, 161, and compare with the career of the American project builder Abraham Levitt, as described in Jackson, *Crabgrass Frontier,* 234–238. For the influence of American products on market research, see Gail Reekie, "Market Research and the Postwar Housewife," *Australian Feminist Studies* 4 (summer 1991): 15–27; Daniel Oakman, Researching Australia: A History of the Market Research Industry in Australia, 1928–1995, M.A. in Public History thesis, Monash University, 1995, chap. 2.

49. *Wheels,* July 1955, 44.

50. Wilbur Smith and Associates, *Future Highways and Urban Growth* (New Haven, Ct.: Wilbur Smith and Associates, 1961).

51. Leonie Sandercock, *Cities for Sale: Property, Politics, and Urban Planning in Australia* (Melbourne: Melbourne University Press, 1975), 155–159.

52. Interviews with Bill Saggers, April 20, 1994, Ted Barton, April 27, 1994, Neil Guerin, May 18, 1994, Joe Delaney, June 1, 1994, John Bayley, May 25, 1994, and Robin Underwood, June 22, 1994.

53. Here I draw in part on Edward Soja, *Postmodern Geographies: The Reassertion of Space in Critical Social Theory* (London: Verso, 1989), chaps. 6–9; David Harvey, *The Condition of Postmodernity* (Oxford: Blackwell, 1989); and for Australian applications, see Alastair Greig, *The Stuff Dreams are Made Of: Housing Provision in Australia* (Melbourne: Melbourne University Press, 1995), 17–28; and Graeme Davison, *The Unforgiving Minute: How Australians Learned to Tell the Time* (Melbourne: Oxford University Press, 1993), chap. 5.

54. For example, Mike Davis, *City of Quartz: Excavating the Future in Los Angeles* (London: Verso, 1990); Jackson, *Crabgrass Frontier,* chaps. 15 and 16; William Schneider, "The Suburban Century Begins," *Atlantic Monthly* (July 1992): 33–44; William Sharpe and Leonard Wallock, "Bold New City or Built Up 'Burb? Redefining Contemporary Suburbia," *American Quarterly* 46, no. 1 (March 1994): 1–30; Brett W. Hawkins and Stephen L. Percy, "On Anti-Suburban Orthodoxy," *Social Science Quarterly* 72, no. 3 (September 1991): 478–490.

55. R. C. Gregory and Boyd Hunter, "The Macro Economy and the Growth of Ghettoes and Urban Poverty in Australia," Discussion paper no. 325, April 1995, Centre for Economic Policy Research, Australian National University.

56. For a cautionary appraisal of recent American models, see Mark Peel, "Fearing Los Angeles: Australia's Postmodern Urban Nightmare," *Political Expressions* 1, no. 2 (1996): 1–20.

References

Banham, Reyner. "The Machine Aesthetic." *Architectural Review* (April 1955).

———. *Los Angeles: The Architecture of Four Ecologies*. London: Allen Lane, 1967.

———. "Speed the Citizen." *Architectural Review* 136 (August 1964): 103–108.

———. *Theory and Design for the First Machine Age*. London: Architectural Press, 1960.

Bell, Philip, and Roger Bell. *Implicated: The United States in Australia*. Melbourne: Oxford University Press, 1993.

Blainey, Geoffrey. "The New Australia: A Legend of the Lake." *Meanjin* (December 1967): 368.

Boyd, Robin. "The Boyd/Gropius Letters." *Transition* 38 (1992): 121.

———. *The Australian Ugliness*. Melbourne: Penguin, 1960. First published in the *Age,* September 21, 1957.

Bureau of Highway Traffic: Yale University, Biennial Report and Roster of Graduates, 1963–1964. New Haven, Ct.: Yale University Press, 1964.

Calder, William. *Report on His Investigations of Road Problems in Europe and America during 1924*. Melbourne: Government Printer, 1925.

Cohen, Lisabeth. "From Town Center to Shopping Center: The Reconfiguration of Community Marketplaces in Postwar America." *American Historical Review* 101, no. 4 (October 1996): 1056–1060.

Davies, A. F. *Essays in Political Sociology*. Melbourne: Cheshire, 1972.

Davis, Mike. *City of Quartz: Excavating the Future in Los Angeles*. London: Verso, 1990.

Davison, Graeme. *The Unforgiving Minute: How Australians Learned to Tell the Time*. Melbourne: Oxford University Press, 1993.

Fairfield, John D. "The Scientific Management of Urban Space: Professional City Planning and the Legacy of Progressive Reform." *Journal of Urban History* 20, no. 2 (February 1994): 179–204.

Garden, Don. *Builders to the Nation: The A. V. Jennings Story*. Melbourne: Melbourne University Press, 1992.

Gregory, R. C., and Boyd Hunter. "The Macro Economy and the Growth of Ghettoes and Urban Poverty in Australia." Discussion paper no. 325. April 1995. Centre for Economic Policy Research, Australian National University.

Greig, Alastair. *The Stuff Dreams are Made Of: Housing Provision in Australia*. Melbourne: Melbourne University Press, 1995.

Hamer, David. *New Towns in the New World: Images and Perceptions of the Nineteenth Century Urban Frontier*. New York: Columbia University Press, 1990.

Harvey, David. *The Condition of Postmodernity*. Oxford: Blackwell, 1989.

Hawkins, Brett W., and Stephen L. Percy. "On Anti-Suburban Orthodoxy." *Social Science Quarterly* 72, no. 3 (September 1991): 478–490.

Herald. October 3, 1960.

Jackson, Kenneth. *Crabgrass Frontier: The Suburbanization of the United States.* New York: Oxford University Press, 1985.

Jakle, John, Keith Sculle, and Jefferson Rogers. *The Motel in America.* Baltimore: Johns Hopkins University Press, 1996.

Johnson, R. J., and P. J. Rimmer. "The Competitive Position of a Planned Shopping Centre." *Australian Geographer* 10, no. 3 (1966): 160–168.

———. "A Survey of Chadstone Shopping Habits." *Australian Planning Institute Journal* 4, no. 3 (July 1966): 75–77.

Kingston, Beverley. *Basket, Bag, and Trolley: The History of Shopping in Australia.* Melbourne: Oxford University Press, 1995.

Manning, Ian. *The Open Street: Public Transport, Motor Cars, and Politics in Australian Cities.* Sydney: Transit Australia Publishing, 1991.

Marshall, Alan. *The Gay Provider: The Myer Story.* Melbourne: Cheshire, 1961.

McCahon, George. *A Regional Shopping Centre at Chadstone: Progress Report to Mr. A. H. Tolley, December 1958.* Coles-Myer Archives.

McCormack, W. T. B. *Report on His Investigation of Road Problems in the United States and Canada in 1937.* Melbourne: Government Printer, 1937.

Mickle, D. Grant. *Melbourne's Traffic Problem.* City Development Association. Melbourne, October 1954.

"Motels." *VPRS* 1163/1174. re Cyril Lewis to Henry Bolte, January 16, 1956, Bolte to Arthur Fadden, March 8, 1956, Fadden to Bolte, March 22, 1956.

Mumford, Lewis. *The Culture of Cities.* London: Secker and Warburg, 1938.

———. *The Highway and the City.* New York: Harcourt, Brace and World, 1963.

Oakman, Daniel. Researching Australia: A History of the Market Research Industry in Australia, 1928–1995. M.A. in Public History thesis. Monash University, 1995.

Odell, Arthur. "The Architect, Civic Development, and Society." *Architecture in Australia* 54, no. 2 (June 1965): 72–75.

Peel, Mark. "Fearing Los Angeles: Australia's Postmodern Urban Nightmare." *Political Expressions* 1, no. 2 (1996): 1–20.

Pratt, Ambrose. *Sidney Myer: A Biography.* Melbourne: Quartet Books, 1978.

Radiator. February 16, 1949, 7; January 18, 1950, 13; June 14, 1950, 4; September 20, 1950; September 19, 1951, 4.

Reekie, Gail. "Market Research and the Postwar Housewife." *Australian Feminist Studies* 4 (summer 1991): 15–27.

Richardson, John. "Movies under the Stars: Drive-ins and Modernity." *Continuum: An Australian Journal of the Media* 1, no. 1 (1987): 111–115.

Sandercock, Leonie. *Cities for Sale: Property, Politics, and Urban Planning in Australia.* Melbourne: Melbourne University Press, 1975.

Schneider, William. "The Suburban Century Begins." *Atlantic Monthly* (July 1992): 33–44.

Serle, Geoffrey. "Austerica Unlimited." *Meanjin* (September 1967): 240.

————. "Other Places." *Meanjin* (June 1967): 121.

————. *Robin Boyd: A Life*. Melbourne: Melbourne University Press, 1995.

Sharpe, William, and Leonard Wallock. "Bold New City or Built Up 'Burb? Redefining Contemporary Suburbia." *American Quarterly* 46, no. 1 (March 1994): 1–30.

Soja, Edward. *Postmodern Geographies: The Reassertion of Space in Critical Social Theory*. London: Verso, 1989.

Sparke, Penny, ed. *Design by Choice*. London: Academy Editions, 1981.

Spearritt, Peter. "Suburban Cathedrals: The Rise of the Drive-in Shopping Centre." In *The Cream Brick Frontier: Histories of Australian Suburbia*, no. 19. Edited by Graeme Davison, Tony Dingle, and Seamus O'Hanlon. Melbourne: Monash Publications in History, 1995.

Wallace-Crabbe, Chris. "Melbourne." *Current Affairs Bulletin* 32, no. 11 (October 1963): 168.

Weber, Adna. *The Growth of Cities in the Nineteenth Century: A Study in Statistics*. Ithaca: Cornell University Press, 1963 (1899).

Wheels. January 1955, 34; July 1955, 44.

White, Richard. "'A Backwater Awash': The Australian Experience of Americanization." *Theory, Culture, and Society* 3 (1983): 110.

————. *Inventing Australia*. Sydney: Allen & Unwin, 1981.

Wilbur Smith and Associates. *Future Highways and Urban Growth*. New Haven, Ct.: Wilbur Smith and Associates, 1961.

12

The Creation of Australian Space

ALAN FROST, LA TROBE UNIVERSITY

CANADA, UNITED STATES, MEXICO, Uruguay, Argentina, South Africa, Australia, and New Zealand—those countries which Alfred Crosby has termed the "Neo-Europes"—share a number of geophysical and demographic features. They lie largely in the temperate zones, so that they have roughly similar climates (i.e., warm-to-cool temperatures and precipitation rates of 150–50 cms per year). They have very extensive grasslands, suitable either for pastoral production or large-scale agriculture. They have (or have had) rich mineral deposits. They have all been sites of European colonization in the past five hundred years, and their indigenous human populations, fauna, and flora have been unable to resist the invaders, who have brought with them "a scaled-down simplified version of the biota of Western Europe" which took vigorous root.[1]

This is not to say, though, that the histories of these emergent nations have run exactly parallel. For example, the vice-regal system meant that extensive state controls were established earlier in Mexico than in the United States or Canada; Australia has no distinct population group as the Quebeçois of Canada; in Mexico, indigenous populations and food resources have had greater influence than in some of the other countries. However, the similarities are sufficiently strong and broad for me to be able to use the case of Australia to develop a paradigm of the creation of national space in a neo-Europe—or, more directly, to describe the creation of Australian space.

The first step in the awesome process of the definition of national space in a neo-Europe involved its being brought within European systems of time, space, and imagination. The first European sightings of the shores of "New Holland" were made by Dutch navigators from the beginning to the end of the seventeenth century. The British explorer James Cook's charting of the entire eastern coastline of New South Wales followed in 1770. Having a few years earlier established the insularity of Tasmania, between 1802 and

1805 Matthew Flinders circumnavigated and charted the whole continent and gave it its modern name. Since it had been anticipated by the older expectation of *Terra Australis,* this delineation of a southern continent did not carry with it the astonishment that the discovery of the New World occasioned; and the assimilation of the fact of the Americas made comparatively much easier that of a second "New World."[2] Then, the Europeans needed to take possession—symbolic and effective—of the region. Cook did the first when, on August 21, 1770, with the way to the East Indies clear, he landed on an island in Torres Strait:

> Having satisfied my self of the great Probabillity of a Passage, thro' which I intend going with the Ship, and therefore may land no more upon this Eastern coast of *New Holland,* and on the Western side I can make no new discovery the honour of which belongs to the Dutch Navigators; but the Eastern Coast from the Latitude of 38° South down to this place I am confident was never seen or viseted by any European before us, and Notwithstand[ing] I had in the Name of His Majesty taken posession of several places upon this coast, I now once more hoisted English Coulers and in the Name of His Majesty King George the Third took posession of the whole Eastern Coast from the above Latitude down to this place by the name of *New South Wales,* together with all the Bays, Harbours Rivers and Islands situate upon the said coast, after which we fired three Volleys of small Arms which were Answerd by the like number from the Ship.[3]

The British government rendered this symbolic occupation effective when, in 1788, it sent Captain Arthur Phillip with one thousand people to establish a colony at Sydney. Subsequently, the British settled about other harbors— Hobart in 1804, Brisbane in 1824, Perth in 1829, Melbourne in 1835, Adelaide in 1836. In 1829, the imperial government claimed the whole continent.

The creation and filling of space is central to European culture. (Consider, for example, how the Spanish built their towns in Mexico about the zócalo). With the great space of the future nation delineated, smaller spaces might be defined and filled. On the coasts there were port towns to be founded, with their wharves and water supply, adjacent hospital, government buildings, officers' dwellings, and workers' cottages. Then, at various removes about these cities were the agricultural and pastoral spaces needed for subsistence—farms with central buildings surrounded by gardens, orchards, small-scale animal yards. (One of the striking differences between Mexico and to some extent the United States on the one hand, and Canada and Australia on the other, in the first years of colonization was the Europeans' utilization of food resources created by indigenous populations.)

As more colonists came or were born, they extended agriculture and increased their herds and flocks. In 1823 the commissioner sent to inquire into the state of the settlements concluded that the production of fine wool "appear[ed] to be the principal, if not the only source of productive industry within the colony, from which the settlers can derive the means of repaying the advances made to them from the mother country, or supplying their own demands for articles of foreign manufacture."[4] This recommendation led to a particular definition of Australian space. Explorers probed the interior in search of grasslands, and pastoralists soon followed them with sheep (and to a lesser degree, cattle). By 1850 Europeans and their animals had occupied a broad arc behind the Great Dividing Range, stretching from the Burnett Valley north of Brisbane to Adelaide. In the second half of the nineteenth century, northern exploration revealed other pastoral areas, which proved much more suitable for cattle rather than for sheep.

An expanding colony needed order, organization, regulation. In 1823 the British government created a Legislative Council in New South Wales, with a Supreme Court. In 1826 the colony was surveyed and nineteen counties delineated, with one-seventh of the land being reserved for a Church and Schools Corporation. In 1842 the Legislative Assembly was reformed (with one-third of its members being nominated, and two-thirds elected on a property franchise). In 1855 came responsible government, with a fully elected lower house. As these advances reached the other colonies, their spaces were progressively refined. Simultaneously, the first settled port cities became both administrative sites and the points of interchange between the distant world and the vast interior, so that what had begun as peripheries of metropolitan power themselves became centers with their own peripheries.

Unlike Mexico, Australia's indigenous people had established no inland urban centers which the colonizers might appropriate. With one partial exception, as not in the United States and Canada, Australia lacks water courses giving access to the interior. Therefore, there are no very large inland cities in Australia. Nonetheless, there was a significant European peopling of the bush in the second half of the nineteenth century, which came mostly as a consequence of mineral discoveries—of copper in South Australia, Queensland, New South Wales, and Tasmania between 1860 and 1900; of silver in New South Wales in the 1880s; but above all of gold: in New South Wales and Victoria in the 1850s, in Queensland in the 1860s, 1870s, and 1880s, in Western Australia in the 1890s. The gold discoveries brought hundreds of thousands of new migrants. Victoria's European population increased sevenfold between 1850 and 1860; and that of Australia as a whole rose from about 400,000 to about 1,200,000. Disappointed diggers demanded farming land; and colonial legislatures obliged with Selection Acts. The widespread cultivation of wheat in Australia dates from the middle decades of the century, as farmers expanded agriculture.

With the growth and spread of population and the increase in economic activity, communications networks grew. Metropolitan authorities extended road- and bridge-building programs. By the 1850s there were regular mail services in all the colonies. Upon the discovery of gold, coaching services expanded rapidly. By the 1870s Cobb & Company's coaches traveled 28,000 miles per week in South Australia, Victoria, New South Wales, and Queensland, harnessing 6,000 horses a day. By the late 1860s, all the major ports were linked by regular steamship services, and there were also services to and from Europe and Asia. In 1875 a service opened between Sydney and San Francisco, where travelers might take the transcontinental railway to New York and cross to London by steamer, for a total traveling time of forty-one days. Paddle steamers began plying the Murray-Darling waterways in the mid-1850s. By 1900 they traveled from South Australia up to the Queensland border, providing cheap carriage for wool, wheat, and people. The first railway line was laid in 1850. By the 1880s there were networks in all colonies. The first telegraph line was laid in 1854. In 1858 Sydney was linked to Adelaide via Melbourne. Tasmania and the mainland were linked in 1859, Sydney and Brisbane in 1861. With the completion of the Adelaide-Darwin line in 1872, Australia was connected to Europe via Singapore.

These developments acted both to truncate and to consolidate Australian space. In the mid-1880s, for example, it became possible to travel by rail from Sydney to Melbourne in eighteen hours. Escaping the monsoon, people on sugar plantations in Far North Queensland might travel by steamer south to Brisbane or Sydney in one or two weeks. The results of the 1888 Melbourne Cup were known in Auckland, New Zealand, before the judge had posted the winning numbers. In 1902, returning from England on a British India liner, the pastoralist Robert Christison looked for cables at Colombo, Batavia, and other ports that might tell him if the five-year-long drought in eastern Australia had at last broken.[5]

The mid-nineteenth-century population increase brought other changes. Refugees from the Irish potato famine and the failed revolutions of Europe demanded political reforms. Male adult franchise for lower house elections was granted in Victoria in 1857 and in New South Wales in 1858. Women obtained some voting rights in South Australia in 1861 and full suffrage in 1894. In Western Australia women obtained full suffrage in 1899 and in the other states early in the twentieth century. In 1902 the federal government enfranchised all adult men and women who were citizens. By the end of the nineteenth century, too, all the colonies had instituted "free, compulsory and secular" primary education. The Land Selection acts passed by the democratic majorities in the colonial legislatures reduced the hegemony of the old pastoralist class. An increasing division between capital and labor created a climate conducive to unionism. Building workers in Sydney and Melbourne won an eight-hour day in the later 1850s. Mining workers unionized in 1872, maritime workers in 1874, and shearers in 1886. A comprehensive Australian Workers Union emerged in 1894.

A better-educated population with leisure to read and the opportunity to participate in political processes, one brought increasingly together by modern communications, began to entertain a sense of national rather than colonial identity. The use of the names "Australia" and "Australians," first adopted by Governor Macquarie in 1817 to identify the continent and its inhabitants, became progressively more widespread as the nineteenth century extended.[6] The native-born William Charles Wentworth named the newspaper he began publishing in 1824 the *Australian.* In 1835 the *Sydney Herald* defined the rhythm of "The Australian Year" for its readers, announcing among other things that in January, which is "generally the hottest month of the year," . . . "the wheat harvest ends . . . [and] fruits [are] plentiful"; and that in May, which is "the finest month in the year," the weather is "clear, cool, and bracing; the sun sets and rises in a cloudless sky for weeks together, and the scenery of the heavens at night is sublime beyond description."[7] In 1836 the pert adolescent daughters of Hannibal Macarthur told the visiting Charles Darwin, "Oh we are Australians & know nothing about England."[8] In 1838 the *Sydney Herald* described the celebrations of the fiftieth anniversary of British settlement thus:

> Towards ten o'clock the shops were all either totally or partially closed, and the streets of Sydney presented every appearance of an approaching festival. Numbers of all grades in society might be perceived proceeding in crowds to the harbour—some to go on board the steam vessels—others to embark in the various pleasure boats which skimmed the surface of the waters—and more to enjoy a sight of the gay and lively scene which lay before them. At eleven the steamboat *Australia,* "which was engaged by four Australians," having taken on board the persons invited, proceeded slowly from the stairs in the domain to the centre of the stream. After she had lain stationary for a few minutes, the *standard,* adopted by the natives of the Colony, was hoisted on the stern, amidst the most deafening and enthusiastic cheering. It was with no ordinary feelings of gratification that we looked upon an ensign which, in all probability, will, before fifty years hence be seen in every port and on every sea—the emblem of an independent and a powerful empire.[9]

In 1893 the English journalist Francis Adams announced that behind the continent's Pacific slope, west of the Great Divide, a national "type," the "Australian," was emerging—"where the marine rainfall flags out and is lost, a new climate, and, in a certain sense, a new race begin to unfold themselves."[10]

Aware of this gathering common identity and pondering the problems posed by six separate administrations within the confines of a continent, in the 1880s and 1890s politicians concluded that more comprehensive political, administrative, judicial, and defense structures were needed. The Commonwealth of Australia was inaugurated on the first day of the new century (January 1, 1901).

The twentieth century has seen both the continuation of those older processes which have acted to define national space, and some newer ones. For example, the states have continued to surrender rights to the federal government—in defense, taxation, education, law, industrial relations, and social welfare—so that the Commonwealth has progressively become the dominant geopolitical and social entity. This process has been much assisted by the building of Canberra as the federal capital, with its highly symbolic monumental buildings. Large-scale migration has continued, but while the numbers of people living in the interior have increased somewhat, the bulk of Australia's population continues to inhabit the coastal cities. Advances in communications—telephone, radio, television, electronic data networks—have continued to truncate space. When I was a boy in Far North Queensland (in the late 1940s and the early 1950s), the summer monsoon would cut road and rail links with the south for weeks at a time, and the first warning we had of an impending cyclone was a red flag flying at the Post Office. Now, people from Cairns to Sydney to Hobart, from Rockhampton to Alice Springs to Port Hedland, can hear the same broadcast of a cricket match, and on television see satellite photographs of tropical depressions forming in the Coral Sea. Company offices from Perth to Darwin, Melbourne to Cairns, can reach each other instantly by phone, fax, or e-mail, so that gone are the days of executives absenting themselves from regional offices because the fish are running.

One of the new factors to operate in the twentieth century has been war. Australia followed Britain slavishly in foreign affairs until the circumstances of World War II forced a fundamental reconsideration. Its subsequent attachment to the United States lessened as a consequence of the Vietnam War. Its present (more or less) independent stance and its increasing economic orientation to Asia and the Pacific Rim are signs of its passage from colonialism to nationalism. Another new factor is the tourism that has developed as a consequence of cheap air travel. With the reaches of the continent only three to five hours away from the major centers of population, large numbers of Australians have traveled—to Kakadu and the Kimberleys, to Uluru (Ayer's Rock) and the Olgas, to the Daintree rain forest and the uplands of Tasmania—so that we now incorporate our wild, untrammeled places into our Australian space.

* * * *

So far, I have been considering the formation of Australia's national space from geographical and political points of view. We should also, I think, understand that a time axis informs national space, which because of the different extensions it can take renders that space multidimensional. The first extension is personal. Unless and until they traveled, the children of European parents knew only their Australian colony, which was to them home. The blue of those children in New South Wales, for example, was pale but intense in spring, whitish with heat in summer. Their stone was the pale Sydney sandstone. Their pets were kangaroos, parrots, and possums. Their parents' houses, more often than not, were long, lean structures with verandahs on three sides. These dwellings were the sites of those "associations connected with the roof under which we spent the happy hours of our childhood which no other dwelling could possess."[11] Charles Harpur, whose convict parents had a farm on the banks of the Hawkesbury River northwest of Sydney, infused his poems with the brown of summer, "sun-parched hills," with the "crimson streaked with pink and gold" of clouds lit by the rising sun, with the green of fields of maize, the yellow of blossoming wattle.[12] When the Macarthur sons, whose parents had a farm by the Nepean River to the west of Sydney, traveled to England, one of the things they did was to undertake a walking tour of the Wye Valley, evoked so powerfully by Wordsworth in Tintern Abbey. "As we proceeded down the river," James wrote, "[the] scenery increased in magnificence, the banks were rocky on both sides & reminded me somewhat of the dear Nepean."[13]

The second extension of the time axis is public. As a European population spread over the bush and economic activity quickened, people traversed the length and breadth of the continent. Migratory labor patterns emerged. Bullock drivers urged their straining teams between the coastal ports and the inland runs. Spending the other half of the year working in cities or on small selections, shearers began their season in Queensland sheds in June and worked down through New South Wales to finish in Victoria and South Australia in October. Stockmen drove hundreds of thousands of animals over thousands of miles to railheads and cities. On July 16, 1888, the telegraph office in Barcaldine, western Queensland, announced one such drive: "800 bullocks, Munnigrub Station for Melbourne, Clancy of the Overflow in charge."[14] Mounted outlaws struck over vast distances. With their skills, freedom and fecklessness, mateship and egalitarianism, these bush workers and bushrangers became the stuff of story and song.

> *I had written him a letter which I had, for want of better*
> *Knowledge, sent to where I met him down the Lachlan,*
> *   years ago,*
> *He was shearing when I knew him, so I sent the letter to him,*
> *Just "on spec," addressed as follows, "Clancy, of The Overflow."*

And an answer came directed in a writing unexpected,
(And I think the same was written with a thumb-nail
  dipped in tar)
'Twas his shearing mate who wrote it, and verbatim *I will quote it:*
"Clancy's gone to Queensland droving, and we don't know where
he are."

In my wild erratic fancy visions come to me of Clancy
Gone a-droving "down the Cooper" where the Western
  drovers go;
As the stock are slowly stringing, Clancy rides behind
  them singing,
For the drover's life has pleasures that the townsfolk never know.

And the bush has friends to meet him, and their kindly voices
  greet him
In the murmur of the breezes and the river on its bars,
And he sees the vision splendid of the sunlit plains extended,
And at night the wond'rous glory of the everlasting stars.[15]

This mythologization then extended to the nation's soldiers. To the official historian of Australia's role in World War I, the young men whom he saw fight and die on the beaches of Gallipoli and later in the mud of Flanders possessed those qualities—physical beauty, courage, improvisation, egalitarianism, mateship—that he had earlier admired in the bushmen. And April 25, 1915, the day the Anzacs landed at Gallipoli on the Turkish peninsula, became our day of national remembrance, remembrance that progressively encompassed other campaigns:

Softly and humbly to the Gulf of Arabs
The convoys of dead sailors come;
At night they sway and wander in the waters far under,
But morning rolls them in the foam.
Between the sob and clubbing of the gunfire
Someone, it seems, has time for this,
To pluck them from the shallows and bury them in burrows
And tread the sand upon their nakedness.[16]

The national identity that this mythologization gave rise to was one almost exclusively white and male. It was also one effectively lawless, for to it the restraints of communal living and family responsibilities were strangers. Gradually, however, writers and artists extended their vision to comprehend women.

While the processes I have been describing had generally been present in the formation of national space in each of the neo-Europes, they have, of course, occurred at different points in time and at different rates. For example, Mexico, the United States, and Canada experienced war earlier than Australia; and each of the North American countries had national governments (and monumental architecture) before Australia.

However, two other processes which have also been significant in the formation of national space have proceeded simultaneously in all four countries. Each again involves a time axis. First, over the past two hundred and fifty years (i.e., from the time of the spread of the Linnaean system of classification), European science has collected, classified, and determined distributions of species. In any case, this process has been important in the delineation of national space—for example, A. R. Wallace's work was instrumental in locating the limits of fauna and flora in the East Indian archipelago, and thus in defining the "Australian" biosphere. But when geological investigation was added to collection and classification, an immense time axis was activated. Now we know Australian space to comprehend the igneous rock strata of the Kimberleys, formed some four thousand million years ago; the breakup of the supercontinent Gondwana three hundred million years ago; the evolution of unique sets of flora and fauna; the shaping of the continent by upheaval and subsidence, by ice and sea, wind and rain.

Second, this scientific reconnaissance has also brought us knowledge of the human depth of our space. Partly because the sites that they would have first settled have been buried by the rising of the seas subsequent to the recession of the last Ice Age, no one knows precisely when humans first reached Australia: certainly 40,000 b.p., perhaps as much as 50,000 or 60,000 b.p. There were likely several migrations rather than a single one. But however these things were, what we may now know is that through millenia, throughout the continent people gave space human attributes. Of their cultures most often we have only tantalizing glimpses. On the now-desolate, but once fertile shore of Lake Mungo in western New South Wales, for example, by 30,000 b.p. people had developed elaborate mortuary rites that involved cremation, smashing the skeleton, and sprinkling it with red ochre.

In all the neo-Europes, I think, after being briefly an object of curiosity to the colonizers, the indigenous human Other was reviled, dispossessed, and decimated. Then, in the nineteenth century that Other became an object of scientific inquiry. However unfortunate some of the consequences of this curiosity were, it did mark the beginning of the recognition of the Other's humanity, a recognition furthered in the second half of the twentieth century by social conscience and political pragmatism. In 1967 the (European) Australian people voted "Yes" to two propositions: that Aboriginal people should for the first time be included in census; and that the Commonwealth government should be able to legislate in matters pertaining to them (previously the prerogative of the states). From these decisions have flowed full citizenship rights, including most recently land rights, for Aborigines.

As this has happened, the Other has been incorporated into the Self, so that the white Australian imagination now comprehends black Australian space. Interestingly, this process has also run in the other direction, with black writers and artists using European-derived media. The next century will see significant extensions of this process, as people of Asian origin locate themselves in Australian time and space.

Australia's national space, then, has developed in time and racially, as well as geographically and politically. In doing so, publicly, it now offers materials for important political and cultural renewals and evolutions; and privately, as its vibrant literature, art, and music show, it offers materials for "new, tremendous symbol[s] for the soul."[17]

Notes

1. Alfred W. Crosby, *Ecological Imperialism: The Biological Expansion of Europe, 900–1900* (New York: Cambridge University Press, 1986), 2–7, 89.

2. See Stephen Greenblatt, *Marvelous Possessions: The Wonder of the New World* (Chicago: University of Chicago Press, 1991).

3. *The Journals of Captain James Cook on His Voyages of Discovery*, ed. J. C. Beaglehole (London: Hakluyt Society, 1955–1967), I, 387–388.

4. [J. T. Bigge], *Report on the State of Agriculture and Trade in the Colony of New South Wales* (London: House of Commons, 1823), 18.

5. M. M. Bennett, *Christison of Lammermoor*, 2nd ed. (London: Alston Rivers, 1928), 235.

6. See Macquarie's letters in *Historical Records of Australia*, 1st series (Sydney: Government Printer, 1914–1925), IX, 356, 404, 477, 726.

7. *Sydney Herald*, January 8, 1835.

8. F. W. Nichols and J. M. Nichols, *Charles Darwin in Australia* (Cambridge: Cambridge University Press, 1989), 64.

9. *Sydney Herald*, January 29, 1838.

10. Francis Adams, *The Australians: A Social Sketch* (London: T. Fisher Unwin, 1893), 9–13, 144.

11. James Macarthur to John Macarthur, May 17, 1827, quoted in Hazel King, *Elizabeth Macarthur and Her World* (Sydney: Sydney University Press, 1980), 131.

12. Charles Harpur, "The Cloud," "Dawn and Sunrise in the Snowy Mountains," "Early Summer."

13. James Macarthur, Journal, quoted in Robert Dixon, "Nostalgia and Patriotism in Colonial Australia," in *Studies from Terra Australis to Australia*, ed. John Hardy and Alan Frost (Canberra: Australian Academy of the Humanities, 1989), 215.

14. Quoted in *Australians: 1888,* ed. Graeme Davison, et al. (Sydney: Fairfax, Syme & Weldon, 1987), 104.
15. A. B. Paterson, "Clancy of the Overflow."
16. Kenneth Slessor, "Beach Burial."
17. Judith Wright, "The Harp and the King."

References

Adams, Francis. *The Australians: A Social Sketch.* London: T. Fisher Unwin, 1893.

Beaglehole, T. C., ed. *The Journals of Captain James Cook on His Voyages of Discovery.* Cambridge: Hakluyt Society, 1955–1967.

Bennett, M. M. *Christison of Lammermoor.* 2nd ed. London: Alston Rivers, 1928.

Bigge, J. T., *Report on the State of Agriculture and Trade in the Colony of New South Wales.* London: House of Commons, 1823.

Crosby, Alfred W. *Ecological Imperialism: The Biological Expansion of Europe, 900–1900.* New York: Cambridge University Press, 1986.

Davison, Graeme, et al., ed. *Australians: 1888.* Sydney: Fairfax, Syme & Weldon, 1987.

Dixon, Robert. "Nostalgia and Patriotism in Colonial Australia." In *Studies from Terra Australis to Australia.* Edited by John Hardy and Alan Frost. Canberra: Australian Academy of the Humanities, 1989.

Greenblatt, Stephen. *Marvelous Possessions: The Wonder of the New World.* Chicago: University of Chicago Press, 1991.

Historical Records of Australia. 1st series. Sydney: Government Printer, 1914–1925.

King, Hazel. *Elizabeth Macarthur and Her World.* Sydney University Press, 1980.

Nichols, F. W., and J. M. Nichols. *Charles Darwin in Australia.* Cambridge: Cambridge University Press, 1989.

PART IV

Government

13

Australian Democracy and the American Century

JAMES WALTER, GRIFFITH UNIVERSITY

ABSTRACT

American observation has shaped Australian social analysis for most of the twentieth century. The high point in the American influence on Australia was arguably between the 1940s and the 1980s. The way this shaped reflection on Australian political science can be traced in the work of an insightful interpreter of the Australian polity, A. F. Davies (1924–1987). This paper traces the intellectual journey Davies took from his landmark early work, *Australian Democracy* (1958), via "Politics in a Knowledgeable Society" (1972), to a late manuscript, *Small Country Blues*—unpublished after his premature death. Davies' early work had illuminating parallels with the influential developments in American political science which issued in the "civic cultures" debates of the 1960s. His *Australian Democracy* can be seen as an anticipatory exercise on a "civic culture." In the 1970s explicit application by Davies of American social theory to the Australian instance became manifest. By the 1980s the complexities of American society for Davies formed the backdrop to assessing the dynamics of a "small country's" predicament. The tensions between "knowledge criteria" and "political criteria"; between bureaucracy as a "stain" and as the best means of delivering equalizing outcomes; between the necessary skills of "program professionals" and the demands of broad participation; and ultimately between American modes and the Australian experience were at the core of his work. Testing his propositions ten years after his final work shows that Davies accurately foreshadowed the essentials of what he designated "the steady evaporation of politics." Davies' reflection on Australia was productively shaped by dialogue with America as *the* metropolitan culture of the late twentieth century. His insistence that the comparative framework and an interpretative sense of political cultures should inform political analysis remains an important message as we address the problems of the 1990s.

I want to comment on social science—and in particular political science—as a reflective practice, and on the shaping of Australian intellectual agendas by engagement with and responses to American influence. I will use as a touchstone the work of the late A. F. Davies for three reasons: his text *Australian Democracy* was one of the first postwar attempts to combine institutional description with comment on the patterns of Australian political culture; he was, more than most of his peers, concerned with self-reflection as an integral element in political science; and he was acutely attuned to U.S. debates and the U.S. comparison in his analysis of the Australian predicament. Davies' intellectual journey from *Australian Democracy* (in the late 1950s) through "Politics in a Knowledgeable Society" (in the early 1970s) to *Small Country Blues* (a book begun in America and unfinished at the time of his death in 1987) illuminates quite a lot about Australian political science in the American century.

AMERICAN INFLUENCE ON AUSTRALIAN SOCIAL AND POLITICAL ANALYSIS

While it is the case that "political science in Australia, as in most other countries, is best thought of as a scholarly development of the years after the Second World War," it is a mistake to ignore the earlier precursors of Australian social sciences.[1] Australia, predominantly a British settler society until the 1940s, modeled its universities on their British counterparts, and (as in Britain) political science was slow to gain a foothold (p. 2). It is nonetheless significant that U.S. influence and U.S. interchange between the wars was to some extent a catalyst for what was to follow. In the first decade after federation, the American Victor Clark was among those foreign observers who came to witness the Australian social experiment and whose lengthy commentary provided a first "take" on Australian national politics. In 1914 R. F. Irvine, professor of economics at the University of Sydney, returned from a tour of North American universities to report on "The Place of Social Sciences in a Modern University"—using as his model American sociology.[2] The first sociological evaluation of Australia was produced in 1918 in Columbia's faculty of political science by an expatriate Australian, C. H. Northcott (who had gone there from Sydney to work with F. H. Giddings) (pp. 49–50). The book claimed as the first comprehensive work on the Australian social condition, Meredith Atkinson et al., *Australia: Economic and Political Studies* (1920), shows the influence of American, as well as British, social theory (p. 52). That American developments were the object of Australian attention is manifest in the careers of Australians such as Elton Mayo, C. H. Northcott, Herbert Heaton, and Griffith Taylor, who left in the 1920s to pursue distinguished careers in America (pp. 60–66). The American Institute for Pacific Relations was to inflect the British empire orientation of the Australian Institute for International Affairs by the injection of Rockefeller Foundation funding for empirical research—with lasting effects on Australian scholarship in international relations.[3] The model for a synthesizing, contemporaneous text on Australia might be thought to be the American C. Hartley Grattan's *Introducing Australia* (1942), commissioned by the Carnegie Corporation—and whose penultimate chapter attempted an overview of "Australian Democracy."

It is important to make these points to counter the received wisdom about Australian political science, which is that "British ways of approaching questions of politics and government were most influential," and influential to the extent that U.S. connections and influences could be ignored.[4] Davies' *Australian Democracy* was not only a description of political institutions but also an analysis of political culture—and the nature of this latter exercise cannot be understood without knowing of the American interwar catalysts and the climate of American political science in the 1950s. Davies' text speaks for its moment: it acknowledges the British stamp on Australian institutions and the American dominance of the present. His determinedly bifocal approach had its impetus in his conviction that "the compelling and organising centres for . . . writing were far distant, and what local work there was limped along discontinuously at their very margin."[5] Thus his mischievous comment:

> Even English and American writing has contributed far more [than local] to our understanding of our own society and politics. We learn about our civil service by reading C. P. Snow, about our intellectuals from Saul Bellow's *Herzog,* about our working class from Lawrence's *Sons and Lovers.* English social criticism of the forties carried us through the fifties, and American social criticism of the fifties carried us through the sixties. (p. 32)

Yet this mordant mood does less than justice to Davies' own pioneering work.

BUREAUCRACY AS A "CIVIC CULTURE"

Davies' *Australian Democracy* efficiently covered the rudiments of federal, state, and local government, legislatures, executive government, the civil service, electorates, and parties. But, more than simple institutional description, Davies' purpose was to uncover a style: "Learning a country's politics is a matter of getting to know the general style in which the 'gates' are 'kept,' the regional differences, and the special methods of initiation, persuasion or decision in each principal department of social life."[6] Davies skillfully synthesized historical influences (the lingering effects of colonial patterns of administration) with pragmatism (the limits of federalism on reform governments) and a sort of Fabian despair about the paralysis of the state. But he was above all concerned to show how particular traits, consistent with the origins of a settler society, dictated "the general style in which the 'gates' are 'kept'": Australians, he said, "have a characteristic talent for bureaucracy" (p. 4).

In this statement Davies was doing two things. First, and on the surface, he was making a claim based on observation. Second, as a careful reading of his book shows, he was bringing together the work of many of his contemporaries—Noel Butlin and A. G. L. Shaw on economic history; Henry Mayer, Don Rawson, and L. F. (Fin) Crisp on parties; R. S. Parker and R. N. Spann on institutions and public administration—and drawing out a pattern to show how a settler society's (and a new federation's) preoccupation with institution building led to a politics and social milieu infused with bureaucratic styles of "gatekeeping." In insisting that the signs of our bureaucratic penchant were all around us, Davies broke with the radical nationalist historians (e.g., Russel Ward) who, at that same time, were claiming a rough and ready improvisational heritage in the pioneer history of the nineteenth century (and, incidentally, again drawing on American models—in this case F. J. Turner's "frontier theory"—to do so).[7] Davies' response was explicit:

> This [talent for bureaucracy] runs counter not only to the archaic and cherished image of ourselves as ungovernable, if not actually, lawless people, but also to our civics of liberalism which accords to bureaucracy only a small and rather shady place. Being a good bureaucrat is, we feel, a bit like being a good forger. But in practice our gift—to be seen *in statu nascendi* at any state school sports—is exercised on a massive scale in government, economy and social institutions. Of course bureaucracy pervades most modern societies—it is the price of complex organisation—but Australian demands for security and equality have been unusually strong.[8]

I well remember a symposium in the late 1970s where another distinguished political scientist complained vehemently that Davies' idiosyncratic assertion lacked any empirical base. This criticism ignores the careful use of the primary work of others in Davies' book and overlooks the implicit reference in the statement above to Weber (on complex organization) and to W. K. Hancock, F. W. Eggleston, and N. G. Butlin (on demands for security and equality). Yet Davies, characteristically, would have fought such objections on the ground of observation—the behavior to be seen at state school sports days! Thirty years later, however, another generation of political historians has vindicated Davies' seemingly impressionistic assertion—see, for instance, Alastair Davidson's *The Invisible State* (1991).

It is Davies' linking of political practice with political culture that is important. *Australian Democracy* has to be read as part of the efflorescence of the postwar intelligentsia and its concern with a national culture. It has to be read, that is, alongside the "Godzone" debates in *Meanjin*, the radical nationalist histories themselves, Serle's mapping of high culture, *From Deserts the Prophets Come* (1973), and the texts of a more self-analytical people: Porter's *Watcher on the Cast Iron Balcony* (1962), Johnston's *My Brother Jack* (1964), Hughes' *The Art of Australia* (1964), Covell's *Australia's Music* (1967), Horne's *The Lucky Country* (1964), Clark's *A History of Australia* (vol. 1, 1964), and so on. But Davies should also be read as a parallel, and a response, to the American interest in social systems and comparative politics. There is no reference in *Australian Democracy* to American social theory—with the exception of a comment on Robert Lane's early work on social attitudes. Given Davies' focus on style, gatekeeping, and attitudes, it is perhaps surprising that there is no explicit reference to, say, David Easton (1953) or the early essays of Gabriel Almond (1956)—on which Davies would later comment.[9] To be fair, the major American works on comparative political cultures would not appear until the mid 1960s.[10] Nonetheless, it is clear that Davies, in *Australian Democracy*, was engaged in an anticipatory exercise in analyzing a civic culture. And, given his lifelong attention to the "far distant . . . compelling and organising centres for . . . writing," there can be little doubt that he was attuned to the climate of American social sciences, and well aware of emerging American debates on civic cultures, as he did so. Indeed, it is difficult to read Davies' final criticism of the depreciation of Australian politics, the professionalization of political activism, and the apathy of the people without being strongly reminded of the arguments of Lane, Lipset, Almond, and Dahl about the relative autonomy of elites and the tide of popular apathy in democratic systems.[11]

POLITICS IN A KNOWLEDGEABLE SOCIETY

As Davies persisted with teasing out the implications of the Australian "talent for bureaucracy," he was drawn more and more to American political and sociological theory. This was most manifest in an essay of the early 1970s, "Politics in a Knowledgeable Society." Asking what happens to democratic politics when specialist knowledge is demanded and bureaucratic dominance is impelled by the complexity of modern organization, Davies looked almost exclusively to American debates—borrowing from Lane (1966) for his title, Wilensky on professionalization (1964) and organizational intelligence (1967), Etzioni on the active society (1968), Hofstadter on anti-intellectualism (1964), Bell on post-ideological politics (1969), and Wright-Mills and Dahl on elitism versus pluralism (1967).[12] Not only, however, was the translation of American theory into the analysis of Australian democracy now explicit but also American society was used as the benchmark: the harbinger of the modern organization of knowledge, and the manifestation of what Australia might become.

Davies, having been, as we have seen, concerned since the late 1950s with "the great grey plain of administrative routine . . . the depreciation of politics *vis-a-vis* administration," now found in American society, and in American social science discourse, a case "for the thesis of a steady evaporation of politics . . . In the policy process, itself, objective or 'knowledge' criteria seem broadly, where they are at odds with political criteria, to have an edge"[13] Davies was addressing the problem of modernism in full flower: "the belief in progress, of which the visible aspect . . . [is] a fundamental change in the 'policy' task of the administration, which is now less concerned with regulating the present than with creating the enabling conditions of the future. The 'future orientation' of public policy is the root cause of the extension of the official information base" (p. 5).

The difficulty this posed for democracy Davies put in this way:

> The knowledgeable society clearly threatens the social spheres fruitfully organisable by the parties or raw political groups in general; it arms the official against the politician; it elevates the professional expert and dispenses with the amateurs, gifted or otherwise. Does it also fatally narrow the participant base of democratic politics? (p. 6)

In surveying the knowledge workers, Davies arrived at a more complex and ambivalent view of bureaucratic specialization. Certainly there were problems: the submission of the specialist not to large organizations but to rationalism itself; regulatory agencies always in competition to keep on top by being more knowledgeable than their clients; oligarchy and centralization in work arrangements; a growing gap between "two cultures: one designed for those who enjoy and seek rapid change, and one designed for those who are made anxious and inadequate by it."[14] And yet there *are* benefits: "a general sharpening of methods of organisational steering: collecting the right information, seeing that it reaches decision-makers, allocating resources more rationally and with better budget and control techniques monitoring the system";[15] the emergence of what Wilensky hailed as the "program professional . . . whose professional competence and commitment are beyond question, but whose commitment to particular programs . . . is just as strong . . . these men [*sic*] . . . constitute an important link between professional culture and civic culture";[16] and even, finally, the possibility that "the new knowledge workers . . . should be more alive to problems and less ideological and power-oriented and they may even be somewhat altruistic (from the long discipline on the way to professional status)."[17] This surely was a more complex and less negative view of what Davies had earlier described as "the bureaucratic mode . . . [which] has invaded private life . . . which becomes increasingly tidy, passionless and 'pre-ended.'"[18] Yet the worry about the evaporation of politics remained, and Davies in his conclusion remarked, "what I do fear is the waste of those whom knowledge politics leaves right out."[19]

SMALL COUNTRY BLUES

In the 1980s Davies returned to his concern with the nature of the Australian polity. The stimulus in part was a stint as Visiting Professor of Australian Studies at Harvard University, where, he said, the first task was to decide "what should be stressed today [when] . . . talking to people in a distant country who want . . . a succinct view of Australian politics?"[20] He subsequently took the readings he had identified as central, and his commentary on them, back into his Australian undergraduate teaching. In a piecemeal way, he began to fashion these materials into a book. There was also a second stimulus: his own dissatisfaction with *Australian Democracy* as a book where institutional description was predominant and political culture was a subtext. He wanted now, a quarter of a century later, to redress the balance: to put ideas and cultural practices at the center in explaining how social formations work.

Davies' introduction to the manuscript, whose working title was *Small Country Blues,* took Lucien Pye's work on China, Burma, and Thailand as examples in "looking for the links between the general culture and the political tradition of the nation" (p. 4). He described his own notion of political culture as

> caught . . . in a couple of metaphors: political culture can be seen as an envelope containing a people and its politics—a large and invisible envelope . . . taken totally for granted; or looked at from the individual outwards, it can be seen as a set of lenses or filters which help one perceive the key meanings in social events and at the same time distorts what one sees in the act of perceiving it. And one can add the final point that . . . different societies will, in the nature of things, have unique political gifts and handicaps. (p. 4)

The manuscript has a valedictory tone: implicitly referring back to the confidently declarative *Australian Democracy,* Davies referred to his present work as

> an asking, not a telling book, as befits an author who has gratefully outgrown the dogmatism and assurance of his youth and can see, as

he cleans out his desk, that with his own chance of finding answers now past, the best he can do is bring one last polish to his questions in the hope that one or two of them will catch the eye of younger workers. (p. 5)

The text was not about Australian institutions but about how observers have interpreted those institutions, with chapters on those he called (borrowing from Brian Fitzpatrick) "the inspectors"—Trollope, Dilke, the Webbs, Metin, Clark, and Bryce—and on historians—Hancock, Hartz, and Emy (with one historical figure, Cobbett, included as indicative of the "common man" temper translated to Australia). Equally, the book was not about politics but about how Australians *learn* their politics, with chapters on childhood socialization and the differentiated learning settings of locality, class, ethnic community, and generation. The book, therefore, had two aims: to show how the "envelope" of political culture had been seen from the outside and to show how it was constructed from within. At the core, however, were two chapters most germane to my purpose here, one crystallizing Davies' thoughts on Australian political culture and another (giving the book its title) on the problems of a "small country."

At the broad level of political culture, "the overarching environment with its lesson that certain things are unthinkable, and certain others go without saying" (p. 57), Davies focused on three themes: the ambiguous regard in which politics is held; Australia's commitment to equality; and the politics of smallness.

In relation to the first theme, Davies surveyed the fluctuation in Australians' regard for political leaders, noting intense interest in the "mobilizing" periods of 1880–1914, 1941–1949, and 1970–1975. He noted, too, that Hancock had long ago said "both that Australians were apt to demand too much of politics, and that they zig-zagged between cynical resignation and mad reforming zeal" (p. 69). While establishing that the "appetite for high politics is intermittent," and there is "irritable uncertainty about [its] worthwhileness," Davies nonetheless pointed out that

> people have a need, deeper than perhaps they know, to attach themselves to a political order, to be incorporated into some sort of national frame that highlights and gives a context to their everyday activities, to defer to and applaud those carrying out the hard tasks at the centre of the institutional system . . . Here, in this vital, central sphere of any society, is where people believe creative and portentous things are done in a way that is characteristic of "us," in accord with "our" special national values and understanding. (pp. 67–68)

Davies was drawing here on Edward Shils.[21] High-definition politics, Davies argued, rarely provided such a center because Australians formed their society without a sense of mission or other worldly justifications [the implicit contrast, surely, is America?], without native historical traditions, and without common religious sentiments. So Australian nationality has habitually been defined in terms of some elusive quality residing in Australians and in the social relations of people in their common dealings.[22]

Where, then, is the center? Despite the state being accorded no more than an instrumental function, Davies reverted again to the "knowledge workers" of the public sector as those holding the center. There had, he said, been "steady, cautious and constant experimentation at what might be called the bureaucratic growing edge." He remarked on the surprising scope of the Australian public sector and the high proportion of public sector employment (compared with America); the relatively free hand given to bureaucrats in running their enterprises; the reliance on experts, rather than ministers, leading to some senior officials being better known than their political masters; a high level of bureaucratic innovation; and a pattern of resort to bureaucratic initiative when parties are deadlocked or have run out of ideas. Yet Australian bureaucrats, he suggested, have managed to keep the state off a pedestal: They have "a conscious gift for the democratic style of administration, making it look as if a consensus directs things . . . tempering bureaucracy with a personal modesty of style. . . [I]ts very familiarity and pervasiveness must also work to keep [the state] unpretentious."[23] Clearly Davies had reverted to his insistence of twenty-five years earlier on the characteristic talent of Australians for bureaucracy. Yet this is a considerably more positive picture than that earlier image of bureaucracy as a stain, invading even private life.

Turning to the commitment to equality as a leading trait in the political culture, Davies reviewed both historical records and contemporary research to demonstrate the importance of the ethic of "a fair go." But how, he asked, might we distinguish this trait from the American "belief in equality"? The distinction, he suggested, was that while in the United States there is greater emphasis on and practice of equal citizen rights, in Australia there is greater uneasiness about inequality of life chances. So Australians have devoted their energies to equalizing projects. Taking four instances—the relative distribution of income; the mediation of the balance of advantage between different economic groups; the regional equalization achieved through federal programs; and the near universalization of educational access and standards—Davies demonstrated the commitment to equality in play. Further, he sought to show that the achievements of relative equality, and hence of social integration, had been delivered by the bureaucratic order responding to the commonly shared belief that it is "the Government's responsibility to make sure everyone has a good standard of living" (pp. 58–66).

At last, one might have thought, the characteristic of "the knowledgeable society" and of the Australian "talent for bureaucracy" had come fruitfully together—until, that is, one understood one further feature: "the politics of smallness." This section of Davies' argument, the only part of the uncompleted manuscript to have been published, as an article entitled "Small Country Blues," was about the effects of scale on politics. America, with its size and complexity, was the backdrop. In comparison, "small countries [like Australia] blot out the recognition that their society lacks differentiations, complexities and competencies vital to the functioning of major powers . . . refus[e] to contemplate an external society richer in any detail than the known small world."[24]

Davies made four points in elaboration. "First," he said, " . . . a small social system implies a strained and probably under-equipped elite." The knowledgeable society, whatever its size, must fill out a complex system of leading roles. The intense competition for such roles in large societies is replaced in the small by "unfenced ambition," self-nomination, posts filled by overpromotion or very approximate fit. "A second source of small country discomfort lies in the imbalance and tension between imported and local ideas." The ritual jousting between cultural "importers" and "protectionists," of which he provided instances, manifested "chronic and painful doubt about the achievable quality of life in the small country." Third, however, small countries may have a better chance of solving their problems: the scale and cost even of radical solutions may not be prohibitive. In contrast, the average nation-state, as Daniel Bell had remarked, "has become too small for the big problems of life and too big for the small problems of life . . . The problem, sociologically, for the end of this century and the beginning of the next, is the matching of scales."[25] Fourth, the converse of the third hypothesis, small countries may prove more vulnerable to small shocks (especially demographic change).

> Field by field, the discomforts and tensions . . . demand individual mapping. In politics, for example, the desired local quotient is high in the first place, foreign models and novel expedients quite accessible, most skills not marketable abroad, and the national sphere fairly comfortably contains ambitions. In science, technology and business the portentous knowledge tends to be severely metropolitanised—work at very advanced levels of skill is simply not done at the periphery . . . While many in arts and humanities still look to England, the social sciences are now thoroughly Americanised . . . complaints of . . . the difficulty of contributing from the periphery to international colloquy are . . . common. (p. 246)

I take Davies in the end to be saying that "the knowledgeable society" cannot be fully achieved in Australia because of the problem of scale, but that the jousting within our political culture is shaped in part by denial: denial that our elites are overstretched; denial that we are in fact at the periphery. Here, then, is where the "talent for bureaucracy" reaches its limit: with a limit on the pool of talent, with denial of scale and complexity and with a preoccupation with "the politics of being central" in a small society.[26] Behind it all is a sense of American scale and complexity as the proper benchmark.

My purpose in this discussion to date has been less with whether Davies was right or wrong than with teasing out not only his increasing resort to American social theory but also the implicit use of America as comparator and benchmark in his thinking about Australian democracy. This is a case study of how reflection on America has informed reflection on Australia. But let me remind you of the contours of his argument before returning to one or two of his questions and asking how we would answer them in the decade since *Small Country Blues*.

A constant in Davies' thinking was that the Australian "talent for bureaucracy" explained much about our politics. At first this was for him a point of criticism: politics, indeed *Australian Democracy* itself, being vitiated by administration. Yet his attitude gradually changed. When, in the 1970s, his analysis turned to what would be required for "the knowledgeable society"—an essay deeply influenced by American social theory of the time—the systematic approach of "knowledge politics" to problem solving gave a new resonance to a facility for complex organization. Granted, there were still major problems: not only the way specialization might erode the participant base of democratic decision making but also the way "political criteria" might be swept aside when at odds with "knowledge criteria." By the 1980s the bureaucratic talent was applauded not only as the means of delivering on core values (such as equality) and a source of innovation when parties become deadlocked or dry up but also as the talent that held the center, that shaped how the "portentous tasks" were done. Yet here, he argued, we might nonetheless be defeated by the politics of scale—left bickering over imported ideas (and irrelevant fashions); at the mercy of ill-equipped, thinly stretched, and overpromoted elites; and unable, finally, to realize "the knowledgeable society." As this discussion developed, Davies' writings within themselves manifested what he described as the "Americanization" of the social sciences—though he never lost sight of the Australian evidence, of the contemporaneous work of his local peers, nor of the insights of "the inspectors." In the end, however, the "small country blues" thesis makes sense only in terms of a dialogue between Australian experience and American benchmarking.

SMALL COUNTRY BLUES: TEN YEARS ON

Looking again at Davies' concerns, ten years later, how have his observations weathered the changes? He did not, I think, fully foresee the force of the Anglo-American preoccupation with liberal internationalism and its impact on Australia. But his concerns with the way specialism would erode the participant base of democracy and "knowledge criteria" would override "political criteria" have been borne out. And the metaphor, "small country blues," goes some way to explaining why there were no critical barriers to those Anglo-American versions of market fundamentalism that would—in the name of small government—erode the "talent for bureaucracy," and with it the capacity for innovative programs to equalize life chances.

Davies was, I think, right in his overall depiction of the small-country dynamic, but wrong about the element of denial which, he suggested, pushed Australians toward an illusion of "completeness." The sense of conscious vulnerability has been very much what the Australian importers of ideas have traded on. Our political elites have told us for a hundred years that we are a slumberous, inward-looking nation, inattentive to the imperatives visited on us from abroad. Thus, as I have recently argued, we are always entreated to be alert to the imperatives defined by "the great elsewhere."[27] The politics of the 1980s cohered around the message voiced by Prime Minister Bob Hawke in this way: "If the world decides it does not trust you, then it can ruin you."[28]

The ground for politics since Davies' final work appears to have been that articulated in the early 1990s by Francis Fukuyama. He argued that the ineluctable triumph of liberal economics (which he claimed to be self-evident and internationally recognized) had put an end to the dialogue (and conflict) between different ideologies which had constituted modern history. History is therefore at an end, and the mobilizing ideas that had fueled past politics will wither away: "idealism will be replaced by economic calculation, the endless solving of technical problems . . . there will be neither art nor philosophy, just the perpetual caretaking of the museum of human history."[29] Social interaction is reduced to economic interaction and politics thus reduces to disputes about management. Fukuyama's thesis about the homogenizing effects of the international free market seems at odds with the new forms of conflict and fragmentation (often fueling local wars) characteristic of the post–Cold War order. This might explain why—though fashionably prominent and widely quoted between 1989 and 1992—his visibility was relatively brief. Yet his underlying contention remains strongly alive, particularly in the Australian mass media where politics is still reduced almost entirely to the discussion of economic management and the impediments local policy might introduce into the beneficial spread of the international free market. When economists themselves recant (like Fred Argy) or take a critical position (like John Nevile)—suggesting that implementing the deregulatory liberal order in Australia has had adverse effects on social equity, income distribution, and community sovereignty—the only response is that any other option is unthinkable. So strong is the grip of this mindset, that important books suggesting that other options are of course think-able—Emy (1993) on the social market, Langmore and Quiggin (1994) on work for all, Stretton and Orchard (1994) on the state's capacities, for instance—have had nothing like the critical notice and discussion they deserve. They cannot be admitted to an agenda shaped by the conviction that: "in the universal homogeneous state, all prior contradictions are resolved and all human needs are satisfied . . . what remains is primarily economic activity."[30]

There have, of course, been other national approaches to the challenges of economic globalization. The Asian "economic miracle" (dependent on state interventions) and the persistence of welfare regimes within European economies showed the potential for managed capitalism rather than market fundamentalism, even within a globalizing context. Such lessons were ignored in Australia, showing the dominance of the Anglo-American mind-set. But what happened was also a playing out of the way "knowledge criteria" overrode "political criteria"—and economic knowledge was all that counted.

In the 1970s politicians in all the market capitalist societies (but especially in the settler societies like Australia whose economies were already highly dependent on world markets) confronted the effects of high modernity without understanding its causes. People experienced an almost intolerable increase in the pace of change, with the ability of transnational business and finance to generate movements of capital, resources, and peoples across national boundaries without regard for intranational sensibilities. Political leaders saw the effects of the rapid circulation of capital eroding the ability of the state to control the nation's affairs. What they understood to be happening was that state agencies themselves were failing: *this* was the "crisis of the state." The people expected political remedies for their dislocation, economic uncertainty, and suffering: the politicians became convinced that the old solutions no longer worked. It is significant for my story here that, in Australia, the Chicago School (rather than, say, the London School of Economics) was seen as the repository of new wisdom. But let's be clear, economic rationalism flourished, because it fulfilled three essential purposes. It explained that dislocation was an aftereffect of the old order, the price that had to be paid for inappropriate state activities. It justified the processes of internationalization. And it allowed politicians to disclaim responsibility for what happened: it was a rationale for divestiture of state responsibilities ("the market" would solve what politicians had been unable to).

Once committed to this techno-specialism, politicians became more and more prey to their advisors, and less reliant on their parties, the grass roots, or the community, none of whom could be expected to understand "the economy." Often, by eliding market and society, they lost the ability to conceptualize the community: as one Australian leader, John Hewson, graphically showed in 1993, they lost the sense of who to address, or how.

Was this not precisely what Davies had feared as the downside of "the knowledgeable society"? Belief in applied knowledge has stimulated an increasing resort to specialists who speak not from their knowledge of the community or of politics, but from their expertise. The "program professionals" have been drawn into the center, with perceptible effects on the public culture. In part, "experts" have been drawn in by the pressure on politicians to appear attuned to the complex intellectual demands of the modern world. Informal practices by leaders of creating "private office" families for personal support have everywhere become institutionalized.[31] This was only one face of the resort to specialist advice. In Australia the public service more broadly was transformed in the 1980s to promote managerial and economic efficiency and in ways that accentuated the particular intellectual agenda sketched above.[32] Suddenly people with narrow specialisms had considerable sway, not just at the ministers' sides, but in the public service generally. The specialisms most frequently favored were management and economics.

A process that commenced with informal networks has ended with the dominance of institutionalized, in-house, technical specialists. The needs for informed decision making and for specialist skills in a modern polity are clear. But when every political problem is seen as demanding a technical solution, the shortcomings become evident. Instead of listening to the community and attempting to respond to its needs, political leaders swing to telling the community what it should have or do. In Australia the swing, increasingly, away from persuasion—Robert Menzies' call to the "forgotten people," Gough Whitlam's call to the "men and women of Australia"—to prescription—Paul Keating perhaps most famously on the "recession we had to have"—in modern political rhetoric has been remarkable.

It's not that politicians have been at the mercy of their advisors. Rather, it has been a symbiotic process, where politicians who are too caught up in the exigencies of combat politics to devise solutions have been provided with ready-made answers by the dominant American intellectual movement of the day. That this is a moment when everything is seen to hinge on a specialist form of economic knowledge, and one apparently devoid of any sense of history or of the collective interest, reveals the potential shortcoming of the intellectuals. They can be too specialized, too much the creatures of their context and their political masters, incapable of taking the long view.

Paradoxically, the Australian talent for "experimentation at . . . the bureaucratic growing edge" has been lost in this process. In part, it has been because the new "program professionals" themselves have been wedded to market rather than state solutions: they have been involved in winding back (rather than defending) the public sector. In part it is because the new specialists do not have the gift of old-order Australian bureaucrats: the "gift for the democratic style of administration." So, as Davies feared, the participant base of democracy has been eroded.

On one side there is deep disquiet and corrosive cynicism about Australian politics.[33] On the other, those who have been left out by the "knowledge elites," those who "are made anxious and inadequate" by change, are prey to extremist nonsense—and so fringe groups who are against liberal society and, above all, opposed to received knowledge, emerge to "explain" the world in a different way. Will the Australian propensity, noted by Hancock and Davies, to zigzag from "cynical resignation" to "mad reforming zeal" save us this time?

Notes

1. D. Aitkin, "Political Science in Australia: Development and Situation," in *Surveys of Australian Political Science,* D. Aitkin, ed. (Sydney: Allen & Unwin, 1985), 1, 2.

2. H. Bourke, "Social Scientists as Intellectuals: From the First World War to the Depression," in *Intellectual Movements and Australian Society,* ed. B. Head and J. Walter (Melbourne: Oxford University Press, 1988), 48.

3. S. Alomes, "Intellectuals as Publicists, 1920s to 1940s," in *Intellectual Movements and Australian Society,* ed. B. Head and J. Walter (Melbourne: Oxford University Press, 1988), 81.

4. Aitkin, "Political Science in Australia," 4.

5. A. F. Davies, *Essays in Political Sociology* (Melbourne: Cheshire, 1972), 33.

6. A. F. Davies, *Australian Democracy: An Introduction to the Political System,* 2nd ed. (Croydon: Longmans, 1964), 4.

7. R. Ward, *The Australian Legend* (Melbourne: Oxford University Press, 1958), 238–269.

8. Davies, *Australian Democracy,* 4–5.

9. See Davies, *Essays in Political Sociology.*

10. G. Almond and S. Verba, *The Civic Culture* (Princeton, N.J.: Princeton University Press, 1963), and L. W. Pye and S. Verba, *Political Culture and Political Development* (Princeton, N. J.: Princeton University Press, 1965).

11. Davies, *Australian Democracy,* 139–142.

12. A. F. Davies and S. Encel, "Politics," in *Australian Society: A Sociological Introduction,* ed. A. F. Davies and S. Encel (Melbourne: Longman Cheshire, 1965), 96–113; Davies, *Essays in Political Sociology,* 3–20; W. E. Connolly, *Political Science and Ideology* (New York: Atherton Press, 1967), 21–50.

13. Davies, *Australian Democracy,* 142; Davies, *Essays in Political Sociology,* 3.

14. D. N. Michael, *The Unprepared Society* (New York: Basic Books, 1968), 26.

15. Davies, *Essays in Political Sociology,* 12.
16. H. L. Wilensky, "The Professionalization of Everyone?," *American Journal of Sociology* (1964): 158.
17. Davies, *Essays in Political Sociology,* 20.
18. Davies, *Australian Democracy,* 142.
19. Davies, *Essays in Political Sociology,* 20.
20. A. F. Davies, *Small Country Blues,* unpublished manuscript, 163 pages, n.d., 58.
21. E. Shils, *Center and Periphery: Essays in Macrosociology* (Chicago: University of Chicago Press, 1975).
22. Davies, *Small Country Blues,* n.d., 70–71; and see G. Nadel, *Australia's Colonial Culture* (Cambridge, Mass.: Harvard University Press, 1957).
23. Davies, *Small Country Blues,* n.d., 69–70.
24. A. F. Davies, "Small Country Blues," *Meanjin* 44, no. 2 (1985): 243–252.
25. Quoted in Davies, "Small Country Blues," 246.
26. See A. F. Davies, "The Politics of Being Central," *Island Magazine* 28 (1986): 24–35.
27. J. Walter, *Tunnel Vision: The Failure of Political Imagination* (Sydney: Allen & Unwin, 1996), chap. 3.
28. R. J. L. Hawke, *The Hawke Memoirs* (Melbourne: Heinemann, 1994), 175.
29. F. Fukuyama, *The End of History and the Last Man* (London: Penguin, 1992), 23, 24–25.
30. F. Fukuyama, "The End of History," *Quadrant* 34, no. 8 (1989): 16.
31. J. Walter, *The Ministers' Minders: Personal Advisers in National Government* (Melbourne: Oxford University Press, 1986).
32. J. Walter, "Prime Ministers and Their Staff," in *Menzies to Keating: The Development of the Australian Prime Ministership,* P. Weller, ed. (Melbourne: Melbourne University Press, 1992), 28–63.
33. H. Mackay, *Reinventing Australia: The Mind and Mood of Australia in the '90s* (Sydney: Angus & Robertson, 1993).

References

Aitkin, D. "Political Science in Australia: Development and Situation." In *Surveys of Australian Political Science.* Edited by D. Aitkin. Sydney: Allen & Unwin, 1985, 1–35.

Almond, G. "Comparative Political Systems." *Journal of Politics* 18, no. 3 (1956): 391–409.

Almond, G., and S. Verba. *The Civic Culture.* Princeton, N.J.: Princeton University Press, 1963.

Alomes, S. "Intellectuals as Publicists, 1920s to 1940s." In *Intellectual Movements and Australian Society.* Edited by B. Head and J. Walter. Melbourne: Oxford University Press, 1988, 70–87.

Atkinson, M., ed. *Australia: Economic and Political Studies.* Melbourne: Macmillan, 1920.

Bell, D., ed. *Towards the Year 2000*. Boston: Beacon Press, 1969.

Bourke, H. "Social Scientists as Intellectuals: From the First World War to the Depression." In *Intellectual Movements and Australian Society*. Edited by B. Head and J. Walter. Melbourne: Oxford University Press, 1988, 47–69.

Connolly, W. E. *Political Science and Ideology*. New York: Atherton Press, 1967.

Davidson, A. *The Invisible State*. Melbourne: Cambridge University Press, 1991.

Davies, A. F. *Australian Democracy: An Introduction to the Political System*. 2d ed. Croydon: Longmans, 1964.

———. *Essays in Political Sociology*. Melbourne: Cheshire, 1972.

———. "The Politics of Being Central." *Island Magazine* 28 (1986): 24–35.

———. "Small Country Blues." *Meanjin* 44, no. 2 (1985): 243–252.

———. *Small Country Blues*. Unpublished manuscript, 163 pages. n.d.

Davies, A. F., and S. Encel. "Politics." In *Australian Society: A Sociological Introduction*. Edited by A. F. Davies and S. Encel. Melbourne: Cheshire, 1965, 96–113.

Easton, D. *The Political System*. New York: Knopf, 1953.

Emy, H. *Remaking Australia: The State, the Market, and Australia's Future*. Sydney: Allen & Unwin, 1993.

Etzioni, A. *The Active Society*. New York: Collier-Macmillan, 1968.

Fukuyama, F. "The End of History." *Quadrant* 34, no. 8 (1989): 15–25.

———. *The End of History and the Last Man*. London: Penguin, 1992.

Grattan, C. H. *Introducing Australia*. 1st Australian ed., 1944. Sydney: Angus & Robertson, 1942.

Hawke, R. J. L. *The Hawke Memoirs*. Melbourne: Heinemann, 1994.

Hofstadter, R. *Anti-intellectualism in American Life*. London: Jonathan Cape, 1964.

Lane, R. E. "The Decline of Politics and Ideology in a Knowledgeable Society," *American Sociological Review* (1966): 249–262.

Langmore, J., and J. Quiggin. *Work For All: Full Employment in the Nineties*. Melbourne: Melbourne University Press, 1994.

Mackay, H. *Reinventing Australia: The Mind and Mood of Australia in the 90s*. Sydney: Angus & Robertson, 1993.

Michael, D. N. *The Unprepared Society*. New York: Basic Books, 1968.

Nadel, G. *Australia's Colonial Culture*. Cambridge, Mass.: Harvard University Press, 1957.

Pye, L. W., and S. Verba. *Political Culture and Political Development*. Princeton, N.J.: Princeton University Press, 1965.

Serle, G. *From Deserts the Prophets Come*. Melbourne: Heinemann, 1973.

Shils, E. *Center and Periphery: Essays in Macrosociology*. Chicago: University of Chicago Press, 1975.

Stretton, H., and L. Orchard. *Public Goods, Public Enterprise, Public Choice: Theoretical Foundations of the Contemporary Attack on Government*. London and New York: St. Martins Press, 1994.

Walter, J. *The Ministers' Minders: Personal Advisers in National Government*. Melbourne: Oxford University Press, 1986.

————. "Prime Ministers and Their Staff." In *Menzies to Keating: The Development of the Australian Prime Ministership.* Edited by P. Weller. Melbourne: Melbourne University Press, 1992, 28–63.

————. *Tunnel Vision: The Failure of Political Imagination.* Sydney: Allen & Unwin, 1996.

Ward, R. *The Australian Legend.* Melbourne: Oxford University Press, 1958.

Wilensky, H. L. *Organizational Intelligence: Knowledge and Policy in Government and Industry.* New York: Basic Books, 1967.

————. "The Professionalization of Everyone?" *American Journal of Sociology* (1964): 137–158.

CHAPTER

14

Civilizing Capitalism? Game Over, Insert Coins

PETER BEILHARZ, LA TROBE UNIVERSITY

*T*HE WORLD CHANGED, according to Virginia Woolf, in or around December 1910. Probably she only half meant it, for the impact of aesthetic modernism on a highly traditionalistic culture was as likely remarkable as it was marginal. Leonard Woolf, more hedgehog than fox, for his part put it differently; the world changed irrevocably with the Great War. Karl Marx, in a different setting, warned us earlier, in 1848, that change was our fate; in the beginning was change, and we moderns were doomed to be the sorcerer's apprentices, fated to start more than we could possibly finish. More recently, Eric Hobsbawm, like many others, has taken Leonard Woolf's cue, locating the great change in 1914 or more precisely in 1917, and opening a new, colder, global epoch with the fall of the Berlin Wall in 1989.[1] We are only just leaving the world of the shadows of 1914, and all its consequent symbols and markers, 1917, 1929, 1933, 1939, 1941, the long boom, the rise and fall of capitalism's Golden Age and its concomitant age of reform.

Hobsbawm's short twentieth century is the history of the October Revolution and its effects. This is a significant view, but it is also one that is highly particularistic, because autobiographical; and it is perhaps more evocative read globally than it is in terms of domestic social policy and cultural life within developed capitalist countries. The younger historian Donald Sassoon suggests a distinct temporality and a different orientation in his monumental study, *One Hundred Years of Socialism,* echoing Garcia Marquez; as though one hundred years of solitude now stand before us. Sassoon's neat century opens in 1889 with the formation of the Second International and closes with the collapse of communism into 1989.[2] Sassoon's curiosity is closer to my own, in books like *Transforming Labor* and *Postmodern Socialism.* For the "West," for Europe, North America, and its annexes, the twentieth century was in this view perhaps less emphatically the century of communism than it was the century of capitalism and social democracy. What has changed today is the uncoupling of this century-long relationship of master and slave, where socialism was a perpetual if subordinate presence in modernity.

The terms of reference themselves are not new, but the sense of epochal shift or transformation is. In 1938 Joseph Schumpeter was regretfully awaiting the internal socialization of capitalism or even its cultural implosion via the forces he, following Marx, called "creative destruction." In 1949 T. H. Marshall viewed the struggle between power and democracy as even, at best. By the 1980s we are witness to the extraordinary sea change in which this project of civilizing and socializing capitalism comes unstuck.[3]

My own sense of chronology here is a little looser than that of Hobsbawm or Sassoon. My sense is that we have inhabited a century of more or less liberal or social democratic consensus, which opened discernibly into the 1880s and closed into the 1980s. Obviously the idea of consensus is difficult, for it is variously contested and subject to shifts and changes, and in some places or regions it never really bites at all. My claim, however, is that the idea of national, reforming politics acted as the key informing project for industrializing countries from Mexico and Brazil to Australia and Canada and elsewhere.[4] As Sassoon observes, and to amplify, the impossible model for industrializing or modernizing countries was modernity as Americanism; more explicitly, the imaginary ideal throughout Western Europe became something like an American base and a Swedish superstructure. The politics of national modernization, civics in mass education, the formation of a national culture and literature, and import-substitution and protection in economics became the received utopia of modern, and modernist, aspirants.

There were some Australian peculiarities in this process, though they also seem to echo through the experience of South America more than North America. Australia in effect developed a kind of capitalist culture without much of an industrial capitalist economic structure to hold it up. We acquired a culture where somehow in the cities at least consumption seemed to rule over production. Now Marx, of course, knew about Australia, and even wheeled us into the final chapter of *Das Kapital,* though the apocryphal story is that this was a device to mislead the censors. But what would he have made of this uneven development? A national experience by no means peculiar in the South American context, where the superstructure somehow drove the base rather than the other way around? Imaginably Marx, in good company with generations of other old Europeans, would have put this down to the absurdity of our location—topsy-turvy, upside down.

The consequences are more serious than this line of speculation might suggest. As Jack Lindsay cryptically expressed it, ours became a bourgeois culture without a bourgeoisie, without the virile modernizing elite which so impressed culture and economy elsewhere.[5] Entrepreneurial culture came late. Ours was a statist culture. Where a middle class prospered it was arguably a state-located or related middle class (folks like us), for here the state was pri-

mordial if less than gelatinous. The labor movement was arguably the dominant class actor across Australian culture into this period, and its ethos was
laborist and often rural rather than aggressively modernizing in the way, say,
that the French labor movement's was. One consequence of these peculiarities of Australia's formation is that intellectual life and criticism has until
recently been dominated not directly by labor intellectuals so much as by the
left intelligentsia who have behaved as though they were the natural representatives of the labor movement.

This constellation of forces raises some interpretative puzzles of considerable difficulty, partly because in Australia as elsewhere the sociology of
intellectuals has largely remained a field of embarrassed silence. No surprise
that it was East Europeans like Ivan Szelenyi who revived the old fear anticipated by Machajski, that Socialism inter alia could be a mask for the intellectuals on their road to power in worlds where the bourgeoisie did not
reign.[6] In imagining themselves as organic intellectuals or representatives of
the labor movement, various leading Australian figures, including potentially Bob Connell and Terry Irving in *Class Structure in Australian History,* have
argued as though Australian capitalism essentially reflects Marx's two-class
model; as though there is no middle class.[7] I want to suggest to the contrary
that, by virtue of its statist imperial heritage and its late industrial revolution
after World War II, modern Australian history has largely been coordinated
by a state middle class that is now under threat of extinction.

How could this be so? My postulated century of liberal-labor consensus
is perhaps more clear in Australia (or in New Zealand) than elsewhere,
though it is also plainly dependent on, and derivative of, the British experience in civilizing capitalism. On a transnational scale of comparison, the
1880s result in the formation of the Second International, Chamberlain's
Radical Program, the ALP and Rerum Novarum, various responses to the
Fabian impulse which picks up on the often Christian imperative to reform,
driven by the Statistical Societies and others from the 1830s on.[8] The
Fabians turned the procedure implicit here into a theorem: research, measure, and agitate, privately or publicly; then legislate. The first Fabian
Society pamphlet of 1884, *Why Are the Many Poor?* was an ambit claim that
this problem could be solved following the procedure that the theorem indicated. This impulse is evident then from the Blue Books through the 1911
National Health Insurance Act and the Beveridge Report, which confirmed
the British Welfare State; in Australia its expiring breath is in the delivery of
the Henderson Commission of Inquiry into Poverty in 1975.

The post–World War II period is important not only because
reformism becomes established. It also seeds the beginning of the end for
communism. Polycentrism, the recovery of national roads to socialism, in
effect feeds radical forces back into social democracy, for Social
Democracy rules. In Australia, as elsewhere, the Communist Party collaps-

es back into the Labor mainstream five years before the fall of the Wall. The larger theme is apparent. Across the period, say 1880–1980, there spread a commonsense that capitalism generated social problems or economic dysfunctions which could be and ought to be solved politically. For the political actors and social critics of the late nineteenth century, the Social Question was emphatically a question; it had an answer. Socialism or social reformism was the answer to the Social Question, even if the latter was best conceived as an ongoing process with a conditional, incremental, civilizing answer. In our own times, in comparison, social problems have become phenomena which bewilder us, beyond comprehension let alone resolution. This is the sea change. The sense that capitalism could be and ought to be civilized is going, or gone; we are left with a different message, that it is in fact capitalism which civilizes, again in the classical sense; that civilization depends on violence and inequality. Civilization is again seen less as our task, more as something which an economic dynamic generates or does to us (or at least to others).

The problem about economic globalization is that it is effectively an attack on social democracy. Social democracy is a national project, a nation-building tradition; citizenship and rights, identity formation, and belonging, remain primarily national. Cultural globalization, inasmuch as we can make the distinction between cultural and economic globalization, is a process that most of us would celebrate. Economic globalization is less easy to celebrate, unless we presume that it now solely motivates the civilizing process. For modern Australia has always been involved in cultural globalization, indeed, as Bernard Smith has shown, it was established in that process, and the cultural traffic, which proceeds across the Atlantic, Pacific, and Indian Oceans, has arguably made us incomparably richer in cultural terms.[9] But if the state-based middle class has sponsored the civilizing process in places like the antipodes, this is also why we now hear strident or else mournful responses to globalization and its political embrace by Australian politicians and opinion makers.

What we are departing from is a century where middle-class actors have been privileged or have privileged themselves, where the pursuit of nation-building has advantaged us over others. Globalization, in comparison, is authorized by a newly emerging middle class, a culturally and geographically mobile middle class with less national loyalty than the civil service or local intellectual traditions once had. Robert Reich's great contribution in *The Work of Nations* in this regard is to proclaim this point, to revive thereby indirectly both the ailing sociology of intellectuals and the even more desperate sociology of the middle classes, to open up again those central yet marginalized areas of self-reflection bracketed out by years of habitual social ventriloquism, where we act for others as though we are them, as though it were exclusively and selflessly the interests of others—the workers, the downtrodden, the weak and oppressed—that we represent. For the state middle class, the "symbolic analysts," in Reich's language, represent a particular interest as a general one and deny their own interests in the process.[10]

My claim, then, is that we face several anomalies concerning the representation of the modern Australian experience. We face relatively uninvestigated or undertheorized phenomena such as a bourgeoisie small and culturally conservative or quiescent, a working-class movement together with its invisible middle-class representatives, the latter working in and around the state (and now increasingly the media, for "public" intellectuals are in fact "media" intellectuals), and we confront a relation of social ventriloquism between this middle class and its others—and it is this assemblage or historic compromise that is under threat of extinction in the face of globalization. What we face is an experience now decadent, yet never quite fully bourgeois. Ours is not a torn country; it is a hybrid culture, or better, a culture formed in traffic which is now, as ever, in transition.

So now, finally, we face the end of the century; *fin-de-siècle;* end of the millennium as well as the end of history; the end of Labor in Australia?; the end of communism in Eastern Europe and of reformism globally. Endism rules. What we are seeking to make sense of is more modest than this; what we puzzle over is the end of the world as we have known it, the failure of political imagination—as we have known it. The new world, the new century, rests on both a cultural and a structural shift, the extent of which is yet to become clear. In this context, the liberal intelligentsia has lost or is losing its influence, because its voice is local and its vocabulary is dead or dying. Of course there are other voices, born-again Durkheimians like George Soros, liberals and communitarians arguing elsewhere, and these may become more influential rather than less with the passing of time, into the new epoch. In the meantime the risk is that, as was the case in Australia under Whitlam, the left intelligentsia will disappear into a politics of resentment against a world too stupid to heed its admonitions.

Globalization comes together with the postmodern, together with senses of increasing speed, fragmentation, and uncertainty about what can be known let alone what might be done. Further shifts of power into media seem to confirm longer-term trends to the economization of politics. In this setting, it is not so much a matter of "if it ain't broke, don't fix it" as it is one of the erosion of the capacity to distinguish what works and what doesn't. What, for example, is a city that "don't work"? The late-twentieth-century answer to this kind of question is likely to be rather different to that offered a century ago. This is the change we encounter.

The argument I have put forth in *Transforming Labor* is that ultimately Keating lost the measure of a fine task, that of balancing tradition and modernity. Labor's success in 1983–1996 was in this sense Pyrrhic. My conclusion in *Postmodern Socialism*, which in a sense is a global, second-order reflection on the same phenomena, is that we now rediscover the under-world, sometimes literally under our cities, more often on their edges or physical extremities.[11] Globalization is also a dualization of the world. As we remain closed into relations of domination, so was socialism held together in tension with capitalism. The capitalist Prometheus would not be bound, but could not be unbound. This story is not over. Residual components of the reform project remain intact and evident in urban culture. The problem here, as I see it, is that once the will to reform revives, its funding or tax base will have disappeared into distant data banks. It is not the case that the reform-ing imagination is lost forever; the problem is rather that the conditions of its reconstruction into the new century will raise challenges hitherto beyond us.

So where might this leave us? The intellectual tasks and challenges to imagination are abundant. They include revaluation of the old world we are departing, for one issue here, begot of nostalgia, is that, having denied its cultural and economic achievements by radical criteria through the seven-ties, the temptation now is for intellectuals to overvalue what was achieved from Menzies to Whitlam. Yet if we lost opportunities, opportunities they nevertheless were, and they need to be revalued. In revaluing old worlds, we need also, I think, to remain open to new worlds. Australian intellectuals, in my mind, need to rediscover the experience of Spanish-American modern-ity which is also such an apparent current in the experience of the United States. If we encounter modernity as the relentless imperatives of change, then we also negotiate traditions and anticipations of the future as we con-struct senses of the present. If we encounter history as the inextricable com-bination of gains and losses, if we encounter modernity as the ambivalence which is us, then the prospect of the new century is as promising as it is threatening. Civilizing capitalism? The game is not over, not yet, even if the rules are changing, and, like Hegel, we need some distance to allow the swirl to settle before we begin to think modernity anew.

Notes

1. Eric Hobsbawm, *Age of Extremes* (London: Michael Joseph, 1994).
2. Donald Sassoon, *One Hundred Years of Socialism* (London: Tauris, 1996).
3. J. A. Schumpeter, *Capitalism, Socialism, and Democracy* (London: Allen & Unwin, 1943); T. H. Marshall, *Citizenship and Social Class* (Cambridge: Cambridge University Press, 1950).
4. P. McMichael, *Development and Social Change* (Thousand Oaks, Calif.: Pine Forge, 1996).
5. Jack Lindsay, *Life Rarely Tells* (Ringwood: Penguin, 1982).
6. George Konrad and Ivan Szelenyi, *The Intellectuals on the Road to Class Power* (Brighton: Harvester, 1979).

7. R. W. Connell and Terry. Irving, *Class Structure in Australian History* (Melbourne: Longman, 1988); Peter Beilharz, "Theorizing the Middle Class," *Arena* 72 (1985).

8. Peter Beilharz, *Labour's Utopias—Bolshevism, Fabianism, Social Democracy* (New York: Routledge, 1992).

9. Peter Beilharz, *Imagining the Antipodes—Culture, Theory, and the Visual in the Work of Bernard Smith* (Melbourne: Cambridge University Press, 1997).

10. Robert Reich, *The Work of Nations* (New York: Vintage, 1992).

11. Peter Beilharz, *Transforming Labour—Labour Tradition and the Labour Decade in Australia* (Melbourne: Cambridge University Press, 1994); Peter Beilharz, *Postmodern Socialism—Romanticism, City, and State* (Melbourne: Melbourne University Press, 1994).

References

Beilharz, Peter. *Imagining the Antipodes—Culture, Theory, and the Visual in the Work of Bernard Smith.* Melbourne: Cambridge University Press, 1997.

———. *Labour's Utopias—Bolshevism, Fabianism, Social Democracy.* New York: Routledge, 1992.

———. *Postmodern Socialism—Romanticism, City, and State.* Melbourne: Melbourne University Press, 1994.

———. "Theorizing the Middle Class." *Arena* 72 (1985).

———. *Transforming Labour—Labour Tradition and the Labour Decade in Australia.* Melbourne: Cambridge University Press, 1994.

Connell, R. W., and Terry Irving. *Class Structure in Australian History.* Melbourne: Longman, 1988.

Hobsbawm, Eric. *Age of Extremes.* London: Michael Joseph, 1994.

Konrad, George, and Ivan Szelenyi. *The Intellectuals on the Road to Class Power.* Brighton: Harvester, 1979.

Lindsay, Jack. *Life Rarely Tells.* Ringwood: Penguin, 1982.

McMichael, P. *Development and Social Change.* Thousand Oaks, Calif.: Pine Forge, 1996.

Marshall, T. H. *Citizenship and Social Class.* Cambridge: Cambridge University Press, 1950.

Reich, Robert. *The Work of Nations.* New York: Vintage, 1992.

Sassoon, Donald. *One Hundred Years of Socialism.* London: Tauris, 1996.

Schumpeter, J. A. *Capitalism, Socialism, and Democracy.* London: Allen & Unwin, 1943.

15

The Australian-American Curriculum
for the Past and the Next Twenty Years

HON. E. GOUGH WHITLAM

*M*Y MOST RECENT BOOK, *Abiding Interests,* was published in June 1997. It happens to cover the twenty years since the establishment of the Chair of Australian Studies at Harvard. One suggestion for its title was "Preoccupations of an Octogenarian." Since some Eurocentric historians already identify the period 1914–1991 as the "short twentieth century," I first thought of calling this paper "Prognostications of a Centenarian." Last August I settled on "The Australian-American Curriculum for the Past and the Next Twenty Years"—if you like, a short half-century.

There may, of course, be a certain convenience in defining and confining this century between the fall of the Russian, German, Austrian, and Ottoman empires and the fall of the Soviet Empire. There is, indeed, a "fearful symmetry" from Sarajevo to Sarajevo. Yet even in strictly European terms, the truncation involves a serious distortion of history. For example, any political interpretation of the events in southeastern Europe in the 1990s would have to go back at least to the Congress of Berlin in 1878.

The narrow European chronology is even less appropriate when it comes to understanding the tremendous events of the past twenty years. The Eurocentric view, or its North Atlantic version, failed to foresee the collapse of the Soviet Union; it equipped us poorly to deal with the aftermath. It is even less relevant in helping the United States and Australia form our response to the most important development involving our common interests, the emergence of the Western Pacific as the world's most dynamic region.

This global transformation was already taking shape twenty years ago. It was a significant consideration in my government's response to President Nixon's invitation to help celebrate the bicentennial of the American War of National Liberation. On July 4, 1975, I announced that the Australian government would endow a Chair of Australian Studies at Harvard University.

In 1977, the year of the agreement establishing the Chair, U.S. trade with Asian countries for the first time exceeded U.S. trade with Europe. The importance of the Pacific community provided the theme and the title for the three public lectures I gave here in April 1979 as the third Visiting Professor of Australian Studies. In 1981 my lectures were published in an unmatched Harvard University Press book by the Australian Studies Endowment in collaboration with the Council of East Asian Studies.

In my first year as prime minister, I visited Indonesia, India, Japan, and China, in that order. The Pacific community has continued to be the dominant factor shaping Australian policy over the past twenty years. The U.S.-Australian relationship itself will be increasingly modified by our respective relationships with China, Japan, Indonesia, and Vietnam. I have no doubt that the new reality will influence the U.S.-Australian curriculum over the next twenty years. In May 1997 the first U.S. ambassador arrived in Vietnam.

Before I proceed to develop the Pacific thesis, I would like to comment on four aspects of contemporary Australia which may bewilder Americans: our elections, our budgets, our head of state, and our Aborigines.

The United States was the model for federation in Australia. The worst features of politics in Australia did not arise from those features of the U.S. Constitution which Australia has adopted. They flow from features of the U.S. Constitution which Australia has not sufficiently adopted or developed. Throughout this century presidents, governors, mayors, members of Congress, state legislatures, and local governments have been elected for fixed terms. Whether their terms are for six, four, or two years, they all face the electors on the Tuesday after the first Monday in November in even-numbered years. In some cities, for example New York, mayors and local governments are elected on the Tuesday after the first Monday in November in odd-numbered years. The joint election date is not prescribed by the U.S. Constitution but has evolved in a cooperative process. In Australia, however, simultaneous federal and state elections are proscribed by a section of the Federal Electoral Act inserted in 1918. No federal government has since sought to repeal this provision. The states can hold elections on the same date but even contiguous states have rarely done so. When Australians commit themselves to the clear and definite goal of reducing the frequency of elections and promoting the synchronization of elections, they will reduce the discord between the houses in their bicameral legislatures and reduce the federal/state buck-passing in their election campaigns.

There was a *coup d'état* in Australia in 1975 because, after the Constitution of Australia was enacted by the British Parliament in 1900, Australians have not taken steps to clarify a feature which still operated in the British Parliament in 1900 and which had operated in the legislatures of the six colonies in Australia to which Britain granted self-government last century. In the United States the president, the Senate, and the House of Representatives often produce different budgets; ultimately the budgets are reconciled without the president or either House or both Houses being forced to elections. Annual budgets were introduced in Australia's colonial assemblies but could be and sometimes were rejected in the Legislative Councils. The Constitution of Australia declares that budgets shall not originate in the Senate, but it does not expressly declare that the Senate shall not reject them. The Senate has never rejected a budget, but the Senate's threat to reject the 1975 budget led to the *coup d'état*. The financial power of upper houses is no longer part of the "Westminster system." The House of Lords lost it in 1911, the Legislative Council of New South Wales in 1934, and the Legislative Councils of Victoria and South Australia in 1984. The legislatures in Queensland and the two Territories are unicameral. The position is unresolved in Western Australia and Tasmania. The senators are unlikely to transgress again.

The U.S. president is both head of state and head of government. In Australia, in accordance with British tradition, the head of government is not the head of state. When the Australian Parliament gave a luncheon in honor of President Clinton in November 1997, our prime minister proposed the toast, "The President of the United States." Thereupon the president, with a straight face, had to propose a toast, "The Queen of Australia." Queen Elizabeth II is the head of state of the United Kingdom and of fifteen other Commonwealth countries, including Australia. In all her kingdoms other than the United Kingdom, her functions are discharged by fallible deputies. When she herself visits countries of which she is not the head of state, she represents the United Kingdom alone; she is accompanied by a British minister, and she promotes Britain's diplomatic and commercial objectives. There is naturally a preponderant view among Australians that a resident of Australia should be the Australian head of state. To achieve this objective, the Constitution of Australia has to be altered. Under the Constitution there is only one way that it can be altered. First, members of the Federal Parliament must pass a proposed law for the alteration of the Constitution and, secondly, the electors of Australia must approve the alteration at a referendum. Only members of the Australian Parliament can initiate such a referendum. If a referendum is not held during the reign of Queen Elizabeth, Prince Charles will automatically succeed her as King of Australia. This is because the Constitution requires every member of Parliament—every time he is elected and before he takes his seat—to swear or affirm that "I will be faithful and bear true allegiance to Her Majesty Queen Victoria, her heirs and successors according to law." The Constitution notes that "the name of the King or Queen of the United Kingdom of Great Britain and Ireland for the time being is to be substituted from time to time."

There is at present a raucous controversy about land rights for Australian Aborigines. In the U.S. Constitution, Congress was given the power "to regulate Commerce with foreign Nations, and among the several States and with the Indian Tribes." In the Constitution of Australia, however, Aborigines were mentioned in two contexts, both negative. First, "the aboriginal race in any State" was excluded from the Federal Parliament's power to make laws with respect to the people of any race for whom it is necessary to make special laws. Secondly, "aboriginal natives" were excluded from any reckoning of the people of the Commonwealth, or of a state or other part of the Commonwealth. These two exclusions were removed at a referendum in 1967. Thus, for the first two-thirds of this century, the Federal Parliament was denied crucial jurisdiction concerning Aborigines. Not until the 1980s were Aborigines able to have cases brought before the High Court of Australia and then only pursuant to my government's enactment in 1975 of the 1965 International Convention on the Elimination of All Forms of Racial Discrimination. In 1982 the High Court for the first time handed down judgments on the basis of evidence tendered by or for Aborigines. Professional historians who had failed to research Aboriginal history and state politicians who had continued to neglect the welfare of Aborigines now vilify justices of the High Court as interlopers. Until the 1970s, appeals from Australian courts could still be heard by the Judicial Committee of the British Privy Council. Thus, the High Court was long inhibited from keeping in step with its counterparts, the Supreme Courts of the United States and Canada.

While Americans may be bewildered by these domestic obsessions among Australians, Australians are bewildered by the obsessions among Americans about Australia's largest Asian neighbors. I examine just one instance, which occurred in April 1997. The UN Commission on Human Rights has considered the situation of human rights in China and in East Timor several times since protesters were killed in Beijing on June 4, 1989, and in Díli on November 12, 1991. The Commission consists of fifty-three members, fifteen from African states, twelve from Asian states, five from Eastern European states, eleven from Latin American and Caribbean states, and ten from Western European and Other states (WEOG). The United States has always been a member of the Commission, and Australia served a fourth term on the Commission from 1991 to 1996.

Resolutions coming before the Commission, which operates under the rules of the UN Economic and Social Council, can be sponsored not only by states that are members of the Commission but also by states that attend the sessions of the Commission as observers. In April 1996, when the resolution on China came before the Commission for the sixth time, it was sponsored by twenty-three states, namely all ten members from WEOG (Australia, Austria, Canada, Denmark, France, Germany, Italy, Netherlands, the

United Kingdom, and the United States), one member from the Asian states (Japan), fourteen observers from WEOG, and one observer from the Eastern European states. The Commission, however, carried a no-action motion.

On April 10, 1997, a resolution on China again came before the Commission. The number of sponsors had dropped to fifteen, namely six members from WEOG (Austria, Denmark, Ireland, Netherlands, the United Kingdom, and the United States) and nine observers from WEOG. Conspicuously, the resolution was not supported by the other four WEOG states which were still members of the Commission—Canada, France, Germany, and Italy. A no-action motion was carried by twenty-seven votes to seventeen, nine members abstaining. The only Asian state that voted against the no-action motion was Japan. The Philippines and the Republic of Korea abstained. The other nine Asian states voted for the no-action motion.

Later on the same day, a resolution on East Timor came before the Commission and gained the support of twenty of its fifty-three members. In previous years the Commission had also passed a no-action motion on East Timor. This year the resolution was sponsored by twenty-two states, twelve members of the Commission (Austria, Canada, Denmark, France, Germany, Ireland, Italy, Netherlands, and the United Kingdom from WEOG and Angola, Cape Verde, and Mozambique from Africa) and ten observers from WEOG (the four other Nordics, two Dutch neighbors, Switzerland, Portugal, Spain, and Greece). Since only fourteen members of the Commission voted against it, the resolution was carried. There were eighteen members that abstained. The resolution was opposed by ten of the twelve Asian members; Japan and the Republic of Korea abstained.

It will be noted that the United States sponsored the resolution on China but was the only member from WEOG that did not support the resolution on East Timor. The different outcome of the two resolutions came about because the United States informed Portugal that it would support Portugal in condemning Indonesia if Portugal continued to support the United States in condemning China. In July 1996 Portugal and six former colonies formed the Community of Portuguese-Speaking Countries (CPLP). On April 10, 1997, Angola, Cape Verde, and Mozambique voted for no-action on the China resolution and Brazil abstained, while all four voted for the resolution on East Timor. An editorial a week later in the *Sydney Morning Herald*, Australia's oldest and most prestigious newspaper, observed that this behavior brings international bodies into disrepute. The foreign editor of Rupert Murdoch's *The Australian,* the only newspaper that is published in every state capital, wrote that "it is vastly hypocritical for the Commission on Human Rights to criticise Indonesia but not China." He deplored "a grotesque insouciance by Washington in its policy towards Indonesia."

U.S. influence is dominant in New York, where a large and skilled staff is continually engaged at UN headquarters. U.S. influence fluctuates at the European headquarters of the UN specialized agencies in Geneva, Vienna, Rome (FAO), and Paris (UNESCO). In UNESCO, where I was a permanent delegate and then a member of the Executive Board between 1983 and 1989, it was embarrassing to see the lack of U.S. experience and capacity; in the eleven years before the United States withdrew, successive administrations appointed seven permanent delegates to the Executive Board, where terms are expected to last for four years. The Commission on Human Rights operates in Geneva; the United States cannot play an effective and consistent role if it depends on high-profile amateurs who are brought in for brief sessions.

Australia, being no longer a member of the Commission, could not vote on either resolution in April 1997. Although Australia was still an observer, the Australian government chose not to sponsor either resolution. Australia is confused by the variable signals which come from the U.S. administration and Congress about two of Australia's neighbors which have the largest and the fourth largest populations in the world. Today, even more than twenty years ago, it is the Pacific that makes Australia relevant to the United States and the United States relevant to Australia.

As we approach 2000, one cannot fail to detect a degree of pessimism, even a loss of self-confidence, in the West. Setting aside any apocalyptic premonitions associated with the end of the millennium, the current mood is the more surprising in the light of the West's remarkable recovery since 1945; its technological ascendancy, surpassing anything achieved in the nineteenth century; and the outcome of the Cold War.

There is, for example, a striking comparison, and contrast, to be found in the work of the distinguished Harvard historian and political scientist, Samuel P. Huntington. In 1991—the year after the fall of the Berlin Wall and the year before the fall of the Soviet Union—Professor Huntington, as director of the John M. Olin Institute for Strategic Studies, published his important study, *The Third Wave—Democratization in the Late Twentieth Century.* In 1996 he published *The Clash of Civilizations and the Remaking of World Order.* It was reviewed in the *Times Literary Supplement* and *The Spectator* on April 11 and 12, 1997. The latter describes it as "one of those rare books from academe which will shape the times as well as reflect them," a compliment perhaps more gratuitous than gratifying for a Harvard professor.[2]

The Third Wave was, in the words of the Introduction, "about an important, perhaps the most important, global political development of the late twentieth century: the transition of some thirty countries from non-democratic to democratic political systems. It is an effort to explain why, how, and with what immediate consequences the wave of democratization occurred between 1974 and 1990."[3] Professor Huntington scrupulously avoided the triumphalism that characterized much of the Western response to the astonishing events in Eastern Europe and the Soviet Union at that time. Nevertheless, his general optimism was expressed in the last sentence of his penultimate paragraph when he wrote: "Time is on the side of democracy" (p. 30). Five years later he is far less optimistic.

In his 1991 book, Professor Huntington foreshadowed the central thesis of his 1996 book. He examined the argument—George Kennan's argument—that democracy was "appropriate for north-western and perhaps central European countries and their settler colony off-shoots." He found "the Western culture thesis impressive, if not totally persuasive" (p. 299). "Conceivably Islamic and Confucian cultures pose insuperable obstacles to democratic development" (p. 310).

Several reasons exist, however, to question the severity of these obstacles. He pointed, for example, to the altered role of the Catholic church in Latin America and the new influence of Protestantism there; elements favorable to democracy in both Islamic and Confucian cultures; and the dynamics of change within those cultures themselves.

Professor Huntington concluded *The Third Wave*:

For a century and a half after Tocqueville observed the emergence of modern democracy in America, successive waves of democratization washed up on the shores of dictatorship. Buoyed by a rising tide of economic progress, each wave advanced further and ebbed less than its predecessors. History, to shift the metaphor, does not move forward in a straight line, but when skilled and determined leaders push, it does move forward. (p. 316)

In *The Clash of Civilizations and the Remaking of World Order*, however, Professor Huntington states:

Spurred by modernization, global politics is being reconfigured along cultural lines.[4]

And later:

Cultural communities are replacing Cold War blocs and the fault lines between civilizations are becoming the central lines of conflict in global politics.

Undoubtedly, Professor Huntington's analysis contains much food for thought for those involved in drawing up the curriculum for the next twenty years. Neither embracing nor rejecting his thesis, however, I must say this much: the most significant and cohesive regional grouping in our neighborhood, crucial in the region for the past twenty years and for the next twenty, is the Association of Southeast Asian Nations (ASEAN). Yet the racial, religious, cultural, and political diversity of its members is greater than that of any comparable grouping in the world. Thirty-five years ago it was quite accurate for me to describe Southeast Asia as "the world's most deprived and turbulent region." Nobody would now entertain such a description. The cohesiveness of ASEAN has been a major factor in the transformation.

This much, however, is certain, and to this extent I accept the Huntington thesis:

> Over the next 20 years, the broad cultural issues will be more significant in the relations between States than the political issues which have pre-occupied us for the past 20 years.

The challenge for Australia has been well summarized in another new publication, *Is Australia an Asian Country?* by Dr. Stephen FitzGerald, whom I appointed Australia's first Ambassador to the People's Republic of China in 1973. He writes:

> The future will not be one in which the United States, or any other power with which we have shared cultural heritage or political philosophies or processes or institutions, is the determining force in the part of the world in which we live. The dominant political force and cultural influence will be something like the coalition of East Asian States which emerged for ASEM [i.e., the ASEAN-Europe meeting in March 1996, from which Australia was excluded], in turn under the pervasive and dominant influence of China. This will be an utterly new experience for Australia and there will be no certainty that we will be able to handle it in a way which protects fundamental features of our society which make it attractive to us, and to hundreds of thousands of people from the countries who seek to settle here.[5]

In assessing China's likely course over the next twenty years, we could do worse than heed the words of Thomas Jefferson, who, it seems, is again as controversial a figure as he was two hundred years ago. I quote from another recent publication, Theodore Draper's *A Struggle for Power: The American Revolution.*

> In 1774, Thomas Jefferson explained the Boston Tea party in terms of a new power relationship: "An exasperated people, who feel that they possess power, are not easily restrained within limits strictly regular."[6]

The element of exasperation cannot be discounted when we presume to judge China, not only a regime, but a proud and powerful people, never again to be humiliated. This will be particularly relevant in assessing the actions of the People's Republic in Hong Kong after June 1997. The measure of China's good faith will not be the so-called Patten reforms, which it has never accepted, but the Deng-Thatcher accords of 1982, by which it accepted the "one China, two-systems" formula. This understanding is one part of the Thatcher legacy that should have been restored in the first month of the Blair government in Britain and the last month of the British Empire in Asia.

Australia's place in its region cannot, of course, be defined exclusively in terms of a dominant China. Australia, after all, is the country whose closest neighbor, Indonesia, is the world's largest Islamic nation and whose major trading partner—and it is a substantial partner—is Japan, the world's second largest economy. These are the realities, and not just the realities of geography, on which the answer to Dr. FitzGerald's question, "Is Australia an Asian country?" must be based.

By contrast, Professor Huntington scorns "futile efforts to make Australia Asian." He writes:

> Instead of defining Australia as an Asian power, Australia's leaders could define it as a Pacific country. . . If Australia wishes to make itself a Republic separated from the British Crown, it could align itself with the first country in the world to do that, a country which, like Australia, is of British origin, is an important country, is of continental size, speaks English, has been an ally in three wars [actually four] and has an overwhelming European, if, and also like Australia, increasingly Asian, population. Culturally, the values of the July 4th 1776 Declaration of Independence accord far more with Australian values than do those of any Asian country.[7]

The description is elegant; but the professor's prescription is irrelevant. For he then writes:

> Economically, instead of attempting to batter its way into a group of societies from which it is culturally alien and who for that reason reject it, Australian leaders could propose expanding NAFTA into a North American–South Pacific arrangement including the United States, Canada, Australia, and New Zealand. (p. 154)

As I have recalled, my own public lectures from the Chair in 1979 were published under the title that expressed this theme, *A Pacific Community*. To envisage a Pacific community limited to or based on the four English-speaking democracies is at best an exercise in nostalgia. In reality, it is a recipe for Australian stagnation and stultification.

Nevertheless, I am grateful to Professor Huntington, because, in a timely and scholarly work that commands international attention, he has attempted to set forth the alternative to the policies pursued by successive Australian governments, beginning with my own; but in doing so he has demonstrated that the alternative is simply no alternative at all.

The partial failure of our efforts so far has not been because the concept of Australia's Asian role is fatally flawed. Stephen FitzGerald pinpoints the reason. He writes:

> The Australian commitment to Asia was not one of the mind. It was not informed by deep knowledge. It was not thought out or conceptualised within an understanding of the elemental forces at work within Asian societies. It was in this sense not an intellectual engagement; it was not intellectualised.[8]

Here surely is a major subject for the curriculum of the Chair of Australian Studies at Harvard over the next twenty years. As the United States refashions its own role in the region, as Australia fashions its very future, there could be no more valuable contribution to our common interests than the promotion of an intellectual engagement with Asia. There could be no better place to promote it than Harvard, an outstanding center of the intellectual excellence of Western civilization.

Notes

1. *Sydney Morning Herald,* April 18, 1997; Editorial, *The Australian,* April 22, 1997.
2. *Times Literary Supplement,* April 11, 1997; *The Spectator,* April 12, 1997.
3. Samuel P. Huntington, *The Third Wave: Democratization in the Late Twentieth Century* (Norman: University of Oklahoma Press, 1991).
4. Samuel P. Huntington, *The Clash of Civilizations and the Remaking of World Order* (New York: Simon & Schuster, 1996).
5. Stephen FitzGerald, *Is Australia an Asian Country?* (Sydney: Allen & Unwin, 1997), 5.
6. Theodore Draper, *A Struggle for Power: The American Revolution* (New York: Times Books, 1996), 512.
7. Huntington, *Clash of Civilizations,* 153, 154.
8. FitzGerald, *Is Australia an Asian Country?*

References

Draper, Theodore. *A Struggle for Power: The American Revolution.* New York: Times Books, 1996.

FitzGerald, Stephen. *Is Australia an Asian Country?* Sydney: Allen & Unwin, 1997.

Huntington, Samuel P. *The Clash of Civilizations and the Remaking of World Order.* New York: Simon & Schuster, 1996.

———. The Third Wave: *Democratization in the Late Twentieth Century.* Norman: University of Oklahoma Press, 1991.

Contributors

PETER BEILHARZ is Reader in Sociology at La Trobe University, and is founding editor of the international journal of social theory, *Thesis Eleven*. He has written or edited nine books, most recently *Imagining the Antipodes* (1997) and *Fabianism and Feminism* (1998). He will hold the appointment as Visiting Professor of Australian Studies at Harvard University for the academic year 1999–2000.

GEOFFREY BLAINEY successively held chairs of economic history and history at the University of Melbourne between 1968 and 1988. He is now an emeritus professor of that university and Chancellor of the University of Ballarat. Professor Blainey has also served in federal government posts, being at various times the chairman of the Australia Council, the Australian Literature Board, the Commonwealth Literary Fund, and the Australia-China Council. He has written twenty-six books, mostly on Australian history. Professor Blainey was Visiting Professor of Australian Studies at Harvard during the academic year 1982–1983.

HAROLD BOLITHO is Professor of Japanese History and Chair of the Australian Studies Committee at Harvard University. Professor Bolitho, a native of Australia, was educated at the University of Melbourne and received his Ph.D. from Yale University. He held teaching positions at the University of Melbourne and Monash University, as well as visiting positions in Great Britain, Australia, and Japan, before coming to Harvard in 1985. He has served as President of the Japanese Studies Association of Australia and as Director of the Edwin O. Reischauer Institute of Japanese Studies at Harvard. Professor Bolitho has published extensively on his primary research interest, the Tokugawa Period of Japanese History.

GRAEME DAVISON is Professor of History at Monash University in Melbourne and occupied the Harvard Chair of Australian Studies in 1988–1989. His publications include *The Rise and Fall of Marvellous Melbourne* (1978), which was jointly awarded the Ernest Scott Prize, and *The Unforgiving Minute: How Australia Learned to Tell the Time* (1993). His latest book, *The Use and Abuse of Australian History*, will appear later in 1998 as will *The Oxford Companion to Australian History*, of which he is a co-editor.

ALAN FROST holds a Personal Chair in History at La Trobe University, Melbourne. Among many other works, he is the author of *Convicts and Empire* (1980), *Arthur Phillip, 1738-1814: His Voyaging* (1987), *Botany Bay Mirages* (1994), *The Precarious Life of James Mario Matra* (1995), and *East Coast Country: A North Queensland Dreaming*, published by Melbourne University Press.

KEVIN HART is Professor of English and Comparative Literature at Monash University in Melbourne, Australia. His principal publications are *The Trespass of the Sign* (Cambridge University Press, 1989), *A. D. Hope* (Oxford University Press, 1992), *The Oxford Book of Australian Religious Verse* (Oxford University Press, 1994), *New and Selected Poems* (1995), and *Economic Acts: Samuel Johnson and the Culture of Property* (Cambridge University Press, forthcoming, 1998).

L. R. HIATT was Reader in Anthropology at the University of Sydney until he retired in 1991. He was President of the Australian Institute of Aboriginal Studies, 1974–1982. His most recent book is *Arguments about Aborigines: Australia and the Evolution of Social Anthropology*. Professor Hiatt held the Chair of Australian Studies at Harvard during the academic year 1990–1991.

RHYS JONES holds a Personal Chair at the Institute of Advanced Studies at the Australian National University in Canberra. Dr. Jones holds a B.A. and an M.A. from Cambridge University and a Ph.D. from the University of Sydney. A prominent Australian anthropologist and archaeologist, he speaks several Australian Aboriginal languages and has done extensive fieldwork in Australia, Papua New Guinea, Indonesia, Europe, and Antarctica. Dr. Jones held the Chair of Australian Studies at Harvard during the 1995–1996 academic year.

DAME LEONIE KRAMER is the Chancellor of the University of Sydney, a post she has held since 1991. Her current positions include Chair of Quadrant Magazine Management Committee; member of the World Book Encyclopedia Advisory Board; member of the Board of Studies, NSW; member of the International Council of the Asia Society (New York); member of the NSW Council of Australian Institute of Company Directors; and Chair of Operation Rainbow Australia Limited. Dame Leonie was Professor of Australian Literature at the University of Sydney from 1968–1989; a member of the Universities Commission, 1974–1986; Chair of the Australian Broadcasting Commission, 1982–1983; Director of the Australia and New Zealand Banking Group Limited, 1983–1994; Director of the National Road and Motorists Association, 1984–1995; and Commissioner of Pacific Power, 1988–1995. She was Visiting Professor of Australian Studies at Harvard during the academic year 1981–1982, and an Honorary Fellow at St. Hugh's College, Oxford in 1994.

JOHN MULVANEY, Visiting Professor of Australian Studies from 1984–1985, was educated at Melbourne and Cambridge Universities. He was appointed Foundation Professor of Prehistory in the Faculty of Arts at the Australian National University in 1971, retiring in 1985. From 1989–1996, he served as Secretary to the Australian Academy of the Humanities. He has published widely on Australian history, archaeology, and anthropology. His books include *The Prehistory of Australia* (1969, 1975), *So Much That is New: Baldwin Spencer 1860-1929* (1985), *My Dear Spencer: The Letters of F. J. Gillen to Baldwin Spencer* (1997, edited with H. Morphy and A. Petch), and *Exploring Central Australia* (1996, edited with S. R. Morton).

JILL ROE is Professor in History at Macquarie University, Sydney. Her field is Australian cultural history, including alternative religious histories, and she has a particular interest in women's biography. She is a graduate of the University of Adelaide and of the Australian National University. In 1992 she was elected a Fellow of the Academy of the Social Sciences in Australia and is currently a member of the Academy's Executive. She also serves as Chair of the Editorial Board of the *Australian Dictionary of Biography* and as Vice-President of the Australian Society for the Study of Labor History. Her publications include *Beyond Belief: Theosophy in Australia 1879-1939* (1986) and *My Congenials: Miles Franklin and Friends in Letters* (2 vols., 1993). In addition to projects on the life and work of Miles Franklin, she is presently engaged in further research on Australian women in America. Professor Roe was the Visiting Professor of Australian Studies at Harvard for the academic year 1994–1995.

JAN SENBERGS, painter and printmaker, has exhibited regularly in Australian galleries since 1960. He has shown work in various international group exhibitions, including representing Australia at the São Paulo Biennale in Brazil in 1973. His public art commissions include a large-scale mural for the High Court of Australia, Canberra. Mr. Senbergs taught at the Royal Melbourne Institute of Technology, Melbourne, in the 1970s; was a Creative Arts Fellow at the Australian National University, 1975–1976; an Artist Trustee at the National Gallery of Victoria, Melbourne, 1984–1989; and was awarded Doctor of Arts, *Honoris Causa*, from the Royal Melbourne Institute of Technology in 1986. He is represented in Australia in the Australian National Gallery and all the state galleries. In the United States, he is represented in the Museum of Modern Art, New York; the National Gallery, Washington, D.C.; the Wadsworth Atheneum, Hartford, Connecticut; the Museum of Fine Arts, Houston, Texas; and in private and corporate collections in Australia and the United States. Mr. Senbergs held the Australian Chair at Harvard during the academic year 1989–1990.

PETER STEELE, who is a Jesuit priest, was educated in Australia. He has been a Provincial Superior of the Jesuits there, and has long taught at the University of Melbourne, where he has a Personal Chair. He has published books on Jonathan Swift, on modern poetry, on autobiography as an art, and on Peter Porter. He has published two books of poetry and many articles on literature in its various modes. He has been a visiting professor at a number of universities.

CHRIS WALLACE-CRABBE worked at various jobs in Melbourne before becoming Lockie Fellow in Australian Literature at the University of Melbourne in 1961, where he is now Professor Emeritus in The Australian Centre. He has been Harkness Fellow at Yale (1965–1967), Visiting Professor at the University of Venice (1973), and held the Chair of Australian Studies at Harvard (1987–1988). His *Selected Poems 1956–94* (Oxford University Press) won the D. J. O'Hearn Prize for Poetry and the *Age* Book of the Year Prize. His most recent critical work is *Falling into Language* (Oxford University Press, 1990) and a new book of verse, *Whirling,* which appeared in May 1998.

JAMES WALTER teaches Australian Studies at Griffith University in Brisbane, Australia. He is a former Head of the Sir Robert Menzies Centre of Australian Studies at the University of London and is currently Pro-Vice-Chancellor at Griffith University. He has published widely on Australian political culture, leadership, biography, and intellectual history. His latest book is *Tunnel Vision: The Failure of Political Imagination* (1996).

E. GOUGH WHITLAM was the leader of the Australian Labor Party from February 1967–December 1977, and the Prime Minister of Australia from 1972–1975. After resigning from Parliament in 1978, Whitlam was a National Fellow at the Australian National University. He was a member of the World Heritage Committee from 1983–1989. From 1983–1986 Whitlam was ambassador to UNESCO, of which Australia and the United States were foundation members. His latest book, *Abiding Interests* (1997), covers his activities after Parliament.

Index

Permissions Acknowledgments

Publishers have generously granted permission for the following:

"A Walk by the Charles", copyright © 1993, 1955 by Adrienne Rich, from *Collected Early Poems: 1950-1970* by Adrienne Rich. Reprinted by permission of the author and W. W. Norton & Company, Inc.

"A Week's Grace" from *Sometimes Gladness*, 5th edition, Bruce Dawe; Addison Wesley Longman Australia Pty Ltd.

"Walking Across the Atlantic" and "Etymology" from *The Apple that Astonished Paris* by Billy Collins. Reprinted with permission from University of Arkansas Press.

Extract from "Australia" from *Collected Poems* by A. D. Hope. Reprinted with permission from HarperCollins Publishers, Australia.

"To the Bobbydazzlers" from *New and Selected Poems* by John Forbes. Reprinted with permission from HarperCollins Publishers, Australia.

Extract from "Beach Burial" from *Selected Poems* by Kenneth Slessor. Reprinted with permission from HarperCollins Publishers, Australia.

"Rain" from *Collected Poems* by David Campbell. Reprinted with permission from HarperCollins Publishers, Australia.

Extract from "The Quest for the South Land" from *Collected Poems* by James McAuley. Reprinted with permission from HarperCollins Publishers, Australia.

Extracts from "The True Discovery of Australia" from *Collected Poems* by James McAuley. Reprinted with permission from HarperCollins Publishers, Australia.

"Porter's Retreat" and extract from "Hand in Hand." Reprinted from *Possible Worlds* by Peter Porter (1989) by permission of Oxford University Press.

Extracts from "Home and Hosed," "South Sea Bubbles," and "Paradis Arificiel." Reprinted from *The Automatic Oracle* by Peter Porter (1987) by permission of Oxford University Press.

Extract reprinted with permission from *The Dream Below the Sun: Selected Poems of Antonio Machado* © 1981. Published by The Crossing Press: Freedom, CA.

"Walkers," from *The Vixen* by W. S. Merwin. Copyright © 1995 by W. S. Merwin. Reprinted by permission of Alfred A. Knopf, Inc.

113029

Portion of "Poem at the New Year" from *Hotel Lautreamont* by John Ashbery. Copyright © 1992 by John Ashbery. Reprinted by permission of Alfred A. Knopf, Inc. Territory: U.S. and Canada and elsewhere throughout the world, excluding the British Commonwealth.

Portion of "Poem at the New Year" from *Hotel Lautreamont* by John Ashbery, 1992. Reprinted with permission from Carcanet Press Limited. Territory: UK/Commonwealth, excluding Canada.

"Pastoral" from *Path of Ghosts: Poems 1986–1993* by Jemal Sharah. Published by William Heinemann Australia, 1994. Reprinted with permission from Margaret Connolly.